BAILE IN SCÁIL

'The Phantom's Frenzy'

Edited by
Kevin Murray

Irish Texts Society
Cumann na Scríbheann nGaedhilge
Volume 58
2004

The Irish Texts Society: Baile in Scáil
Edited by Kevin Murray

First published by the Irish Texts Society
(Volume 58) November 2004
Copyright Kevin Murray
and Irish Texts Society

ISBN 1 870166 58 2

The Irish Texts Society
c/o Royal Bank of Scotland
Drummonds Branch
49 Charing Cross
Admiralty Arch
London SW 1A 2DX

Book design and layout by
Diskon Technical Services Limited, Dublin 8.
and printed by the
Brunswick Press Limited, Dublin 12.

Contents

I gcuimhne ar m'athair

Abbreviations

ACL *Archiv für celtische Lexikographie*, ed. W. Stokes & K. Meyer, 3 vols (Halle, 1898-1907).

AClon. *Annals of Clonmacnoise being the Annals of Ireland from the Earliest Period to A.D. 1408*, ed. D. Murphy (Dublin, 1896).

ACon. *Annála Connacht: The Annals of Connacht (A.D. 1224-1544)*, ed. A.M. Freeman (Dublin, 1944).

ACot. *The Annals in Cotton MS. Titus A. XXV*, ed. A.M. Freeman (Paris, 1929) [= *RC* 41, 301-30; 42, 283-305; 43, 358-84; 44, 336-61 (1924-7)].

AFM *Annála Ríoghachta Éireann: Annals of the Kingdom of Ireland by the Four Masters*, ed. J. O'Donovan, 7 vols (Dublin, 1848-51; 2nd ed. 1856; facs. repr. with Introduction and Appendix by K. Nicholls, Dublin, 1990).

AI *The Annals of Inisfallen (MS Rawlinson B. 503)*, ed. S. Mac Airt (Dublin, 1951).

ÄID *Über die älteste irische Dichtung*, ed. K. Meyer, 2 vols (Aus den Abhandlungen der Königl. Preuss. Akademie der Wissenschaften 6, 10, Berlin, 1913-14).

Ainm *Ainm*: Bulletin of the Ulster Place-name Society.

Anecd. *Anecdota from Irish Manuscripts*, ed. O.J. Bergin, R.I. Best, K. Meyer, J.G. O'Keeffe, 5 vols (Halle / Dublin, 1907-13).

ATig. 'The Annals of Tigernach', ed. W. Stokes, *RC* 16 (1895), 374-419, 17 (1896), 6-33, 119-263, 337-420, 18 (1897), 9-59, 150-97, 267-303; repr. 2 vols (Felinfach, 1993).

AU *The Annals of Ulster (to A.D. 1131)*, vol. 1, ed. S. Mac Airt & G. Mac Niocaill (Dublin, 1983).

BB *The Book of Ballymote*, Photo-lithographic Facsimile, with Introduction by R. Atkinson (Dublin, 1887).

BC *Baile Chuind*.

BFen. *The Book of Fenagh*, ed. W.M. Hennessy, trans. D.H. Kelly (Dublin, 1875).

BS *Baile in Scáil*.

CA 'Cóir Anmann', ed. W. Stokes, *Irische Texte* 3, ii, ed. W. Stokes and E. Windisch (Leipzig, 1897) 285-444.

CGH *Corpus Genealogiarum Hiberniae* 1, ed. M.A. O'Brien (Dublin, 1962; repr. 1976).

CIH *Corpus Iuris Hibernici*, ed. D.A. Binchy, 6 vols (Dublin, 1978).

CMCS *Cambrian (formerly Cambridge) Medieval Celtic Studies*.

CS *Chronicum Scotorum. A Chronicle of Irish Affairs from the Earliest Times to A.D. 1135*, ed. W.M. Hennessy (London, 1866).

DIL *Dictionary of the Irish Language based mainly on Old and Middle*

	Irish Materials (compact ed., Dublin, 1983).
ÉC	*Études Celtiques.*
EIHM	*Early Irish History and Mythology*, T.F. O'Rahilly (Dublin, 1946; repr. 1999).
EIV	*The Early Irish Verb*, K. McCone (Maynooth, 1997).
FAI	*The Fragmentary Annals of Ireland*, ed. J. Radner (Dublin, 1978).
FFÉ	*Foras Feasa ar Éirinn: The History of Ireland by Geoffrey Keating D. D.*, ed. P. S. Dinneen & D. Comyn, 4 vols, ITS 4, 8, 9, 15 (London, 1902-14).
GOI	*A Grammar of Old Irish*, R. Thurneysen (Dublin 1946, repr. 1980).
Harl.	British Library MS Harley 5280.
HBS	Henry Bradshaw Society.
HDGP	*Historical Dictionary of Gaelic Placenames / Foclóir Stairiúl Áitainmneacha na Gaeilge*, Fascicle 1 [Names in A-] / Fascúl 1 [Ainmneacha in A-] ed. P. Ó Riain, D. Ó Murchadha, K. Murray, ITS (London, 2003).
IER	*Irish Ecclesiastical Record.*
IGT	*Irish Grammatical Tracts*, O. Bergin (1916-55) [A Supplement to *Ériu* vols 8, 9, 10, 14, 17].
ITS	*Irish Texts Society.*
JIES	*Journal of Indo-European Studies.*
JCHAS	*Journal of the Cork Historical and Archaeological Society.*
JRSAI	*Journal of the Royal Society of Antiquaries of Ireland.*
LEIA	*Lexique Étymologique de L'Irlandais Ancien*, ed. J. Vendryes, E. Bachellery, P.-Y. Lambert (Dublin, 1959-).
LGen.	*Leabhar Mór na nGenealach: The Great Book of Irish Genealogies*, 5 vols, ed. N. Ó Muraíle (Dublin: De Búrca, 2003).
LL	*The Book of Leinster formerly Lebar na Núachongbála*, ed. R.I. Best, O. Bergin, M.A. O'Brien, A. O'Sullivan, 6 vols (Dublin, 1954-83).
LU	*Lebor na Huidre: Book of the Dun Cow*, ed. R. I. Best & O. Bergin (Dublin, 1929).
MD	*The Metrical Dindshenchas*, ed. E. J. Gwynn, 5 vols, TLS 7-12 (1906-35; repr. Dublin 1991).
Ml.	The Milan Glosses on the Psalms, Bibl. Ambr. C. 301, *Thes.* i, 7-483.
MMIS	Medieval and Modern Irish Series.
MMWS	Medieval and Modern Welsh Series.
NHI	*The New History of Ireland*, 10 vols [under the auspices of the RIA], ed. T.W. Moody, F.X. Martin, F.J. Byrne, W.E. Vaughan et al. (Oxford, 1976-).
O'DG	W. Stokes, 'O'Davoren's Glossary', *ACL* ii, 3, ed. W. Stokes and K. Meyer (Halle, 1903) 197-504.
OnomG	*Onomasticon Goedelicum, Locorum et Tribuum Hiberniae et Scotiae*, ed. E. Hogan (Dublin, 1910; repr. 1993).
PBA	*Proceedings of the British Academy.*

PHCC	*Proceedings of the Harvard Celtic Colloquium.*
PMLA	*Publications of the Modern Language Association of America.*
PNNI	*Place-names of Northern Ireland.*
PRIA	*Proceedings of the Royal Irish Academy.*
Rawl.	Bodleian Library, Oxford MS Rawlinson B. 512.
RC	*Revue Celtique.*
RIA	Royal Irish Academy.
SC	*Sanas Cormaic: An Old Irish Glossary*, ed. K. Meyer, *Anecd.* vol. iv (1912; repr. Llanerch, 1994).
Sg.	Glosses on Priscian, Codex Sangallensis No. 904, in *Thes.* ii, 49-224.
SLH	*Scriptores Latini Hiberniae.*
SnaG	*Stair na Gaeilge*, ed. K. McCone, D. McManus, C. Ó Háinle, N. Williams, L. Breatnach (Maynooth, 1994).
TBC¹	*Táin Bó Cúailnge: Recension 1*, ed. C. O'Rahilly (Dublin, 1976).
TBCL	*Táin Bó Cúalnge from the Book of Leinster*, ed. C. O'Rahilly (Dublin, 1967).
TCD	Trinity College, Dublin.
Thes.	*Thesaurus Palæohibernicus: A Collection of Old-Irish Glosses, Scholia and Verse*, ed. W. Stokes & J. Strachan, 2 vols and suppl. (Cambridge, 1901-3, 1910; repr. Dublin, 1975).
TLS	*Todd Lecture Series.*
Wb.	Glosses on the Pauline Epistles, Codex Paulinus Wirziburgensis, *Thes.* i, 499-712.
YBL	*The Yellow Book of Lecan, a Collection of Pieces (Prose and Verse) in the Irish Language ... Published from the Original Manuscript in the Royal Irish Academy*, Photo-lithographic Plates with Introduction by R. Atkinson (Dublin, 1896).
ZCP	*Zeitschrift für celtische Philologie.*

KEVIN MURRAY

Acknowledgements

Tá an leabhar seo bunaithe ar mo thráchtas dochtúireachta, *Baile in Scáil: The Literary and Historical Perspective*, a chuaigh fé bhráid Ollscoil Náisiúnta na hÉireann i 1997. Is mór an sásamh domsa bheith in ann mo bhuíochas a ghabháil leis na daoine a chabhraigh go fial liom leis an saothar seo.

I received help and encouragement from many friends, particularly Anne Connon, Dr Catherine Kavanagh, Emer Purcell, Hugh Fogarty, Dr Jeremy & Paula Lowe, Mike & Heather Byrnes and Myles Nolan. Additional debts of friendship were acknowledged in the introduction to the thesis; though they are too numerous to reiterate here, the sentiments expressed still hold true.

I wish to thank fellow members of the 'Tara group', particularly Drs Edel Bhreathnach and John Carey, who thrashed out so many of the pertinent issues with me. My thanks also to all the members, past and present, of the Old Irish department in UCD (Dr Patricia Kelly, Prof. Tomás Ó Cathasaigh, Mrs Doreen Carty, Prof. Máirín Ní Dhonnchadha, Mrs Bernie Mac Giolla Phádraig and Mr Dónall Mac Giolla Easpaig) who treated me with such kindness during my student days.

Thanks are due to the Bodleian Library, Oxford, and to the British Library, London, for permission to consult materials in their possession. Furthermore, I wish to acknowledge the kind assistance received from the staff of Special Collections, Q-1, Boole Library, Cork. I am also grateful to the Irish Texts Society for agreeing to include this volume in their series. I wish to thank the Arts Faculty, University College Cork and the National University of Ireland, for providing grants to help defray the costs of publication.

Since coming to University College Cork, my academic life has been greatly enhanced by regular interaction with my colleagues. To Elmarie Uí Cheallacháin, Maude Vernon and Siobhán Ní Dhonghaile (administrative staff, Na Ranna Gaeilge) and to all the staff of Roinn na Nua-Ghaeilge, *míle buíochas*. My sincere gratitude to all members of the *Locus* project, especially Dr Diarmuid Ó Murchadha, Dr Donna Thornton and Emma Nic Cárthaigh. I owe a special debt of gratitude to my colleagues in the Department of Early and Medieval Irish: Dr Caitríona Ó Dochartaigh, Dr Clodagh Downey and especially to my Head of Department, Prof. Máire Herbert.

I have incurred a number of direct academic debts in the production of this work. Firstly, my thanks to the Honorary Editor of the Irish Texts Society, Dr Máire Ní Mhaonaigh, for her extensive comments on the final draft of this book. Secondly, my heartfelt appreciation to Prof. Pádraig

Ó Riain, President of the Irish Texts Society, who re-read the entire text with me and suggested numerous improvements, saving me from many errors and omissions. Lastly, *buíochas ó chroí* to my thesis supervisor, Prof. Próinséas Ní Chatháin, who set me such a splendid example of generosity and learning during my years in University College Dublin; I am delighted to have had the opportunity to work under her supervision.

Finally, I wish to thank my family: my wife Allie and children (Tom, Anna & Alice); my mother, Nancy, my brother, Tomás, and my sisters, Catherine and Máire. My father, Joe, did not live to see this publication: I dedicate the book to his memory.

INTRODUCTION

I.

Baile in Scáil 'The Phantom's Frenzy' (henceforth *BS*) is an important and intriguing medieval Irish text which purports to be a prophecy recited by an Otherworld phantom in the presence of Conn Cétchathach, king of Tara, detailing all the future kings of Tara that would descend from him. Thus, it is a significant text in the areas of history, mythology and literature. As will become evident later, the main thrust of the tale seems to be the assertion of the rights of the Uí Néill to the kingship of Tara.

1.1 The manuscripts

The only complete copy of *BS* is in Rawlinson B. 512 (henceforth Rawl.) ff. 101ra – 105vb, the mainly fifteenth and early sixteenth-century MS which has recently been catalogued comprehensively by Ó Cuív (2001, 223-54).[1] He notes (p. 223) that the MS consists of 'five separate parts whose composition has been obscured by the way in which they are bound at present and by the loss of leaves'. *BS* is the opening tract of the section designated by Ó Cuív as Part I (comprising ff. 101-22, 1-36 and 45-52).[2] As he states (p. 231): 'apart from some later additions, ff. 5-36 and 101-22 seem to be the work of one unnamed scribe whose hand varies greatly both in quality and in size ... although there is no scribal signature a note on f. 33r gives "Baile na Cuilendtrach" as the place of writing'.[3]

---

[1]   The contents of this MS are also listed in Stokes (1887, xiii-xlv) and its composition is described in detail in Best (1928).

[2]   As Ó Cuív points out (pp. 232-5), all the other four sections of the MS may have connections with the Ó Maoil Chonaire scribal family. In this context, it is worth noting (see Murray, forthcoming: ii) that the contents listed as belonging to the Ó Maoil Chonaire 'Book of Cluain Plocáin' are similar to those in part I, section 1 of Rawl. (ff. 101-22).

[3]   Because this section of the MS was connected with the Plunkett family, Ó Cuív has plausibly suggested identifying *Baile na Cuilendtrach* with (1) tl. Cullendragh, p. Killeagh, b. Fore, co. Meath *or* (2) tl. Cullendragh, p. Culmullin, b. Upr Deece, co. Meath *or* (3) tl. Cullentry, p. Rathmolyon, b. Lwr Moyfenrath, co. Meath. In his edition of *Bethu Brigte*, Ó hAodha (1978, ix) plumps for option 3. Walsh (1947, 45-6) believes that it was 'on the shores of Loch Sílenn, in the district known in former times as Plunket's Country'. Since this seems to fit the context best, option 1 above is to be preferred.

The other surviving copy of *BS*, though not complete, is in British Library MS Harley 5280 (henceforth Harl.) ff. 71a – 72b. In his Catalogue, Flower dated the MS to the early part of the sixteenth century (1926, 298-323). The scribe's name is given on fo. 74b of the MS as 'Gilla riabach mac Tuathail meic Taidc caim I Clerich'. On fo. 58b, a blessing is written in the vocative case for a person named Túathal with the wish that he remember the writer of the blessing everytime he looked at it. As Flower argued: 'if the Tuathal here addressed was the father of Gilla riabach, the MS was written in his lifetime before 1512. But the identification cannot be regarded as certain' (1926, 299). The writer of the blessing identifies himself as Fear Feasa mac Conchobair, whom Flower suggests may have been an Ó Maoil Chonaire, as both names were used by that family. On fo. 74b Giolla Ríabhach gives his place of writing as *a Cuirr Lessa Conaill*.[4]

The scribe of Harl. knew that he had not the full text of *BS* (his copy finishes in the middle of two lines of poetry) so he left space (a page and a half) at the end of the story in which to complete it. He may not have had the full text of *BS* in front of him[5] because it seems that he left insufficient space to take down the rest of the tale, unless in a very summarised form.[6] Rawl. and Harl. have twelve works in common. Seven of these pieces (including *BS*) are to be found in Part I, section 1 of Rawl. (ff. 101-22). A handful of shared readings of significance in Rawl. and Harl. (listed in note to l. 163) would point to both copies of *BS* descending from a shared exemplar. The differences would point to either the presence of different intermediary MSS between the common exemplar and the extant versions or to the vagaries of the scribal copying traditions.

---

4   Walsh (1947, 48) identifies this as *Corrlios Conaill*, p. Kilmore, b. Ballintober N., co. Roscommon and points out that there was an Ó Maoil Chonaire settlement here in the sixteenth century; this would tend to strenghten Flower's suggestion. Both MS copies of *BS*, therefore, may have been connected with the learned family of Ó Maoil Chonaire.

5   However, as is suggested in the note to l. 149, it seems that there may have been a complete version of the Harl. text in existence at some point; this possibility is also raised by the fact that Giolla Ríabhach Ó Cléirigh (the Harl. scribe of *BS* and *Baile Bricín*) utilised later sections of *BS* material (not preserved in Harl.) in his copy of *Baile Bricín* (see Murray, 2002, 53-6).

6   It would take at least 2½ pages to take down the rest of the story. (There are 33 lines to the page in Harl. It took 124 lines in Harl. and 429 lines in Rawl to take down the first section of *BS* [the ratio is, therefore, 1:3½]. There are 300 lines of text after this in Rawl. At the same ratio this would cover 86 lines in Harl., i.e. 2½ pages).

1.2 Previous editions and translations

BS has attracted much attention from modern scholars since O'Curry (1861, 385-91) first drew attention to it. O'Curry's discussion of the tale was necessarily incomplete, however, as he was only aware of the truncated version available in Harl., from which he provided a text and translation of the opening eleven paragraphs (1861, Appendix cxxviii, 618-22). Later summaries of the opening section (§§1-9) of the text include those by Dillon (1948, 107-9) and Carey (1996, 190-1); there is also an unpublished translation of §§1-9 by Ó Cathasaigh (1995). Diplomatic editions (without translation) of the text have been printed: the Harl. version was edited by Meyer (1901); the latter part of the Rawl. version is available in Meyer (1918) with corrigenda in Meyer (1921). He later edited the beginning of this text (Pokorny, 1921); this section was re-edited by Thurneysen (1936).

1.3 Summary of story

Conn Cétchathach was on the ramparts of Tara with his three druids and his three poets. He leapt on a stone which cried out under his feet. After a delay of fifty-three days, Cessarnn, his chief poet, explained that the name of the stone was *fál* and that the number of its roars was equal to the number of kings of Conn's seed that would rule over Ireland. Then a great fog descended and a horseman approached who made three casts at them. Upon learning Conn's identity, the horseman invited him to his dwelling. A young girl was in the house in a crystal chair with a golden crown on her head. Beside her was a silver vat full of red ale, with a beautiful phantom alongside on his throne. The phantom identified himself as Lug mac Ethnenn and he told Conn that he had come to relate to him the duration of his kingship and that of every one of his descendants. It is stated in the text that the girl was the Sovereignty of Ireland. While dispensing the ale from the vat she asked to whom each drink should be given. Lug answered her by naming each of the descendants of Conn who would be king of Tara. Cessarnn wrote down this information in *ogam* on four large rods of yew. Then Lug and his house disappeared, but the vat of ale, the dispensing and drinking vessels and the yew rods remained with Conn. This introductory section of the tale is complete in itself. The remaining part of the text is concerned with detailing the kings prophesied by Lug (printed in Murray 2002, 49-50).

2. DATE

The question of the dating of the text has also been addressed by modern scholarship. O'Curry (1861, 419) believed that it was written about 1000 A.D. by the same person who composed *Baile Bricín* (see Murray 2002, 55-6). Thurneysen and Meyer came to no firm conclusions regarding the date of the text in their editions of *BS* though Thurneysen (1936, 218) did note that he thought *BS* was written in deliberately archaic language. Murphy (1952, 150 n.1) argued that 'the basis of all paragraphs of *Baile in Scáil* would ... seem to belong to the late 9th century'.

Byrne (*NHI* 9, 190) has advanced arguments that there was an original text (henceforth referred to as [**X**]) which was composed *c.* 862 but that the text as we have it (henceforth referred to as [**A**]) 'has reached us in a redaction made between 1022 and 1036'. Herbert (1992, 273 n.4) views the dating of the text similarly, believing 'that there is an earlier stratum in the text, possibly of the ninth century' but that 'the final surviving version ... [is] a revision and updating of the early eleventh century'. This is also the position adopted by the present editor (Murray 2002, 54-5). The linguistic analysis printed in Appendix 4 would tend to support this dating, presenting us with a three-fold picture. *BS* contains: (i) many features which can be safely dated to the late O.Ir. period (ninth century); (ii) developments which show re-working and addition of material in the Mid.Ir. period; (iii) a small number of possible archaic forms, perhaps dating to earlier in the O.Ir. period (eighth century?).[7] Byrne chose *c.* 862 as his date of original composition of [**X**] because this was when Máel Sechnaill mac Máele Rúanaid, the subject of §50, died. Up to this point, all the kings are referred to by name. In §§51-65, most of the kings are first identified by vague kennings followed by their names. The kings of history that are readily identifiable end at §57 with mention of Máel Sechnaill mac Domnaill and Brian Bóruma.

Linguistically, there is not much to distinguish §§51-65 from the preceding sections. Even taking into consideration the possibility that §§60-65 may have originally formed part of [**X**] (see below, **3**), it seems that the eleventh-century compiler was also re-working substantial pieces of O.Ir. material in §§51-59. This is clear from a cursory exami-

---

7   Some of these dating features, however, including all the possible archaic forms, are orthographic in nature (and are cited as such in Appendix 4) and thus they might not be truly reliable diagnostic features.

nation of some of the O.Ir. dating features noted in Appendix 4. Later linguistic features appear sporadically throughout the tale, leading one to conclude that the influence of the compiler is, as one might suspect, to be found all through the text, not just in the later sections where he probably had most input. As mentioned above, it is possible that parts of *BS* may contain linguistic archaisms which raises the possibility that the ninth-century author, and perhaps the eleventh-century compiler, may have been drawing on even earlier materials. The existence of the early poem beginning *Lug Scéith Scál Find* (see below, fn. 9) may also point in the same direction.

It has traditionally been assumed that §58 constitutes a claim for Flaithbertach mac Muirchertaig Uí Néill, Cenél nEógain king of Ailech and, thus, that the eleventh-century redactor was at work after the death of Máel Sechnaill mac Domnaill (†1022) and before that of Flaithbertach Úa Néill (†1036). This traditional time-frame fits well with other dating considerations, viz.

(a) It was in the late tenth and early eleventh century that Uí Néill claims to the over-kingship of Ireland came under serious threat for the first time (Herbert 1992, 272);

(b) *BS* seems to have been known to Flann Mainistrech (†1056). He appears to quote its authority regarding Echu Mugmedón in *Ríg Themra dia tesband tnú* (*LL* 15765-8), though this cannot be regarded as certain (text cited in **4.3**(b) below);

(c) According to the heading in Rawl., *BS* was copied from the book of Dub dá Leithe (†1064) who was appointed *fer léiginn* of Armagh in 1046.

On this evidence, the compiler would appear to have been at work in the first half of the eleventh century. The ninth-century *BS* must have had a MS life, however, and some of the extant references may be to this rather than to the later compilation that has survived.

Finally, it may also be worth drawing attention to the brief parallel alluded to in the Notes (ll. 42-3) between *BS* and *In Tenga Bithnua* (Stokes, 1905i). Carey (1998, 276) would date the version of *In Tenga Bithnua* edited by Stokes from the Book of Lismore to 'some point in the ninth century', a dating comparable to that of much of the material in *BS*.

2.1 The verse content

The verse contained in *BS* has been corruptly transmitted. This may be largely due to the fact that it was only one of a number of sources used by the compiler of the text. The poetry, purporting to be part of the historical record, is in seven-syllable rhymed couplets – the metre a mixture of *rannaigecht* and *deibide*. Many of the lines have imperfect metre; words and syllables have been added and omitted, thus leaving us with lines that have both more and less than the required seven syllables. The rhyme is imperfect in many places. There are some instances of alliteration (e.g., *In cath i mBrí Cobthaig Coil. / Coíntit ile, coíntit cóim* §11, *Matan Maigi Mucramai* §11) but it is not common.

Peter Smith has recently examined the evolution of this type of 'historical' verse, which he defines as 'verse which purports to record knowledge of the historical traditions of Ireland' (2001, 327). Based on his analysis he believes that 'the elaboration of a chronological framework for historical verse may have begun as early as the seventh and eighth centuries, but it appears to have been a sporadic and perhaps merely ornamental feature until the tenth century' (2001, 335). He notes, however, a suggestion made by Séamus Mac Mathúna that 'this [tenth-century] date might perhaps be pushed back further in view of the occurrence of versified regnal years in *Baile in Scáil*' (2001, 335 n. 55). The conclusions regarding dating presented here would tend to support Mac Mathúna's suggestion.

3. STRUCTURE

Editorially, *BS* has traditionally been divided into sixty-five paragraphs, a schematism that has been followed in this edition. §§1-9 make up the introductory framework, constituting the story proper (as summarised in **1.3** above), while §§10-65 comprise a separate paragraph on every putative king of Tara to descend from Conn Cétchathach.

My original views regarding the structure of §§51-65 have appeared in print. In this publication I argued (Murray 2002, 52) that in *BS* §§51-58, 'the kennings refer to known historical personages whose names are also given in the text, occasionally as glosses. From §59 to the end (§65), however, the names associated with the kennings in *BS* cannot be married with any confidence to historical personages, while some of them, e.g. Áed Engach (§62) and Flann Cinuch (§65), seem to be obvious literary creations'. Recent re-examination of the material, however, leads me to put forward a different proposal; this has no important implications for the dating of the text, but it considerably modifies my original beliefs regarding its structure.

As is well known, the kingship of Tara rotated between Cenél nEógain of Ailech and Clann Cholmáin of Mide from 734 (with the accession of Áed Allán mac Fergaile) until 1022 (with the death of Máel Sechnaill mac Domnaill), with two exceptions, viz. Congalach Cnogba mac Máele Mithig (944-56) and Brian Bóruma (1002-14). It seems that this political reality may be acknowledged in §59 with a claim to the kingship for Murchad from Assal (which is in the heart of Clann Cholmáin territory). This Murchad may be a reference to Murchad Rúad (†1049), son of Máel Sechnaill mac Domnaill; however, I think it more likely that it refers to Murchad (†1033), son of Máel Sechnaill Got, successor to Máel Sechnaill mac Domnaill as king of Clann Cholmáin. If this is deemed likely, then this would narrow the work of the compiler to the years between 1022-25, when Flaithbertach was king of Ailech and the father of his putative successor was king of Mide. If it is deemed more likely that Murchad Rúad is the person in question here, then the date of operation of the compiler would probably move to 1032-36 while Flaithbertach was still king of Ailech (restored in 1032 after abdicating in 1030) and Murchad Rúad became the oldest surviving son of Máel Sechnaill mac Domnaill (with the death of his older brother, Conchobor, in 1030).

Where does this leave §§60-65? It is my supposition that these six paragraphs constituted the concluding part of the original text [**X**] and that the names added as glosses represent efforts made to attach the kennings therein to members of royal families who were alive in the second half of the ninth century. Thurneysen (1936, 217) has already suggested that §65 (Flann Cinuch) was part of the original text and it is my belief, following Thurneysen, that Flann Cinuch was already being presented as the hypothetical last ruler of Ireland by the late ninth century; thus, no effort was made to link him to any historical figure. In the case of the rulers listed in §§60-64, however, the following tentative identifications may be made:

(a) §60, Óengus from Óenach Fánat: this may be a reference to Óengus mac Máele Dúin, *rígdamna in Tuaiscirt*, who was killed in 883 (*AU* 883.8);

(b) §61, Murchad from Ailech: this might refer to Murchad mac Máele Dúin, who was Cenél nEógain king of Ailech from 879-

887;

(c) §62, Áed Engach: the most likely candidate would be Áed Finnlíath mac Néill, though he is the subject of a separate entry in *BS* §51. Perhaps, this enduring popular figure in Irish tradition was a literary creation from the beginning;

(d) §63, Cerball from Uisnech: perhaps a reference to Cerball (*fl.* late ninth / early tenth century), son of Flann Sinna;

(e) §64, Fergal from Ailech: perhaps the Fergal in question here is Fergal mac Óengussa (a member of the Northern Uí Néill army under the command of Níall Glúndub); he was slain by troops from Mide in 914 (*AU* 914.7).

Though there is no way of confirming these suggestions, nevertheless, it seems suggestive that these parallels can be drawn. It must also be observed, however, that the comparable kennings in the Book of Fenagh are taken to represent hypothetical kings (see **6.2** below).

There seems to be a natural break in the text at §40. From this point onwards, at which the Harl. text breaks off, we discover where most of the kings are buried (§§40-55). The relevant phrases, which are always in the past tense, are in Latin (e.g. *sepulti sunt* §40; *sepultus est* §47, §48) and in Irish (e.g. *ro adnacht* §41, §43) and are obviously later additions to the story. In §§47-57 the mothers of the kings are also listed. It seems impossible to determine, however, whether there is any connection between the presence of these additions and the fact that Harl. is missing these concluding sections of the tale.

An ambiguity presents itself in §9; this introductory part of *BS* finishes with the line *Ocus is di sen attá Aislingi ⁊ Echtra ⁊ Argraige Cuind Cétcathaig ⁊ Baile in Scáil* (And it is from that there is 'The Dream and the Adventure and the Journey of Conn Cétchathach' and 'The Phantom's Frenzy').[8] This sentence can be interpreted in two ways. Firstly, it may be argued that it gives us the name by which §§1-9 were known. This seems to be the more probable scenario, especially as it accurately describes the contents of these paragraphs. Alternatively, it may be argued that the sentence literally means that §§1-9 are the back-

---

8   Listing of sub-titles within or at the start or end of stories is common in medieval Irish and Welsh literatures. See, for example, *Fled Bricrenn* (Henderson 1899, 128), *Cath Maige Tuired* (Gray 1982, 24) and *Branwen Uerch Lyr* (Thomson 1986, 17-18).

ground to two separate stories, i.e. 'The Dream and the Adventure and the Journey of Conn Cétchathach' and 'The Phantom's Frenzy'. This can be tentatively supported by arguing that §10 onwards constitutes 'The Phantom's Frenzy' and that 'The Dream and the Adventure and the Journey of Conn Cétchathach' is better known to us as *Baile Chuind* (henceforth *BC*).[9]

3.1 Sources

Thurneysen was the first to point out that *BS*, as it has come down to us, 'appears to be a conflation of two distinct prophecies' (Dillon 1946, 12). He argued (1936, 215):

> Ich habe vielmehr den Eindruck, daß ursprünglich zwei Quellen, zwei Weissagungen ineinandergearbeitet worden sind, eine 'retorische' und eine metrische, besonders die Schlachten aufzählende; aber die zweite wurde nur mit Auswahl verwertet, nur ausgezogen, nicht vollständig aufgenommen.

('I have the impression that originally two sources, two predictions were worked together, a 'rhetorical' and a metrical one, particularly the battle-listing one; but only selected sections of the latter were utilised, it was not all used').

This indeed seems to be the case. For example, in §§10-48 it is quite easy to see the influence of both the metrical source and the rhetorical source, and to distinguish between them, though the presence of the rhetorical source does not become pronounced until §17. The rhetorical source primarily seems to have been composed of two-word, self-contained laudatory semantic units, occasionally alliterating, strung together in varying quantities. From §48 onwards, however, poetry is only sporadically attested though the utilisation of rhetorical material remains consistent. It appears that the compiler of [X] had a metrical source and a rhetorical source from which to fashion his text and that

---

9   *BC* is generally dated to the late seventh or early eighth century. That knowledge of the material contained in the opening section of *BS* was current shortly after the date of composition of *BC* can be further argued on the basis of the existence of an early (eighth-century?) elegy on Labraid Loingsech beginning *Lug Scéith Scál Find* (*ÄID* ii, 23; Pokorny (1923) 4). As Nora Chadwick has argued (1935, 2), this may be an allusion to the opening section of *BS*.

the compiler of [**A**] used various different sources of information to complete the tale. It is worth noting that it is explicitly stated in §61 that more than one source was being utlised: *Sic exemplaria uariantur* 'Thus the exemplars differ'.

4. THE LITERARY CONTEXT

BS has many features in common with other texts.[10] The connections between it and *Tucait Baile Mongáin* have recently been highlighted (Carey 1995, 74-7) and it has also been studied in conjunction with *Baile Berchán* (Hudson 2001, 153-5). The present writer has published on its relationship with *Echtrae Chormaic* (Murray, 2001i) and *Baile Bricín* (Murray, 2002). A note on its most important literary relationship, i.e. with *Baile Chuind*, is at press (Murray, forthcoming: i). Other literary connections are discussed in the following pages.[11]

4.1 *Baile in Scáil* and *Senchas Fagbála Caisil*

Senchas Fagbála Caisil (henceforth *SFC*) is another vision story, similar to *BS*, which contains a prophecy about the future kings of Munster (Dillon, 1952). Indeed, Scowcroft (1995, 131 n. 47) refers to *SFC* as 'a Munster variant' of *BS*. It consists of an eighth-century part (§§1-3) and a tenth-century part (§§4-8) and is very obscure in places. The two stories have the following points in common:

i. Both contain the joining together of two separate sources. However, this amalgamation works much more successfully in *BS*.

ii. In both, there is a vision which tells of a future line of kings.

---

10 For example, comparisons have been drawn (Tolstoy 1985, 108-9, 238-40) between it and the medieval Welsh poem *Kyuoessi Myrdin a Gwendyd y Chwaer* 'The Dialogue Between Myrdin and his Sister Gwendyd' (Skene 1868: i, 462-78; ii, 218-33); remarks have also been made (Tolstoy 1985, 118-22) on parallels between *BS* and *Ystorya Gereint uab Erbin* 'The Story of Gereint son of Erbin' (Thomson, 1997; trans. Gantz 1976, 258-97).

11 *BS* has also been afforded a role within Grail scholarship. Loomis, for example, has argued (1963, 48) that it may be seen as 'a remote source of Perceval's adventure at the Grail castle'. It is not my intention here to engage with this apart from the obvious need to state that the arguments advanced by Loomis seem very tenuous, based as they are on many false assumptions about the nature and structure of *BS*.

iii. The king-list may not be an integral part of either text.
iv. In both stories, drink is dispensed to the rightful ruler
v. Both texts contain notification of the arrival of Patrick.

Differences include:

i. The role played by the sovereignty goddess in *BS* is performed by an angel in *SFC*.
ii. The *druí / fili* ('druid' / 'poet') has a much more prominent role in *BS*; the druid has such a small role in *SFC* that it seems that the swineherd has assumed his functions.[12]

Nevertheless, it appears that the existence of a prophetic tale about the future kings of Tara may have influenced the composition of *SFC*. Perhaps it was composed in response to the reference to Munster in the last few lines of *BC* (Murphy 1952, 146-9):

T*u*snicf*ea* fer fingalach esmbrethach; hīpthuss co derc domain; Saxain imchil, immus- hūa Chorc -ebla (.i. Fland); is ē raethe Mum*an* mārlaithe hi Temuir.

A kin-slaying man, *prone to unjust judgements*, shall app   roach it; he shall drink it to *the pit* of the world; encircling Saxons; he (i.e. Flann) shall drive them from Corc; he is the king of Munster of great lordships in Tara.

4.2 *Baile in Scáil* and other texts designated as *baili*

The different stories entitled *baili* have not been considered in-depth as one genre since O'Curry (1861, 382-434) pioneered discussion of the subject. Medieval commentators categorised *baili* as a tale-type (Mac Cana 1980, 56) in the listing of Irish narratives (List B) embedded in the tale *Airec Menman Uraird maic Coise* (Byrne, 1908). Mac Cana argues that the *baili* are a later addition to this list, which is 'indicated fairly clearly by the fact that *Baile in Scáil* is included among them even

---

12   As Ní Chatháin argues: 'It is unlikely in the evolution of society that a druid would be replaced by a swineherd, but it is not too far-fetched that a shamanistic swineherd would be superseded by a more pretentious and sophisticated druid. This development may or may not take into account the theory of the magical and mystical properties of Munster' (1979-80, 206).

though it occurs also as *Fís Chuind Chétchathaig* .*i. Baili in Scáil* in the older section of the *físi* common to A and B' (1980, 70). However, Toner argues that the form *Fís Chuind* 'was deliberately chosen so as to produce paired alliteration' (next to *Fís Chonchobair*) 'rather than *Baile in Scáil* or *Baile Chuind Chétchathaig* as it is known in manuscripts' (2000, 112). Either way, it seems clear that the native term *baile* could be used interchangeably with the loan-word *fís* (< Lat. *visio*). Mac Cana remarks further that 'the term ... (*baile / buile* 'vision, frenzy') ... itself is old, but its extended use to denote a category of tales may well be a late development' (1980, 75).

There seems to be no single unifying factor which ties together the stories designated as *baili* (list of extant *baili* given in Appendix 3). Further to Mac Cana's argument, it may be asserted in general that the term *baile* is not used to denote a category of tales but is used of stories which contain a vision or a prophecy at their core and which do not readily fit into another category. It is at least arguable that the term *baile* in many of these titles may be best understood as meaning 'prophecy'. Many of these texts have no vision element and it is possible that the incorporation of a vision in other examples is a secondary development, attached to these stories as a way of explaining the presence of the prophetic material. The most notable exception to this, however, is the longest and most famous of all the *baili*, viz. *Buile Shuibhne*. Here, *baile* refers to the frenzy or madness of the central character who is cursed by Rónán of Druim Inesclainn and who subsequently loses his reason at the battle of Mag Roth (AD 637).[13] There are other prophetic texts, however, not designated *baili* and which do not incorporate visions, with which tales like *Baile Bricín* and *BS* have more in common with regard to lists of rulers and length of reigns. A good example of this type of text is that edited by O'Keefe (1934) under the title 'A Prophecy on the High-kingship of Ireland'.

Certainly, what distinguishes a *baile* is difficult to ascertain from the evidence presented by *BS*. The story unfolds like an *echtrae* – being in essence a visit to the Otherworld rather than a vision of it (see Dillon 1948, 107). As Carey (1996, 196-9) has pointed out, in both *BS* and *Echtrae Chormaic* descending mist is used as a sign of Otherworld journeying rather than visionary experience. It may be that the 'lost

---

13   According to *DIL* s.v. *baile*, the range of meanings 'vision', 'frenzy' and 'madness' are linked as conditions 'originally arising out of supernatural revelations'. '

narrative introduction' of *BC*, whose existence was first hinted at by Murphy (1952, 152 n.5) and formally proposed by Carey (1995, 76; 1996, 191-4), gave more explicit indications of what constitutes a *baile*. If the introductory portion of *BS* is directly based on this lost introduction, then it is possible that the title of *BS* was taken over from this earlier material, a title that is open to more than one interpretation. *Baile in Scáil* could refer either to Conn's vision of the phantom or to the vision/prophecy visited upon the phantom that allows him to enumerate the future kings of Tara, an option further highlighted by the gloss in the tale-lists, noted above, i.e. *Fís Chuind Chétchathaig .i. Baili in Scáil*. This ambiguity is not resolved within the text.

4.3 References to *Baile in Scáil* in other texts

BS is quoted and referred to a number of times in various sources. These references are given here in full.

(a) In the tale lists: documented above in **4.2** [date: *c.* 1000].

(b) *LL* 15765-8 [date: eleventh century]:
 Marb iarna rígad don t̑slóg
 Eocho mínglan Mugmed*on*
 ro fírad cid cruth aile
 ro scríbad issin Scálbaile.
 Dead after being made king by the host
 courteous Echu Mugmedón
 it came true in another way
 [as] it was written in the Scálbaile.

(c) *Baile Bricín* (Meyer 1913i, §57) [date: composite; ninth to eleventh centuries]:
 Fri rē Aeda engaig genfius Tibraiti, adbir Baili in Scáil.
 During the reign of Áed Engach, Tipraite will be born, (as) *Baile in Scáil* says.

(d) *Echtra mac nEchdach Mugmedóin* (Ní Dhubhnaigh 2001, 262) [date: eleventh century]
 amail at-fét in Scál Baile .i. Fosgamain Assail, [Donn]ainech Dabaill, Fergal Foltgarb.

13

As the Scálbaile relates, i.e. the fawn of Assal, the brown-faced one of Daball, rough-haired Fergal.

(e) *Echtrae Chormaic* (Stokes 1891, §80) [date: twelfth century?]:
A*ch*t adb*er*aid na h*ec*naidi cach uair notaisbenta taibsi ingnad dona righflathaib anall – am*al* adfaid in Scal do Chund, ₇ am*al* tarfas Tír Thairngiri do Corm*ac* –, *con*idh timtir*ech*t diada tic*ed*h fan samla sin, ₇ *con*ach timthir*ech*t deamnach.
The wise declare that whenever any strange apparition was revealed of old to the royal lords, – as the ghost appeared to Conn, and as the Land of Promise was shewn to Cormac, – it was a divine ministration that used to come in that wise, and not a demoniacal ministration.

(f) NLI MS G 3, fo. 22ra [date of marginal entry unknown; four-teenth / fifteenth-century MS]:
Two quatrains beginning: *Clerig gecha cilli / eol damh a ndogh-enad*; above on the margin is written *.i. baili in sgail*.[14]

(g) *AFM* 773 (i, 378):
I mBuile in Scáil atá an rannsa:
Biaidh co nimbiud accan [accaín] an madan hi Forcaladh.
Ria nDonnchadh Midhe meamhais cath init apail Conghalach.
The following quatrain is in Buile-an-Scail:
There will be increase of lamentation in the morning at Forcaladh.
By Donnchadh of Meath the battle shall be won in which Congalach shall perish.

These references point towards *BS* as having established itself as part of the literary canon in Irish by the end of the Middle Irish period, though their paucity (with respect to the size of the tradition as a whole) may indicate that the story never won for itself a central place in that tradition; the lack of other MS copies of *BS* may point in the same direc-tion.

---

14   I wish to thank Clodagh Ní Dhubhnaigh for bringing this reference to my attention. There does not seem to be any connection between the material on this folio and *BS*.

5. THE MYTHOLOGICAL CONTEXT

Previous commentary on the mythological elements of *BS* is plentiful. It has focussed on issues such as the sovereignty goddess, Lug, the *Lía Fáil* and the Otherworld. This scholarship is ongoing as is witnessed by a recent contribution (Carey, forthcoming), where the supernatural associations of Tara evident in *BS* (among other texts) are examined.

5.1 The sovereignty goddess

The goddess in *BS* sits on a crystal throne in the phantom's abode with a golden crown on her head, wearing a cloak edged with gold. She has a silver vat of red-ale in front of her with a ladle (dispensing vessel) hanging from one handle and a beautiful golden cup from which to drink. The theme of the sovereignty goddess in medieval Irish literature has been much discussed [e.g., Bhreathnach (1982); Breatnach (1953); Doan (1985); Mac Cana (1955-56, 1958-59); McCone (1990, §5.3, §6.5); Ó Cathasaigh (1983, 1989); Trindade (1986)]. Though Sessle (1994), Ní Dhonnchadha (2000, 229-31) and Ní Mhaonaigh (2002, 204) all urge discrimination in the application of the paradigm of the sovereignty goddess, this is not a problem in *BS* as the goddess is explicitly referred to as *flaith hÉrenn* 'the Sovereignty of Ireland'. Herbert has made an interesting contribution to our understanding of the sovereignty goddess in *BS* by pointing to the diminution in her role:

> In this text, it is the king-god, Lug, who instructs his female companion regarding the bestowal of the drink of sovereignty on successive kings. It is his action rather than that of the goddess, therefore, which ultimately designates the ruler. The locus of power has shifted from female to male. In its gender asymmetry the mythic image reveals itself in dialogue with the Irish historical era, when royal rule had become a matter of achievement by male sovereign rather than of assignation by female sovereignty (1992, 269).

The motif of the drink of sovereignty, which the goddess uses to identify future kings, is well known [see, for example, Enright (1996, 260-82) and Scowcroft (1995, 130-7)]. The connection in medieval Irish literature between the dispensing of drink by the goddess and the dispensing of the sovereignty of the territory with which she is linked was first made by Ó

Máille regarding Medb, whose name he explained as meaning 'the intoxicating one' (1927, 144) [see also Thurneysen (1930, 108-10) and (1933)]. O'Rahilly maintained that 'receiving the cup of drink from the goddess, or winning her cup, was tantamount to winning the goddess herself' (1943-6, 16). Thus, this acceptance of a drink from the goddess seems to represent the king's symbolic marriage to his kingdom. These inauguration rites of kingship reflect the importance of the sacred king and concepts of sacral kingship in early Ireland [see Binchy (1958, 134-8) and Dillon (1973)]. This opening part of *BS*, therefore, was not written in a vacuum but was part of a well-established and a well-understood tradition.

5.2 Lug

In *BS* the phantom identifies himself as Lug mac Ethnenn maic Smretha maic Thigernmair[15] maic Fáelad maic Etheuir maic Iríail maic Érimóin maic Míled Espáine. Elsewhere, he is variously called Lug m. Eithnenn (Cethnenn, Deithnend, Eithlend) m. Danann, tracing his heritage back to the eponymous goddess of the Túatha Dé Danann (see *CGH*, p. 676).[16] He is also known as Lug mac Céin and is often given the sobriquet *(sam)ildánach* (see Gray, 1982, 126-7).

The role of the god Lug in Irish literature and tradition has been well documented [see, for example, Chadwick (1935); O'Rahilly (1946, 310-14); MacNeill (1962, 3-10); Ó Riain (1977); Ó Cathasaigh (1983)]. In *Cath Maige Tuired* he takes Núadu's place as king of Tara (Gray, 1982, 42 §74). As Ó Cathasaigh notes, 'in *Baile in Scáil*, he is presented as legitimator of the Dál Cuinn (and hence also of the Uí Néill) kings of Tara' (1989, 31). He further points out that when each of the kings listed will receive the drink of sovereignty from the Sovereignty goddess 'that each of them in turn will be wedded to Lug's consort, and in that important sense take the place of Lug, and be his surrogate for the time being in the kingship of Tara' (1983, 12).

There is a certain ambiguity in the text which allows one to treat the horse-rider who casts at Conn and his *fili* in *BS* as a separate character to the phantom (see Carey 1987, 4). However, it would seem legitimate to

---

15   His name is given in Harl. as Lug mac Ethlend maic Thigernmais. For the possible significance of this variant form, see Murray (2003).

16   On the possible lateness of the formation of the name Túatha Dé Danann, however, see Carey (1981).

identify him too as Lug.[17] At the end of §5 we are told: *Anaid an marcach din díbrucud ₇ feraid fáilti fri Conn ₇ con-gart leis dia threiph,* 'The rider ceased casting and he welcomed Conn and he called him to his house'. In §6, when Conn and his poet enter the house, they see the beautiful girl (who is identified in §8 as *flaith hÉrenn*) and we are told: *Et co n-accatar a scál fadeissin isin taig ara ciund inna rígsudiu* 'And they saw the phantom himself in the house, waiting for them on his throne'. Here the word *fadeissin* ('himself') seems to imply that they had already seen the phantom in his role as horse-rider. The image of a horse-rider approaching out of the mist is perfect for one who is presented as a phantom. If identifying the horse-rider with the phantom is rejected, then we are left with the problem of the identity of the rider and why the phantom is in the house of the horseman instead of his own.

5.3 Máel, Bloc ₇ Bluicne

Conn Cétchathach's three druids in *BS* §1 are named as Máel, Bloc and Bluicne. The names Bloc and Bluicne appear as those of two flagstones next to the *Lía Fáil* in Tara in *De Síl Chonairi Móir*. In this tale, the stones open up to let the chariot through if the driver is destined to hold the kingship of Tara. The text also reads (Gwynn 1912, 134 ll. 27-9):

> Inti nad aurimeth flaith Temrach, ni airslaictis riam na da liaic .i. Bloc ₇ Blugne. Ise mod ticed hochair lame eturru.
> The one who should not receive the sovereignty of Tara, the two flagstones would not open up before him, i.e. Bloc and Blugne. It is the way the side of the hand would go beween them.

This confusion in the literary tradition, regarding whether the names represent stones or druids, is also to be seen in *Dindgnai Temrach* (Stokes 1894, 282-6 §21 [= *LL* 3840-2]):

> Ataat teora clocha beca i tæb Ratha na Senad tuaid .i. teora clocha roláit[h]i forsna dru[id]ib, hit é a n-anmand .i. Móel ₇ Blocc ₇ Bluicne. Moel soir ₇ Blocc fodes ₇ Bluicne fotuaidh.
> Beside the Fort of the Synods to the north stand three small

---

17   This ties in with the traditon noted in *Aided Con Culainn* that 'there were three horsemen who first rode in Ireland *ar srian aeneich* "on the rein of a single horse" … [including] … *Lug Lámfada* while killing the Fomorians at the Battle of Moytura' (Ní Chatháin 1991, 127).

stones, to wit, the stones that were set over the wizards. These are their names: *Moel* and *Blocc* and *Bluicne*. Moel to the east, Blocc to the south and Bluicne to the north.

Another connection between *BS* and this text is the glossing of *Fál* in *BS* §4 with *fo ail .i. ail fo rig* as this exact phrase is used to gloss the word *fál* in *Dindgnai Temrach* (Stokes 1894, 281 §13 [= *LL* 3822-3]). The ambiguity regarding the names Máel, Bloc and Bluicne is also to be observed in the metrical *dindshenchas* of Tara (*MD* i, 18, 73-6). Here it is stated:

> Ó lecht ind abaic sin síar
> Mael, Blouc, Bluicne, borb a cíall,
> forru atáit na tri clocha
> dusfarlaicc Mál mór-Macha.
> Westward from the grave of this dwarf
> are Mael, Bloc, and Bluicne – foolish their wisdom!
> over them are the three stones[18]
> that the Prince of great Macha flung.

It seems from this that the druids may have been changed into stone, or that the three great stones may have usurped their functions, because their wisdom was foolish.

There seems to be no way of assessing which tradition concerning Máel, Bloc and Bluicne came first, i.e. whether their names in origin represent flagstones or druids. For example, the opening section of *BS* (§§1-9) and *De Síl Chonairi Móir* appear to be roughly contemporaneous in date, i.e. from the late O.Ir. period, and yet they present opposing points of view.[18a] Even if one could separate all the texts cited above into chronological order, this would still not be sufficient to demonstrate to conclusion which of them respresents the earlier tradition.

5.4 The *Lía Fáil*

Although, the nature and function of the *Lía Fáil* has been the subject of much debate, no consensus has yet been reached on its role in Irish

---

18   This could also be translated as 'named for them are the three stones'.

18a   Having recently had a chance to briefly examine the edition of this text by M.A. O'Brien ([c. 1954], 1-8) from TCD MS H. 2. 7, it appears to be older than the opening section of *BS* (possibly an eight-century text?)

literature. Ó Broin (1990) contains a note of much of the work done on the subject along with a select guide to some of the sources while Ó Cearúil (2003, 75-81) succintly contextualises the part played by the *Lía Fáil* in Irish traditions concerning the end of the world. *De Síl Chonairi Móir* (Gwynn, 1912) is another early text in which this stone is said to acclaim the true king of Tara. In *BS* §4, Cessarnn, the *fili*, interprets the roar of *Fál* for Conn. He tells him: *'Ro gési íarum Fál fad' chossaib-siu', ol in file, '₇ do-rairngert; a llín ngémind ro géisi, is é lín ríg bias ditt' síl-su for hÉrinn co brád'* ('Then Fál cried out under your feet', said the poet, 'and prophesied; the amount of roars it gave is the number of kings of your seed that will be over Ireland forever'). As Carey (1999) has recently argued, this tradition in *BS* that the *Lía Fáil* was a flagstone may in fact be correct and other traditions which equate the *Lía Fáil* with the pillar stone at Tara (nicknamed *Bod Fhearghusa*) may in fact be secondary.

With regard to the role of the *Lía Fáil* in *BS*, Ó Broin argues that 'through an otherworld interpreter Flathius Érenn supplies the actual names of the kings of his seed who will succeed Conn. The stone and the lady deliver almost the same prophetic message, and it is difficult not to see them as one, both goddesses' (1990, 396). This does not appear to be the best interpretation. Relegating Lug to the role of 'otherworld interpreter' is to argue against the dominant role that he occupies in our text. It also goes against the strong argument made by Herbert (see **5.1**) regarding the lessening of the role of the sovereignty goddess in *BS*.

Within the framework of *BS*, it is hard to see the *Lía Fáil* as a goddess. Rather, it seems that its role is as the primary legitimator of the kingship of Conn and his descendants. The role assigned to Lug (and to a lesser extent to the sovereignty goddess) is to confirm this legitimisation and to provide the details and names that Cessarnn does not supply. Therefore, it can be argued that the *Lía Fáil* usurps the functions of both Lug and *flaith hÉrenn* in our text.

It is worth noting that all of the descendants of Conn are legitimised three times in *BS*. Firstly, by the roars of the *Lia Fáil*; secondly, by being named by Lug and thirdly by receiving the drink of sovereignty from *flaith hÉrenn*. Conn, himself, is legitimised a fourth time by being referred to as a king by Cessarnn and the horse-rider (Lug) in §5. This repeated legitimisation of the kings of the Dál Cuinn (and hence also of the Uí Néill) ties in well with Herbert's thesis that *BS* is 'a statement of advocacy on behalf of the Uí Néill dynasty' (1992, 270).

Fálmag ('The Plain of Fál') is also used twice in *BS* (§§31, 39) to represent Ireland. This is a common and well documented use of the word *Fál* (see *OnomG* 406 s.n.). However, it may be worth noting from the use of *Mag Fáil* ('The Plain of Fál') in §13 that, in the context of *BS*, this plain could be interpreted as the plain around Tara, i.e. the plain around the *Lía Fáil*. In §43, in relation to the reign of Áed Aldán, one of the phrases used is *Fálguba Ulad* which I have translated as 'Royal-lamentation of the Ulaid'. However, the *fál* part of this compound could be taken as referring to the *Lía Fáil* though this would leave us with a problem of translation – 'Mourning Fál of the Ulaid?'. The last reference to *Fál* is in the final paragraph (§65) where it is mentioned of Flann Cinuch that: *Roithfid Fál (.i. cloch) find fo thrí* ('He will set bright Fál (i.e. stone) in motion thrice').

5.5 The Otherworld

The Otherworld of medieval Irish literature has received much scholarly attention [for example, Carey (1982; 1987; 1989; 1991); Chadwick (1967); Mac Cana (1976); Ó Cathasaigh (1977-78); Sims-Williams (1990)]. The locations, terminology, parallels and motifs associated with the Otherworld have been examined in depth. The stories of halls which are reached at night or through a great mist and which later disappear are part of this tradition (Carey 1982, 41 n.22). The function of mist in obscuring/revealing the Otherworld has been remarked upon by Carey who notes that 'the barrier here is not one of distance traversed but of vision obscured' (1987, 5).

Building on this, it may be that this form of introduction to the Otherworld, through a great mist, is used in our text as a balance between obscuring and revealing. The mist obscures Tara but is used to reveal the Otherworld.[19] The mist obscures the *Lía Fáil* which could not relate the names of the future kings of Tara but it reveals Lug who fulfills this function. The mist obscures the rampart of Tara which Conn is ready to defend against the Fomorians and the *síd*-dwellers but it reveals Lug whose prophecy is an assurance to Conn that Ireland will not be overrun by them. Conversely, when the mist disappears the 'real world' is revealed once more while the Otherworld is now obscured.

---

19 Carey (forthcoming) shows how *BS* (among other texts) associates Tara with the supernatural in important ways.

The idea that Conn and his *fili* have foreknowledge of their visit to the Otherworld seems to be implied in *BS*. Cessarnn (exceptionally called *druí*, §4, instead of *fili*) tells Conn that he is not the one destined to list the future kings of Tara for him. This suggests that someone who is destined/empowered to relate these names to Conn will soon meet with him; the journeying of Conn and his *fili* to the Otherworld then comes as no surprise. When Conn finds himself surrounded by the mist, he immediately seems to sense that something very unusual is happening and that he and Cessarnn have moved into unknown lands (*hi tíri anetargnaide*). Thus, once again we are unsurprised when the horseman appears out of the mist. This (implied) foreknowledge seems to me to be a way of stating that the descendants of Conn (and hence the Uí Néill) always know that sovereignty awaits them and that the appearance of Lug and *flaith hÉrenn* offering sovereignty never comes as a surprise. It serves as a device to copper-fasten the stated entitlement of Conn's descendants to be kings of Tara.

5.6 Flann Cinuch and the *roth rámach*

The last king prophesied in *BS* is Flann Cinuch who in other sources is variously called *cinuch / ginach* ('voracious') and *cithach* ('showery'). He appears in a number of other Irish tales as the last prophesied king of Ireland:

i.   In the Book of Fenagh (see **6.2** below);
ii. In *Baile Moling* in *YBL* col. 340;
iii. In a tract on the *roth rámach* in *Leabhar Breac*, p. 242b *i*;
iv. As a gloss in *BC*, though this identification is not certain (see Murray, forthcoming: i);
v.   In TCD H.1.10 (MS 1284), fo. 158b (see **6.2** below).

In numbers iii and v, the arrival of the *roth rámach* ('rowing wheel') occurs at the end of the world, during Flann's reign.[20] This is summarised by O'Curry (1861, 401-2) from TCD H.1.10 as follows:

> This 'rowing wheel' was to be a ship containing one thousand beds, and one thousand men in each bed; alike would this strange

---

20   In *MD* iv, 154.123, the phrase *roth Fáil Flaind* is used.

ship sail on sea and on land, nor would it furl its sails until it was wrecked by the Pillar-stone of *Cnámhchoill*. They would then be met by the brave chief of *Cnámhchoill*, who would cut them all off, so that not one of them should ever cross the sea again. After this there would come a fleet to *Inbher Domhnann*.

Much of this information is paralleled in §65 of *BS*:

i.   Flann Cinuch is called *tigḟlaith hÉrenn,* 'the last ruler of Ireland';

ii.   The invasion at *Inber Domnann* (Malahide Bay) is alluded to;

iii. *Cnámchaill* is mentioned as a place of great slaughter;

iv. *Roithḟid Fál (.i. cloch) find fo thrí* ('He will set bright Fál (i.e. stone) in motion thrice') may be a reference to the *roth rámach* ('rowing wheel') being set in motion during his reign;

v.   In both, the invaders are defeated.

It is clear that the same prophetic tradition runs through both texts.[20a]

At the end of the poem in TCD H.1.10, Colum Cille proposes to leave certain relics to the men of Ireland. There may be a reference to this at the very end of §65 of *BS* where it is stated: *Regaid éc aitti íar sein di chretair chréissin hi Temuir,* 'Death will proceed then from the relic of the believer in Tara'.

6. THE HISTORICAL FRAMEWORK

BS contains a large amount of information regarding those listed as kings of Tara from Conn Cétchathach onwards. The historical kings of Tara are listed in §§18-57 (with the intrusion of Colla Úais in §19).

6.1 The kings of history

In Appendix 1, a table comparing the order and length of reigns of the historical kings given in *BS* with the list compiled by F.J. Byrne (*NHI* 9, 189-94) has been drawn up. The reigns of a number of kings of Tara have been ignored by *BS*. These are:

20a   This material has been the subject of an in-depth study by Ó Cearúil (2000, 259-96).

1. Coirpre mac Néill.
2. Báetán mac Ninnedo.
3. Colmán Rímid mac Báetáin.
4. Máel Cobo mac Áedo.
5. Cellach mac Máele Cobo ⁊ Conall Cóel mac Máele Cobo.
6. Cináed mac Írgalaig (though his death in the battle of Druimm Corcáin is briefly mentioned in §42).

Báetán mac Ninnedo, Máel Cobo mac Áedo, Cellach mac Máele Cobo and Conall Cóel mac Máele Cobo were Cenél Conaill kings, Cináed mac Írgalaig belonged to Síl nÁedo Sláine and Colmán Rímid mac Báetáin to Cenél nEógain. Some of these kings had substantial reigns – Báetán (14 years), Colmán Rímid (6 years in joint sovereignty with Áed Sláine), Máel Cobo (3 years), Cellach and Conall (14 and 16 years) and Cináed (4 years). The situation regarding Coirpre mac Néill is unclear. In all cases, the claims of these royal lines to the kingship of Tara had petered out long before the composition of *BS*.

The joint reign of Díarmait mac Áedo Sláine and Blathmac mac Áedo Sláine is treated as two separate reigns in *BS* while the separate reigns of Fogartach mac Néill and Congal Cinn Magair mac Fergusso are merged as a joint reign. Díarmait, Blathmac and Fogartach were Síl nÁedo Sláine kings and Congal belonged to Cenél Conaill. Correct length of reigns listed in *BS* include:

1. Díarmait mac Cerbaill (§27).
2. Forggus mac Muirchertaig ⁊ Domnall Ilchelgach mac Muirchertaig (§28).
3. Áed Allán (alias Uaridnach) mac Domnaill (§31).
4. Fínsnechtae Fledach mac Dúnchado (§36).
5. Fergal mac Máele Dúin (§41).
6. Domnall Midi mac Murchado (§44).
7. Níall Frossach mac Fergaile (§45).
8. All the kings from §§48-56 with the exception of Congalach (§55).

Length of reigns not given in *BS*:

1. Muirchertach Mac Erca (§24).
2. Diarmait Daithi (§35).

23

6.2 The kennings

From §51 to the end (apart from §§53, 56, 60 & 65), the kings are first referred to by vague kennings before their names are given, often in an incorporated gloss.[21] Up to §58, historical personages are being referred to; from §59 to the end, the names of the kings do not allow for positive identification with any historical persons.

Another version of these kennings is to be found in the Book of Fenagh in a poem attributed to Caillín, son of Níata. After listing the kings of history down to Rúaidrí Úa Conchobair (with a gap between 1022 and 1121), the poem continues as follows (Hennessy 1875, 60-3):

> Derg donn, Aed foltlebair cas,
>   In lam fada 'san cliab glas;
>   Crissalach, sraptine naill;
>   Osgamuin donn oinech Dabaill.
>
> Osnadach Uisnig cen gai
>   Iartru Ailig ar aon chai;
>   Foltgarb, is Fland cithach seng;
>   Ard ri degenach Erenn.
>
> Derg-donn; comely Aedh of the long hair;
>   The Long Hand and the Gray-chest;
>   Crissalach; another Sraptinè;
>   The brown-faced Osgamuin of Dabhall.
>
> Osnadach of Uisnech, without falsehood;
>   Iartru of Ailech in the same track;
>   Foltgarb, and Flann Cithach the slender
>   The last arch-king of Ireland

BS makes no mention of the first three kings listed here – Derg Donn, Áed Foltlebair Cas or In Lám Fata. However, the two texts have the following in common:

---

21   There are also kennings present in §35 & §41; for kennings in later Irish material, see Knott (1960) 57-61.

Book of Fenagh	Baile in Scáil
i. cliab glas.	i. clíabhchless – Flaithbertach (§58).
ii. crissalach.	ii. crissalach – Donnchad (§54).
iii. sraptine.	iii. sroiphtine – Máel Sechlainn (§57).
iv. osgamuin.	iv. ossgamain – Murchad (§59).
v. donn oinech Dabaill.	v. dondainech Dabaill – Áed Engach (§62).
vi. osnadach Uisnig.	vi. ossnadach Uisnig – Cerball (§63).
vii. iartru Ailig.	vii. iartrú Ailig – Fergal foltgarb (§64).
viii. foltgarb.	viii. iartrú Ailig – Fergal foltgarb (§64).
ix. Fland cithach.	ix. Fland Cinuch (§65).

It is obvious that both sets of information are part of the one tradition. Whether or not the Book of Fenagh got this information from *BS* is difficult to ascertain – it is more probable (considering the differences) that they derive separately from the same tradition. This tradition is also represented in the prophetic poem addressed to Baoithín at Iona (beginning *Eisd a Bhaoithīn Bhuain*) and ascribed to Colum Cille in TCD H.1.10 (MS 1284), ff. 157-159a18 (discussed above **5.6**).[22] This poem mentions *Aedh Engach* (158a13), *cliabhghlas* (158b4) and *Flann Ciothach* (158b10).

Three of the kennings have also been borrowed directly from *BS* into *Echtra mac nEchdach Mugmedóin* (see note to l. 149). The kennings in question are *ossgamain Assail* §59, *dondainech Dabaill* §62 and *Fergal foltgarb* §64 (text printed in **4.3**(d) above). In *Baile Bercháin* (Hudson 1996, 36-8) there are references to *in lámfada* (§§88-95) and *in clíabglas* (§§95-7)[23] while in *Baile Fíndachta* (Meyer, 1921, 26-7) mention is made of *in donn derg*. Sections of this tradition seem to have been quite productive; for example, Áed Engach gets repeated mention in Irish literature and his important recurring role has been thoroughly discussed by Ó Buachalla (1989) while Flann Cinuch is regularly presented as the last king of Ireland.

---

22 There are other copies in Bodleian Library, Oxford MS Laud Misc. 615, pp. 82-5 and TCD H.4.13 (MS 1354) fo. 210 and it has also been published in O'Kearney (1856), to which I have not had access.

23 Hudson (1996, 187-8) believes *in lámfada* to refer to Flaithbertach Úa Néill and that the *clíabglas ón Claítig* is a reference to the unknown last king of Ireland in whose reign the Antichrist will come; in *BS* (§58) *clíabchless Clóitige* is glossed Flaithbertach and is taken to refer to Flaithbertach Úa Néill while the epithet *lámfada* is not attested.

6.3 The battles in *Baile in Scáil*

One of the many interesting facets of *BS* is the great list of more than one hundred and eighty battles which the text provides. The main problem regarding the listed battles is that in approximately half of the cases there is no information about them given in the text. Many of these battles, however, are known from other sources though some are difficult to identify. Even when battles are identifiable, the lack of information about them in *BS* means that frequently these identifications do not add much to our understanding of the text. It is obvious that the compiler of the original text [**X**] had access to a great list of battles, especially regarding the kings of pre-history – over half the battles listed in *BS* belong to this period. The number of battles which so far have evaded identification is surprising. Also surprising is the number of battles listed as having taken place during the reigns of Conn Cétchathach (§10) and Art mac Cuind (§11), which are actually the names of later historical battles but which seem to have been pressed into service to recount the exploits of the kings of pre-history.

The battles in the reign of Cormac úa Cuind in *BS* are listed in the exact same order as they appear in *AFM, ATig.* and *AU* (see Appendix 2). The relevant metrical source behind *BS* seems to be the forerunner of this common list as many of the battles form part of the poetry of the text. It is no surprise that a king as famous as Cormac would have a stock list of battles in metrical form associated with him. It is a surprise, however, to see how consistently the information was transmitted in so many different texts.

A significant portion (one-sixth) of the battle-list contained in *BS* is also to be found in the poems in *LL* attributed to Flann Mainistrech,[24] especially two of the four poems about the battles waged by Cenél nEógain of Ailech (*Ascnam ni seol sadal, LL* 23483-574 = MacNeill (1913) 48-54; *Aní doronsat do chalmu, LL* 23575-712 = MacNeill (1913) 58-70). Other battle-lists examined also help throw light on our text; for example, eight of the battles from the *bóraime* battle-list compiled by Ó Buachalla (1961) are named in *BS* and fourteen battles waged by Conall Gulban, listed in Hennessy (1875, 326-30), are also in *BS*.

---

24 *LL* 23344-24196; ed. and trans. MacNeill (1913). These poems were re-edited in Pődör (1999).

6.4 The arrival of Patrick

In *BS*, under the reign of Lóegaire mac Néill,[25] the arrival of Patrick to Ireland is foretold with the words *ticfa táilcend* and it is glossed *.i. Pátraic* and a few lines later in a superscript the words *flaith him bachla* ('a king surrounded by crosiers') are used in connection with the future coming of Patrick. These exact phrases occur in *Bethu Phátraic* (Mulchrone, 1939, 22) and the second time the phrase *ticfat tailcind* is used therein, it is glossed *.i. Baili Cuinn dixit* in the British Library MS Egerton 93 recension. Indeed, there is a somewhat similar prophecy in *BC*, first noted by O'Curry (1861, 386), but these exact words are to be found only in *BS*.[26] Interestingly, Egerton 93 is one of the two MSS which contains *Bethu Phátraic*, the main one is Rawl.

---

25 This passage (§21 in Rawl; §20 in Harl.) has been used by Carney (1961, 11-13) in support of his arguments about the arrival of St Patrick to Ireland; Binchy (1962, 101-2) rejects his conclusions.

26 The *ticfa táilcend* formulation is to be found in Latin (*Adueniet ascicaput*) in Bieler (1979, 76). A similar early prophecy about the arrival of St Patrick is present in *Echtrae Chonnlai* (McCone, 2000, 122; 175-8). The relevant lines read: *Ar is bec ro:saig for mesu artrag máir fírián connil muinteraib ilib adamraib* ('It is in a little while that the Great High King's righteous (and) decent one will reach your judgements with many wondrous followers'). These lines are discussed in depth by McCone (2000) 84-8 (iv.15).

27

6.5 The *Banshenchas* element in *Baile in Scáil*[27]

Between §§47-57 the names of some of the kings' mothers have been inserted,[28] mostly as glosses.[29] They are:

§47 Dúnflaith ingen Flaithbertaig maic Loingsich (mother of Áed Ingor, i.e. Áed Oirdnide).

§§48&49 No mothers are given for Conchobor mac Donnchada[30] and Níall Caille.[31]

§50 Aróc ingen ríg Fer Cúl (mother of Máel Sechnaill).[32]

§51 Gormlaith ingen Donnchada (mother of Áed Olach, i.e. Áed Finnlíath).[33]

§52 Flann ingen Dúngaili ríg Osraide (mother of Flann Sinna).

§53 Máel Mairi ingen Chináeda maic Alpín ríg Albban (mother of Níall Glúndub).

§54 Máel Febail ingen Flaind maic Conaing (mother of Donnchad Donn).[34]

---

27 The information regarding the kings' mothers in *BS* is to be found in the three different published versions of the *Banshenchas* edited by Margaret Dobbs – (1) the metrical version in *LL* (Dobbs, 1930, 288-315); (2) the prose version from the Book of Lecan (Dobbs, 1931, 163-200) and (3) the prose version in the Book of Uí Maine (Dobbs, 1931, 200-234). For information on the manuscript tradition of the *Banshenchas*, see Ní Bhrolcháin (1982).

28 It is interesting that the emphasis here is on the kings' mothers as Connon (2000) has proposed that it is a list of kings' mothers, rather than their wives, which ultimately lies behind the large number of the queens of Tara cited in the *Banshenchas*. It would seem that this information in *BS* either derives directly from the *Banshenchas* or from some list of mothers of kings of Tara which was utilised in its compilation.

29 The extent of glossing increases substantially from §50 onwards.

30 In *BS* it is mentioned that his mother was of the Connachta. Conchobor's mother's name is given in Dobbs (1931, 186) as Fuirseach ingen Chongail of Dál nAraide, though this may be a late addition as she is not mentioned in four of the other MS sources of the *Banshenchas*.

31 Medb ingen Indrechtaig maic Muiredaig [rí Durlais] is named as his mother and the mother of Flann [flaith Brega] in Dobbs (1930, 310). She is named as his mother solely in Dobbs (1931, 225) and as the mother of Domnall [rí Ailig] in Dobbs (1931, 186). Anne Connon informs me, however, that there is some confusion regarding the certainty of this relationship.

32 This gloss has already been incorporated as part of the narrative.

33 His father's name (Níall Caille) is also given in the same gloss.

34 He is referred to as *crissalach* and his name is given as Codail Dond in *BS*.

§55 Lígach ingen Flaind (mother of Congalach Cnogba).[35]
§56 No mother is given for Domnall [úa Néill].[36]
§57 Dúnflaith ingen Muirchertaig (mother of Máel Sechnaill).

The information on the mothers of the kings listed above is correct except for one name. Donnchad Donn's mother's name (§54) was Gormlaith ingen Flaind maic Conaing not Máel Febail ingen Flaind maic Conaing. The only Máel Febail to be found in the *Banshenchas* is Máel Febail ingen Fáelacháin m. Goriatha (Dobbs, 1931, 199 & 231), mother of Cú Faifne mac Congalaig, king of Uí Failgi (†1130). It has been suggested to me, by Anne Connon, that the mistake regarding Máel Febail as the mother of Donnchad Donn may be explained as follows – Donnchad's father (Flann Sinna) had no wife called Máel Febail but he did have a sister of that name and it seems that the glossator confused them here. An obituary for 'Maelfebhail, ingen Maoilsechlainn' is recorded in *AFM* 884 (i, 536). It would seem, therefore, that the names of the mothers of Conchobor mac Donnchada, Níall Caille and Domnall úa Néill were not added to *BS* because there was some confusion regarding their identities.

6.6 Conclusions

It seems clear, based on the assembled evidence, that *BS* was a propaganda document for the Uí Néill. This is further supported, for example, by the fact that it appears that Brian Bóruma was absent from *BS* originally and that the material concerning him is a later addition. Though originally composed in the ninth century, it seems that it was the eleventh-century compiler who fashioned *BS* specifically as a Cenél nEógain text (Thurneysen (1936) 215-6). This interpretation is supported by the following points: (1) There are a substantial number of Cenél nEógain victories listed in the text; (2) In §58 there is a claim to the kingship of Tara for Flaithbertach Úa Néill, king of Ailech; (3) Of the final list of kings (§§60-65), four are stated as coming from Cenél nEógain. The re-use of this propaganda text in the early eleventh century is unsurprising,

---

35 His name in *BS* is first given as Congal Cerna though he is later referred to as Congalach.

36 His mother's name is given in Dobbs (1930, 313) and (1931, 188) as Gormlaith ingen Chuilenáin maic Máele Brigte. Thurneysen (1936, 214) mistakenly suggests that Rawl. does not read *.i. Uí Ertuile* but *.ī. Uí Ertuile* (i.e. *ingen Uí Ertuile*).

for at this period in which Uí Néill claims to the over-kingship of Ireland came under serious threat for the first time, 'the mythic past provided a defensive strategy in a threatening present' (Herbert, 1992, 272).

7. EDITORIAL METHOD

The edition offered here is based on the text available in Rawl. with lacunae filled from Harl. when available. Italics are not used to indicate contractions in the final edition as full diplomatic editions of both MS texts are printed immèdiately after the Notes (with the sole addition of superscript paragraph numbers for ease of consultation). In the diplomatic editions *all* expansions are marked by italics. The extent of editorial intervention (i.e. addition and removal of punctuation, capitals, lenition and length marks) may be gauged by reference to the diplomatic edition from Rawl.; all other departures from this diplomatic text are explicitly noted. To facilitate consultation, long dashes are used in the edition to mark off lengths of reigns and lists of epithets are generally grouped in twos or threes, punctuated by commas.

Many parts of the translation are uncertain and these are highlighted by asterisks. Occasionally, no translation has been attempted; these sections have been marked thus: [...]. Words enclosed by square brackets in the translation are not written explicitly in the Irish text but are implicitly understood. Many of these examples include 'future-tense' translations of 'present-tense' verbs.[37] Common placenames are anglicised in the translation (e.g. Tara, the Alps, the Boyne) while the rest are left untranslated. For ease of reference, the paragraphing follows that laid down in Meyer (1918) and Pokorny (1921)

7.1 Scribal orthography

There are a number of unusual orthographic features utilised by the Rawl. scribe which are worthy of mention here (see Thurneysen, 1936, 218). Sometimes he wrote 'fh' for 'f', e.g. *ar-brisfhi* §12, *fhássach* §13, *firfhit* §13, *fhessair* §14, *du-fhuit* §18. He also often placed the *asper spiritus* above the letter 'f' instead of the *punctum delens*. This feature is marked in the diplomatic text from Rawl. with an italicised *h* (e.g. f*h*ile,

---

37   It is a feature of *BS* that the future narrative tense is often supplied by verbs in the present indicative. This is also the case with regard to other prophetic materials; cf. Jackson's reading of *Immacallam in dá Thuarad* (1934, 68).

§5; dergf*h*laith, §9 etc.) but has been replaced by a *punctum delens* in the edited text.

Another feature of Rawl. is the marking of vowel-length by doubling, (e.g. *laa* §1, *sii* §8 etc.; for further examples of this practice, see *SnaG* III, §2.8). In many cases where *ii* is written for *í*, an acute accent may also be written on one or both vowels (e.g. *ríí, thríi, líí, noíi*, etc.). These have been restored as *ii* in the edited text. The acute slanting stroke on the vowel in these cases may just be a way of marking the minims to distinguish the vowel and not for marking vowel-length. This feature is not uncommon in Rawl. (e.g. *daíl* §9, *aín* §13, *cruaíd* §15). There are a small number of examples of *e* written for *ai*, viz. *rúed* (for *rúaid*) §46 and *búed* (twice for *búaid*) §47.

Rawl. frequently replaces final unstressed *–e* with *–i*: e.g. *sithi* §1, *cluchi* §4, *meti* §6, *aislingi* §9, etc. (many of these exx. are unsupported by Harl.). Occasionally Rawl. represents unstressed final *–e* by *–iu*.[38] Examples include: *bluiccniu* §1, *laithiu* §3, *cath chinn tiriu* §10, *cath mibthiniu* §10, *cethri catha i clairiu* §10, *cath cuiliu caichir* §13, *cath fri cláriu* §57. Final *–e* has been restored in these cases. Rawl. also has frequent recourse to the ligature 'æ'; its use, however, seems to be a stylistic rather than a linguistic feature. It is utilised, for example, to represent (i) the diphthong: *fælad, sægal* §7, *mælcend* §13 / *chadræ* §10, *-fæth* §16; (ii) final ae: *damasnæ, torcasnæ* §8; (iii) final a: *flescæ* §9, *machæ* §10; (iv) final ai: *bliadnæ* §34; (v) final i: *nDaigræ* §51. By contrast, Harl. uses the ligature only once – §6 *fo octæ* (Rawl. *foa ochtaig*). In the edition, the ligature is preserved throughout except in the case of the diphthong which is printed *áe* and in circumstances where its removal is deemed necessary (the original reading is then given in footnotes).

---

38 Harl. has examples of unstressed final *–i* being replaced by *–iu*, viz. *iliu* §21 and *berriu* §39. The replacing of unstressed final *–e* or *–i* by *–iu* is an orthographic feature evident in other texts from Harl., e.g. *Baile Bricín* (Meyer, 1913i) and *Cath Maige Tuired* (Gray, 1982).

31

Note: Liam Breatnach's article on words ending in a stressed vowel in Early Irish (*Ériu* 53, 133-42) was published too late to allow for modification of the edited text (words affected include *de, so, ille, amni*). It is interesting to note that of the more than fifty examples of the prep. *di* + suff. pron. 3rd sg. m./n., two of these are marked long in Rawl. (*dé,* §§19 & 20).

EDITION OF *BAILE IN SCÁIL*

INCIPIT DI BAILE IN SCÁIL INSO AR ṠLICHT ṠENLIBUIR DUIB DÁ LEITHI .I. COMARPA PÁTRAIC

1. Laa ro buí Cond i Temraich íar ndíth dona rígaib at-raracht matin
moch for [rígr]aith[1] na Temrach ría turcbáil gréine[2] ₇ a trí druid ríam .i.
Máel ₇ Bloc ₇ Bluicne; Eochaid ₇ Corbb ₇ Cessarnd in ḟilid[3] ₇ Cond fade-
issin. Fodég at-raiged-som cach día in lín sin arna ragabtais fir ṡithi *uel*
Fomoiri for hÉrinn cen airegud.   5
2. In dúa dia ndécad do grés co fúair cloich and ara chiund foa chosaib.
For-ling in cloich íarum ₇ saltrais fuirri ₇ géisis an chloch foa chosaib co
closs fon Temraig hule ₇ fo Bregmag.
3. ₇ is and sin ro íarfacht Cond din ḟilid cid ro géisi in chloch ₇ cía ainm
₇ can do-ralad ₇ cid no regad ₇ cid frisa táraill Temraig. Is and sin as-pert   10
in file fris ní sluindfed dóu co cenn .l. laithe[4] ₇ treissi fair. In tan íarum
ba lán ind árim sin ro íarfacht Conn a ḟrithisi dond ḟilid, ₇ ro buí-side icc
scrútan co n-écetar a eochra éccsi dóu.
4. "Fál (.i. fo ail .i. ail fo ríg) ém", ol an fili "a hainm na cloche[5] ₇ Inis
Fáil asa torlad ₇ is i Temraig tíre Fáil fo-ruirmed. Tír Tailten hi tairiss hí   15
co bráth ₇ iss ed tír in sein bas óenach cluchi dot' chlaind-siu céin bes
flaithius hi Temraig. Ocus a llá ndédenach di ṡechtmain óenaich Tailten,
flaith ná faigbi, is trú issin blíadain sin. Ro gési íarum Fál fad' chossaib-
siu", ol in file, "₇ do-rairngert; a llín ngémind ro géisi, is é lín ríg bias ditt'
ṡíl-su for hÉrinn co brád." "Atta-féid dam amal sodain", ol Conn. "Ní   20
dam ro thocad a rád fritt", ol in druí.
5. A mbátar and íarum co n-accatar cíaig móir impu cona fetatar
cía do-chótar ar méid in dorcha dus-fánic. Co cúalatar trethan in[6]
marcaig ara cend. "Mór maircc dún", for Cond, "má run-fucca

Title: Rawl. – hsenlib*uir* / coa*r*pa.
1   Rawl. – [...]aith; Harl. – ríraith.
2   Rawl. – gr*é*ni; Harl. – gré*i*ne.
3   Rawl. – mæl ₇ blouc ₇ bluiccniu. Eoch*aid* ₇ corbb ₇ cessarnd in fil*id*; Harl. – maol bloc
       bluicne. et a trii fil*id* .i. ethain corb cesarn.
4   Rawl. – laithiu; Harl. – laithi.
5   Rawl. – clocha; Harl. – cl*oche*.
6   Rawl. – trechan an; Harl – trethan i*n*.

33

25 in cheó-sa hi tíri anetargnaide." La sodain do-léci in marcach[7] trí
haurchuru forru ⁊ is traidiu dus-fánic int erchor dédenuch *quam* in
toísiuch.[8] "Is do guin ríg", ol in file, "cip hé díbercess Conn hi Temair."
Anaid an marcach[9] din díbrucud ⁊ feraid fáilti fri Conn ⁊ con-gart leis
dia threiph.
30 **6.** Do-cótar íarum ass conda-rala assa mag ⁊ bile n-órda ann. Tech foa
ochtaig findruine and .x. traigid .xx. a mét. Lotar íarum issa tech co
n-accatar ingen maccthacht i cathaír glanidi ⁊ barr órdai fora mullach ⁊
brat co srethaib di ór impe. Dabach arcait co cethraib cernaib órdaib ara
bélaib, lán di dergḟlaith, escra óir ara óu. Airideog di ór ara bélaib.[10] *Et*
35 co n-accatar a scál fadeissin isin taig ara ciund inna rígṡudiu. Ocus ropu
mór a delgnaide, ba dethbir són ar ní fríth hi Temraig ríam fer a méti
nach a chaíme ar áille a delba n[ach a] chrotha ⁊ ara inganti.
7. Fri[s-gar]t-sidi dóib íarum ⁊ as-[bert]. "Nímda scál-sa [⁊ nímda]
aurdrach ⁊ is [dom' uirdercus dúib] íar m[bás do-deoch]od ⁊ is de ṡíl
40 Á[daim dom ⁊] is hé mo ṡlonnud, [Lug mac Eth]nen[11] maic Smretha
maic Thigernmair maic Fáelad maic Etheuir maic Iríail maic Érimóin
maic Míled Espáine. Et is dó do-deochad-sa co n-écius duit-siu sáegal do
ḟlatha ⁊ cacha flatha bias húait hi Temraig co brád."
8. Et ba sii ind ingen boí isin[12] taig ara cind flaith hÉrenn ⁊ ba sí do-bert
45 díthait do Chunn .i. damasnæ ⁊ torcasnæ. Cethair traigid fichet fott in
damasnai, ocht traigid eter a thúaim ⁊ talmain. Dá thraig déuc fott in
torcasnai ⁊ cóic thraigid eter a thúaim ⁊ talmain.
9. In tand didiu luid ind ingen don dáil, as-bert friu: "cía dia tibérthar[13]
ind airdech cosin dergḟlaith?" ⁊ fris-gart in scál dí íarum, ó rus-sluinn-
50 sidi íarum cach flaith i ndegaid araile ó aimsir Chuinn co brád. Ba

---

7   Rawl. – marcagh; Harl. – ma*rcach*.
8   Rawl. – tossiuch. Harl. – inas torch*or* toísech.
9   Rawl. – marcag; Harl. – ma*rcach*.
10   Rawl. – airideog nech di ór ara belaib; Harl. – copan di ór f*or*a beolai.
11   Rawl. – f*ri*[...]tisidi doib iar*um* ⁊ as [...]. Nimda scálsa [...] aurdrach ⁊ is f*or* [...]
     muccai iarmu [...]od ⁊ is d*e* hsil a[...] is he mo slon*n*ud [...]nen; Harl. – Prisga*rtside*
     doib ⁊ adb*er*t friu nido*m* scalsa e*m* ⁊ nidom urt*r*ach ⁊ domuird*er*cus duib iar mbas
     dodeochad*us* ⁊ is do ci*n*el adai*m* dau*m*. iss e mo slondad lug m*ac et*hlend.
12   Rawl. – esin; Harl. – isin.
13   Rawl. – tiberthæ; Harl. – tib*er*tar.

trom íarum la Cesarnd filid a ndíchetal[14] sin do thabairt fri oínhúair
co n-ecmaing tre ogum hi cetheóra flescæ iphair, cethir traigid fichet
fott cacha flesci 7 ocht ndruimne cacha flesci. Lotar íar sein hi foscad
an[15] scáil 7 ní arrdraigestair a ndún nach a tech.[16] Fo-rácbad immurgu
la Conn in dabach 7 int escra 7 ind airdech[17] 7 na flesca.[18] Ocus is di 55
sen attá Aislingi 7 Echtra 7 Argraige Cuind Chétcathaig 7 Baile in
Scáil.
10. "Cía fors' ndáilfider ind airdech óir-se cosin dergḟlaith[19] 7 cía nodas-
íbai?" ol in ingen. "Ní anse. Dáil de", ol in scál, "for Conn Cétchadach,
cét cadræ firfidius:[20] cath Breg hÉle, cath Ache, cath Machæ, cath 60
Dubaichi, cath Olarba, cath Daim Deirg, cath Rendai, cath for Seilg,
cath Cinn Tíre,[21] cath Gaibthine, cath Étair, cath Ibair, cath Droma Duib,
cath Moínmaige, cath hi Scaleda, cath Mibthine,[22] cath Roiss, cath
Tortan, cath Gréine, cath Magi Muí, cath for Caimsi, cath for Búais fri
fini, fri anfine, 65
cath i nDrummut co fo thrí,   secht catha Maige Line,[23]
cath i Fremaind, cath i Máil, dá ḟescur Mide, cath Da Dule firfide 7
tromár hi Clochur. Dá chath fichet i nAirb, cethri catha i Cláiriu,[24] canis
firfe? Bid [d]emin, firfid secht catha Cúalngi[25] la deóra der[g]maitni
Femin, cath for Gull, cath for Ergull 7 dubadaig Immair. 70
  Do-foíth Forannán in rí,   do-fóethsat rígrad Adni,
da-fóeth Mane mac Bríathraig 7 Ailill Olgné, Conchobar chena, Fergus,
Óingus Dubaigi,

14   Rawl. – a ndichetail; Harl. – om.
15   Rawl. – a; Harl. – an.
16   Rawl. – a dtech; Harl. – an tec.
17   Rawl. – ind dabach 7 int escra 7 in airdech; Harl. – in dubach 7 int escrai ordao 7 and
     airech.
18   Rawl. – flescæi; Harl. – om.
19   Rawl. – cosin [...]lait; Harl. – cosan derglaith.
20   Rawl. – chet chadræ firfidius; Harl. – ced cathrai brisfius.
21   Rawl. – cath chinn tiriu; Harl. – cath cind tiri.
22   Rawl. – cath mibthiniu; Harl. – om.
23   Rawl. – linéi; Harl. – line.
24   Rawl. – clairiu; Harl. – om.
25   Rawl. – cualgi; Harl. – quailgne.

a comrac im Thipraiti,   cith lethchomnart a n-ude,
75   is hé gignetar a [n]glé[26]   in slúagad im ṡuide.[27]
   Dirsan do Chund Chétcathach   íar n-ár thened tar cech mag,
   géntair[28] íar timchiul cach rois   día máirt i Túaith Imrois
   –cóic ḟichit blíadnae nammá–   doda-cich noda-íba."
   11. "Cía forsi ndáilfider ind airidech óir-se", ol ind ingen, "cosin
80   dergḟlaith?" "Ní anse. Dáil de for Art [n]Óenḟer", ol in scál, "fer cét-
   gretha –.lxxx. catha firfess– cath Sléibe Betha, cath Sléibe Cúa, cath
   Moisten, cath Moín, cath Drúaig, cath Tortíni, cath Irlúachra,
   cath Coidlim, cath Locha Daim,   hi tóethsat in duinechoin.
   Bid scél n-airdircc hi cech taig,   cath ḟesar[29] hi Collobair,
85   cath Dromma [Fi]undglaissi, cath Átha Dairi Duib, cath Senchúa, dá
   chath Liphe, cath Dorcha, cath Dromma Dígais, cath Sláini, cath Roigni,
   cath Argatrois dia mbaat ili, dá chath i Liniu, cath Aidni, cath Leithit
   Lach[t]muige, dá ḟescur hi Saimniu, cath Finnmaigi, cath i Fremuin,
   madan Insi Dorndglaissi.
90   In cath i mBrí Chobthaig Coíl.   Coíntit ile, coíntit coím.[30]
   Dirsan do Ḟothud ad-baill   ₇ Óengus mac Domnaill.
   Matan Maigi Mucramai   so hi tóethsatt mairb ile.
   Ba dirsan do Art mac Cuind   cin mac nAililla Auluim.
   Día dardaín sír íar srath   maidtir la echraid Lugdach
95   –.xx. blíadnae nammá–   doda-cich noda-íba.
   12 "Cía forsi ndáilfider ind airdeog óir-si cosind ḟlaith?" ol in ingen.[31]
   "Ní anse. Dáil de for Lugaid Mac Con", ol in scál, "cini di ṡíl Chuind
   dóu, do-aidlibe
   –.u. blíadnai .xx. nammá–   doda-cich noda-íba.
100 A longas co íath nOrc *uel* Alban. Ar-brisfi .iii. noí catha[32] for túatha
   Orcc. Firfid cath Tuithmi la teóra húargresa[33] hUmail.
   Día domnaig for Áth hIi   da-n-aidli[34] fíacail fidbai."

26   Rawl. – a glé; Harl. – ac dluigi.
27   Rawl. – im suidé; Harl. – na slua*g* bias la ssuide.
28   Rawl. – gentar; Harl. – gont*ar*.
29   Rawl. – fesair; Harl. – *om.*
30   Rawl. – coíntit coím cointit ile; Harl. – *om.*
31   Rawl. – ol in inge*n*; Harl. – *om.*
32   Rawl. – .iii. nói cath; Harl. – cet*ri* morcatha.
33   Rawl. – húarg*re*su; Harl. – *om.*
34   Rawl. – do*n*aidli; Harl. – dia*n*aitbi.

13. "Cía forsi ndáilfider?" ol ind ingen.[35] "Dáil de forsin mórbrethach,
for Cormac úa Cuind
  –.lx. blíadnae nammá–   doda-cich noda-íba.   105
Mórfuitir fine ₇ anfine. Síth n-oll co rían ina ré.
Bid rii Temrach co fo thrii   ara-mbebat ilṡíabrai .i. síthaigi.
A breith dar muir la Mǽlchend i n-aidchi gaim tess Beind Bairchi.
Dúbartach Mide dia ḟessar[36] cath Granairdd, cath i nEuo, cath i nEuth,
cath i Cind Dairi, cath Sruthra, cath Cúal[n]gi, cath Átha Beth, cath Átha 110
Dumai,
  cath Cúile Caichir[37] fa thrí   nípat becca ind lúadri.[38]
  Tothaim dímeis Assail áin   cen Cormac ina rígdáil
  cath hi nDubad co fo thrí.   Matan Dairi follscaide
  cath na Lúachrai all Maig Slecht, cath Eillne, cath Maige Techt,   115
  imdercad Cormaic fo thrí,   bid maircc mac ind ḟubthairi.
  Élúd ríg Temrach íar sein   gubadán mór hi Máenmaig.
  Longass Chormaic dar Mag [Réin]   –.iii. blíadnai– cluinti céin.
  Ticfa íar sein co Mumain,   Cormac fria matin fugail,
  cath Bérri, cath Locha Léin,   cath im Luimnech, cath im Gréin, 120
  a mbudni ola bit[39] máir   dochom Temrach dar Mag Fáil.
Ar-nena gíalla Gaídel ara derccduirr dremna,[40] firfid cath Clasaig. Ár
mór ós Muiriscc, cráudórtad troch,
  ar-túaset Ulaid occa,   do-fóeth hEchaid Tóebḟoda,
  cath Slabrǽ, cath Ardda Caim,   do chlaind Muman nípa moín.   125
Orggain na rígingen, bid scél, bid fássach n-aenré.
  Bid óen di neort na[41] flathǽ   for hAidni na bórime.
  Tóla hÉrend la Cormac   fri Fergus, ardrí Ulad.
  Do-fóeth Fergus sceo Énda   dia mbia slúag dérach dubach.[42]
  Máirt hi Crinda céin ṁbess bith hi foíchret slúaig hÉrend grith.   130

---

35 Rawl. – ingin; Harl. – *om.*
36 Rawl. – fhessair; Harl. – *om.*
37 Rawl. – *cath* cuiliu caichir; Harl. – *om.*
38 Rawl. – luádrí; Harl. – *om.*
39 Rawl. – bidh; Harl. – *om.*
40 Rawl. – araderct duirri dremna; Harl. – *om.*
41 Rawl. – ha; Harl. – na.
42 Rawl. – dupuch; Harl. – de*r*ach dub*ach*.

Fíanda firfit[e] dúbarta, memais in cath ría Cormac. Teóra blíadnai íar
sin co cath Crindæ Fregabuil. Bebaid Cormac caín, marb día máirt hi
tóeb Chletig, ad-coínfet Goídil."
14. "Cía forsi ndáilfider ind airedeog óir-si (.i. *regnum Scottorum*) cosin
135 derclaith?" ol ind ingen.

"Dáil de for fer n-ilair glond,[43]   for Coirpri Liphechair, fer noíbas tond
–.xxx. catha ina ré–   –Biaid .lx. blíadnae–
Dúbairt hÉrenn cotá muir,   cath ḟessar[44] i Liphimaig.
Máirt hi Liphimaig ara-thá,   bebaid and in rígniä."
140 **15.** "Dáil de for Fíachu Sroiphtine.[45] Matan Midi la suide, dá chath hi
Maig Rátha

–.xx.u. blíadnai a ré–   co saigid na bóramai.
Tothaimm Fothaid maic Crúaid,   bid scél mór hi cach túaith.
Teóra blíadnai íarum cen meth,   hi Cnámross bied rígbath.
145 Cétaín Cnámroiss, bid gand glé   hi tóeth Fíachu Sroiphtine."[46]
16. "Dáil de for Muiredach[47] Tírech –.xl. blíadnae hi flaith–
cath hi[48] Mórmaig, firfid glé   fri hUltu, fri Araide.
For brú Dabaill hisin chath   do-fáeth Muiredach[49] Tírech."
17. "Dáil de for Echaig Mugmedóin. Tóebḟota Temra, dúnadach
150 Tlachtgai, dúbartach Feimin, costudach Móenmaigi, cruindársid Liphi,
toichmech Toirrchi.

–.xx.u. blíadnai namá–   doda-cich noda-íba.
Guin Glúinḟind, bid mór int écht.   Guin Conchobair, guin Maic Cécht.
Forus ṅHér[e]nd fo Echaig fria ré, bid forggu maithe. Is húad gignedar
155 co bráth bunad na flaithi.

I nDub Chombair fria[50] ré   bied fotha fingaile.
Na trí Colla glanfait ár   hi tóeth Echu Muigmedán.

---

43   Rawl. – Dail *for* fer iolair glond; Harl. – Dail de *for* fer ila*r* nglon*n*.
44   Rawl. – fhessair; Harl. – fesa*r*.
45   Rawl. – roiphtine; Harl. – raib*tine*.
46   Rawl. – roiph*tine*; Harl. – sroib*tine*.
47   Rawl. – muredagh; Harl. – muire*d*ach.
48   Rawl. – he; Harl. – a.
49   Rawl. – murethach; Harl. – muire*d*ach.
50   Rawl. – fri; Harl. – fria.

18. "Dáil de for Níall Noígíallach .i. cóic géill hÉrend ₇ gíall Albun ₇
Bretan ₇ Saxan ₇ Franc. Nóitfitir tuir, mórfaitir maigi, nensitir géill, fes-
saitir catha, sesaitir slúaig, mórfaitir flathi. Fu-géillfi Níel fo thrí, 160
da-ṅgega flaith   ar bid hé in rí maith.
A cath Muirned hi Forath Lúain,   is and do-fóethsat in slúaig.
Fescur coscrach Dúin Chúair,   tathaimm nAu[r]thuli friss antúaith
–.xxuii. blíadnai namá–   doda-cich noda-íobæ.
Du-fuit íar sen gríb thuile glond⁵¹ ar Druimm nAlban, do-fóeth Níall, 165
bid adbar mairg truimm   i nArddmóin die sathairnd."
19. "Dáil de for Colla nÓss (.i. Úais)
–.iiii. blíadnai namá–   doda-ciig noda-íba,⁵²
Scarfaid fri hardḟlaith, scél nglé do dénum na fingaile."⁵³
20. "Dáil de for Ailill Molt mac Nathí maic Fíachrach. Fer úallach, fer 170
adcuínti sochaidi –.xx. blíadnae namá–
Catha ile 'na ḟlaith   ar bid hé in rí maith.
Cucligid Temra, cumascach Tailten, cath Átha Tálmaig[e]. Dúbartach
Séile, nóithech Aichi, cath Rátha Crúachan. Céim for Sabralla, céim
for Elpa. Togal in tuir. Céim for Eolarcca, cath Sratha Cluithi, fortbe 175
nGeinned. Céim dar Muir nIcht dochum nElpa. Cichsit hÉrendmaig,
réim ndían, ata-cumbat echtraind .uii. mbél fri firu Góedel for Ailill i n-
oín dídin ar Elpai. Bit ili at-ethfat⁵⁴ martrai, ba dirsun do ḟeraib hÉrend,
is mór ara-thá toitimm⁵⁵ la echtranda."
21. "Dáil de for Loígairi, fer ilair glond, mórfait iltíre ilbélrae⁵⁶ –.xxx. 180
blíadnae namá– Tascur dían, ticfa táilcend (.i. Pátraic), fer gráid móir
nóifidius⁵⁷ Día. Mórbreó ad-andaba línfus Érinn⁵⁸ cotá muir. Bebaid
Loígairi (flaith him bachla) for brú Chaissi, mórchaur cicharda do-fortat
táilcind."
22. "Dáil de for Túathal Máelgarb (.i. mac Cormaic maic Coirpri maic 185
Néill) –.xx. (blíadnae)– cath Lúachra Ailbi, cath Detnai, totim nArdgail,

---

51 Rawl. – griba tuile gluind; Harl – Biet ile a gluin*n*.
52 Rawl. – nodaíb; Harl. – nodoibhda.
53 Rawl. – scairfaid f*r*i arddscél do denam na fi*n*gali; Harl. – Scarf*aid* f*r*i ha*r*dflaith scel
    ngle do den*um* na finghaile.
54 Rawl. – athet; Harl. – atheat.
55 Rawl. – artha thoitim*m*; Harl – arathá thoitim.
56 Rawl. – mórfait iltire nilbélras; Harl. – ro aichfi libthi ₇ iltire.
57 Rawl. – nóifidsi; Harl. – noifidi*us*.
58 Rawl. – linf*hus* herend; Harl. – linf*us* eri*nn*.

cath Légi, cath Dromma Arbelaig, cath Bregoind. Fornaidm ngíall nGaídel.[59] Íar sin bid scél hi cach maig, bebaid óenguine namá, Túathal oc Grellaig Eilti. Géntair[60] Máelmór dia dígail hi Túaith Imbroiss."

190 **23.** "Dáil de for Lugaid mac Loígairi –.xxui.– co totim dóu di chúairt for hÉrind tria diúltad táilcind i nEscir Forchai."

24. "Dáil de for Muirchertach Mac Ercci (.i. ingen Loairnd). Rí cathach coscrach atcuínti sochaidi,[61]

fo-nen hÉrind, fir $_7$ mná	ar bid comarbba Temra.
195	Cath Átha Sigi íar sen	línfus co hÉrinn airbiu.
Benaid dúbart hi máirt,	in cáirb coscrach, co Laigniu,

mór atbai,[62] bebaid Muirchertach éc atbai máirt Cletig."

25. "Dáil de for Anmirig, timgéra gíallu cach maigi íar tír cinip tair[63] Truimm, do-fóeth ar daig rúaid,[64] firfitir catha –.iiii. blíadnai namá.–"

200 **26.** "Dáil de for Báetán $_7$ Echaig –.iiii. blíadnai.–"

27. "Dáil de for Díarmait (.i. mac Fergusa Cerrbeóil), dúbartach Tailten, tairngertaig Temra.

Cén mair ina flaith   ar bid hé in rí maith.

Día .uii. mblíadnae íar sein cath fáebrach for Díarmait Dreimni.

205 In slóg do-sia antúaith,[65]   glanfaid[66] in roí co Áth Lúain.

Bérthair a cathbúaid.

Ind aín díten hi Ráith Bic,   díth Díarmata imma-ric

–(.xx. blíadnae).–"

28. "Dáil de for Ferggus $_7$ Domnall, dá mac Muirchertaich Maic Erca[67]

210 .i. Brandub mac Echach ro marb –dí blíadain hi comflaith.–"

29. "Dáil de for Áed [n]Úaridnech[68] mac Domnaill mórfass flaith, fo-nen hÉrind. Flaith fodbach foránach. Firfid forbasa hÉrend. Blíadain íar sein do-tuit Ailill mac Domangairt.   Bied gním hi Temairmaig.

Iurait Laigin[69] a ndáma,   con-bibsat a fírdála.

---

59   Rawl. – ngoidil; Harl. – ngaidel.
60   Rawl. – gentar; Harl. – gentoir.
61   Rawl. – sochaide; Harl. – sochaidi.
62   Rawl. – áttba; Harl. – atbai.
63   Rawl. – cinip a taír; Harl. – cinip tair.
64   Rawl. – ar daig ruád; Harl. – ar daig ruad.
65   Rawl. – antuaith; Harl. – antuaith.
66   Rawl. – glanfait; Harl. – glanfaid.
67   Rawl. – maic ainmirech; Harl. – maic erca.
68   Rawl. – uáredach; Harl. – uaridhnech.
69   Rawl. – laigen; Harl. – laigin.

Bid gargg, bid coscrach a ré co llaithe na tangnachte.[70] 215
In máirt i ndescurt Liphi, is ann at-béla in rii
–.uiii. mblíadnai namá.–"
30. "Dáil de for Áed Sláne. Síth n-oll, flaith Góedel. Caín érnfi fini
Fúata Líamna.
Do-tóeth íar sein Áed Sláne íar lín chatha ina[71] ré 220
–.uiii. mblíadnai namá– Doda-cich[72] doda-íba
.i. coirm catha,[73] *potio*[74] *sompni ut dicebat[ur]*."
31. "Dáil de for Áed [n]Olldáin –.uiii. mblíadnai– doda-cich[75] noda-íba,
dúbartach Fálmaige,[76] gébaid for Liphemaig. Ar-nena gíallu Góedel.[77]
Mór marb, mór átbai. Mórail, at-cuínfet Goídeil." 225
32. "Dáil de for Domnall Mend [n]Ulad –noii mblíadnai déc namá–
Drauc ilair band
firfes dá chath i Maig Roth. Máirt is and tóeth ind rígrad.
Et dergmaten Cruthni. Firfid cath Dúin Chethirnd[78] la cath Rátha al
Machi.[79] Cichis íarum a réim, mórail, at-bath in rii."[80] 230
33. "Dáil de for Subni Mend, drauc ilair band –blíadain coa .uiii. bias a
flaith– fo-nena gíallu cach rois. Cath Dathe firfes in rii.
Is and do-tóeth, nípi gáu, Colmán Mór mac Díarmato."
34. "Dáil de for Blathmac mac Áeda (.i. Sláine) is hé noda-íba –.u.
blíadnæ ara derbḟlaith.–" 235
35. "Dáil de forsin rúanaid (.i. a ruidiud ig gabáil láma Mo Chuta),
for Díarmait Daithi, a cétchath Senchúa, cath Roiss Chorcu Búain,
cath Ossraidi, cath Éile, cath Sléibi etir dá Inda.[81] Firfid .uii.
catha Aidni la cath Seilgi íar nóin. Ara-taat immurgu dercmaitni
Cruthni, bid crúas cuimnech túath in Cuib. Íar sen in mortlaid for hÉrind 240
i mbiat múcna int ṡlúaig."

---

70 Rawl. – tangnechta; Harl. – na tangnacté.
71 Rawl. – na; Harl. – ina.
72 Rawl. – dodacaich; Harl. – dodacich.
73 Rawl. – cath; Harl. – cata.
74 Rawl, – p; Harl. – p.
75 Rawl. – dodacaich; Harl. – dodacich.
76 Rawl. – falmaigie; Harl. – falmoigi.
77 Rawl. – goedil; Harl. – gaidil.
78 Rawl. – dúi*n* cethernd; Harl. – dui*n*e cethirn.
79 Rawl. – almachi; Harl. – almoichi.
80 Rawl. – ind ríí; Harl. – inn rig.
81 Rawl. – doinda; Harl. – *da* inda.

36. "Dáil de for Fínnachta .i. mac Dúnchada maic Áeda Sláni, con-saídfi fri Mumain móir. Firfid cath Cúile Coíláin, scíss hi tóeb Chithamra, fer mochtaidi ad-baill fingail móir i n-aín dídin for Dollud. Duthain a
245 recht, nípa rí Áed (.i. mac Dlúthaig)[82] íarum –.xx. blíadnae namá.–"
37. "Dáil de for Sechnusach mac Blaithmaic –uno anno doda-cich[83]– at-beba éc átbai issind Imbliuch ós Bóaind."
38. "Dáil de for Cend Fáelad –.uii. mblíadnai a flaith– íar sen in cath hi Temuirmaig do-tóeth Cenn Fáelad i ndomnach Chúili Coíláin."
250 **39.** "Dáil de for Loingsech[84] (.i. mac Óengusa maic Domnaill), síabraid for Fálmaig, costudach Liphi. Buidnech Béirri.

Do-tóeth ic lecaib finnaib   lassna fíanna fo minnaib.
Regaid a n-imguin fa thúaith,   memais for ríg Essa Rúaid
.i. ría Cellach Locha Cimbi.
255 Die sathairn cichiss ar chel   etir di Choraind[85] Uinnsen
                                       (.i. cath Coraind)
–.xi. blíadnai namá.–"

40. "Dáil de for Fogartach n-án ₇ for Congal mac Fergusæ Fánat –.xiiii. blíadnai namá– Da-thuittet a ndiis in lúan ría samuin, indala n-aí hi
260 tosuch ind laí, alaili inna deriud." Hi Clúain Irairdd *sepulti sunt, ut Pátríni dixit.*
41. "Dáil de forsin cailech (.i. i n-aín dídin a cath Almaine), for Fergal, clethblugaid hÉrenn, armach Lini, ársid Aí.

Bebaid la Laigniu íarna ré,   Fergal hi cath Almaine,
265 biaid ár mór isin chath   línfus co hÉirinn airbriu[86]
hi tóeth ind rígrad moínech   immon cailech ass amru
–.xii.– i nDermaig ro adnacht Fergal. *Unde dictum est.*

Réna fuiligud hi roí,   tailcc ar-bertad catha clí,
indiu for lár Dermaigi   aicsiu Fergaili ní ní."

270 **42.** "Dáil de for Flaithbertach, ind ré bias, is lais firfidir cath Droma Corcáin fri Temraig antúaid, Cináed húa Conaing[87] (fín fo thalmain). At-coínfed Goídil –.xxui. blíadna bass rí Flaithbertach– Con-beba écu

---

82 Rawl. – (.i. dluthaig); Harl. – .i. mac dluthaigh.
83 Rawl. – dodacaich; Harl. – dotacaith.
84 Rawl. – loingsich; Harl. – loings*ech*.
85 Rawl. – da corand; Harl. – 2 corann.
86 This is where the Harl. text finishes; the rest of the tale survives in Rawl. only.
87 Rawl. – cinæd ainm hua conaing.

atbai[88] fo tháilcentaig .i. i nArd Macha i n-ailithre at-bath *clericus* i n-ailaid na ríg."

43. "Dáil de for Áed [n]Aldén (.i. Altán *noimen loci ubi nutritus est*) 275 –Áed airdrí .x. mblíadnae– Firfid cath coscrach gein catha Sáiltiri arangéba, bid ní dáu na dá chath isind óenlóu, cath Átha Dá Charnda, cath Átha Medóin. Memaid for Cenél Conaill. Glanfaid áru. Fálguba Ulad, memaiss for Áed (.i. Rón mac Béicci Bairche) re nÁed.

Int Áed aurbaig (.i. cath Focharta), formna i fán,[89]   280
                                              leth a anmæ hi muir (.i. rón) már.
Do Maig Laigen gébaid grith,   bid slóged n-aurderc fon mbith.

An máirt hi túaiscirt Liphi, dígail chatha Almaine i n-ebbéla cach amra, firfid ail [n]Uchbad. Gébaid Góedelu co muir etir Cond[achta] is Mumain. Cath Cenindsa,   285
cath i nEochind, da-rii   ara-mbebat tigernai.
Bied mairc mór hi cach taig,   íarsin chath a S[e]redmaig.
Biaid ernbas im rígu   sain chan im cholaind nÁeda.
Do-fóeth in rí ó Srúb Brain   for brú Locha Sailchitain.
Hi Clúain mac Nóiss ro adnacht Áed Aldán."   290

44. "Dáil de for Domnall mac Murchadæ, roínfitir catha (.i. cath S[e]redmaigi) ríam, nóifitir fir i ndarddaín. At-beba Bregaib. Éc atbai hi Tailtentaig .i. i nImliuch [F]ía –.xx. blíadan.–"

45. "Dáil de for Níall Frosach, catha ili 'na flaith. Níba friss firfitir, bebaid éc atbui la fuil.   Bérthair hi tíre dar muir   295
.i. co hÍ Coluim Chilli –.uii. mblíadnai namá– .i. Dondchad *expulsit eum de regno suo.*"

46. "Dáil de for Donnchad. Ticfa flaith Dondchadæ tríuin, coicligid insi Scott, gignidir nach tain.

Is lais do-regat in slúaig,   timchell Cairnd Fíachach[90] antúaith. 300
Íbait fiäig lommæ cróu   for brú Locha Luglochtau.
Tróethbaid Brega borrchathaib. Mórchath airthir Fúata firfes.
Biëd co n-immud[91] acain (.i. cenn)   in maten hi Forcalad.
Ré nDond Midi memais cath   inid-abbaill Congalach.
Cath Srúbrach ara-sela Canán géba[s] mén, ré nDund Midi for fini, for 305
anfine. Géntair táilcend, gním co fíni ara mba Fíachru (.i. mac Cathail).

---

88   Rawl. – éc uatba.
89   Rawl. – forma fan.
90   Rawl. – fíachrach.
91   Rawl. – co nimniud.

Ara bélaib sínit fir,   íar tuidecht ó Laigillib,
di lár Tailten, rúanaid glé (.i. cath Cairnd maic Cáirthind),
            ruínfid riäm hi fochlæ (.i. for Áed nIngor),[92]
310 con-saídfe co cendaib troch   dië domnaich im Chlóenloch.
     Cath Étain Tairb,   biat ili mairb.
     Fomnais (.i. Áed Muinderg) i mBricc Fánat i mbí rii, tress tind [D]uind
tess, ád bodbai. Bid comaimser dó in dondfer, co mag di lár Liphi rúed,
ra-fiastar cách. Cellach [a] ainm –dá n-ocht [m]blíadnae bass ind amsir
315 in duind Midi.
     Ónd húair regus cotá muir,   fírscél gona Follamain
                              (.i. mac Con Congalt).
     Cert .xxx. blíadnae namá   co cend rígi Dondcada.
     Biaid golgairi hi cech maig   hi tossach ind úarerraig.
320 In Dond Mide, bebais aitt   dië máirt fo tháilcentaig
.i. hi Clúain Eraird."
47. "Dáil de for Áed nIngor, forsin [n]gercc –.xxiii. blíadnai a flaith.–
     Is hé int Áed cernach crúaid   coscrach brisfess búed.
     Fomnas da mbúed[93] for Clóitig.   Do-foirtbe firu ceni toíthsat[94] ríg.
325 Fo-dercfa bandæ fo dii,   fris[a] tóethsat slúaig Midi[95]
.i. Fíndachta. Rúaidáir truim, dos-foirtbi.
     At-beba dond Cerna crúaid,   in tan ainfes, bid íar mbúaid.
Citha garcca gaile graphand. Do-fortbi táilcentech[96] .i. termann Aird
Macha. Trénchathach Ceníuil Chonaill. Dergthresach Temarmaigi.
330 Slógindredach Cláiri. Costadach Liphi.
     Slúaig do-regat o Srúb Brain   isin mís íar n-úargaim.
     Is lais íbait fiäich fuil   for seichib ic Derclúachair
                                (.i. Druim Ríg).
     In slúag do-ficfe fri clé,   cúl a catha fri Tlachtge.

---

92   This mistakenly appears as a gloss on *íar tuidecht ó Laigillib* (l. 307) in Rawl. See
       note to l. 309.
93   Rawl. – da na mbued.
94   Rawl. – toithsad.
95   Rawl. – mide
96   Rawl. – tailcentaig.

Áed find⁹⁷ cumma chnes,   memais ríam síardes.   335
In tan sóifes clár fri clé   ara-mbeba Fínachtæ.
I nArd Macha *sepultus est* Áed. Mac Dúnflatha ingeni Flaithbertaig
maic Longsich Áed Ordnidi. Ic Áth Dá Fertæ hi Conaillib at-bath *per
conflictionem* Máel Canaig."
48. "Dáil de for Conchabor mac Donnchada, gébaid Goídelu cotá muir, 340
mac mná Condacht. Caínbreó bruigi Bregmaigi –.xiiii.– Ar thecht a
Temuir, cassra tocaid ina ré. Túaruscbáil tíchtan⁹⁸ geinti.
Ind oín díden, coínti[t] tuir,   ar-tá etsecht⁹⁹ Conchobuir,
hi Clúain Iraird *sepultus est*."
49. "Dáil de for Níall Cailli doda-nesfa (.i. Temair). Firfid cath 345
Crúachan (.i. cath Leithi Caim), cath Dairi Chalcaig for geinti.
Níell hi muir, Níell hi nguin, Níell hi tein. Cumasscach (.i.
hÉrenn). –Teóra blíadnai déc– I nArd Macha ro adnacht Níell íarna
bádud hi Calaind .i. hi Linde Néill."
50. "Dáil de for Máel Sechlainn. Ní fiastar nech rúna a cridiu. Tuitet 350
trí duind elgnæi la dubai a gossa. Is leis firfidir fert fingaile uc Clóin.
Díanfichta fri hechtranda (.i. Gaullu), slúagdórtad Forchai. Fescur tess
(.i. co Mumain),¹⁰⁰ cúaird for hÉrinn ata laídi légfaitir (.i. dúan Pátríni).
Die máirt, rígi Roiss, do-fuit atbai i roí Ruis (.i. Aróc ingen ríg Fer
Cúl, máthair Maíl Sechlainn) –.xui. blíadnai– hi Clúain mac Nóis ro 355
adnacht."
51. "Dáil de forsin cóel crésen (.i. cléirech do-gníd), for Óed Olach (.i.
Finnlíath mac Gormlatha ingeni Dondchada 7 Néill Chailli). Slúagadach
Liphi, crúach Clóitigi. Graiphnech Crúachan. Is leis firfidir cath Leitrech
Daigri (.i. cath Cilli úa nDaigræ) gair ríana díth (.i. óen blíadain réna 360
díth .i. ría éc). Íadaid dorcha mór hi cétaín chétgaimrid –.xui. blíadnai– i
Ráith Adomnæ at-bath Áed. I nArd Macha ro adnachtt."
52. "Dáil de forsin mend mbrécach, for Fland Sindæ firfes bróen fingaile

---

97   Rawl. – findi.
98   Rawl. – tichta*in*.
99   Rawl. – artha étsecht.
100 This mistakenly appears as a gloss on *slúagdórtad* in Rawl. See note to ll. 352-3.

fora bráithri. Tecait airdi ili 'na flaith .i. techt di nim (.i. ailithir ó Róim)
365 dia foicertar ár nGoídel ic Duiblind (.i. ind ailithir). Bás cóel a clú do ríg
Crúachan .i. Áed mac Conchabuir ro marbad isin chath. Na .uii. nduba
Temrach (.i. uii. *anni mali*). Firfid forbais for táilcentaig (.i. Ard Macha)
co n-echtrandaib (.i. Gaill .i. maic Ímair). Brisfid for Bréifnechu. Firfid
cath Grellaigi Eilti, cath Maigi Ailbi (.i. Óengus a mac ro bris ₇ Laigin)
370 co clú. Brécad étaig[101] 'na ré. Grúaca a cennaib, glasmes doíne[102] 'na
ré. Síthflaith (.i. Fland) toiccthech, fris-tercha a chúaine féini friss (.i.
a uii. maic). Bás duimrecht[a] for crésion chád. Domnach Aindin arda-
fich i nderiud in fogmair –.xxx.uii. blíadnai– Flann ingen Dúngaili ríg
Osraide máthair *eius* .lxxui. *etatis suæ anno moritur*, hi Clúain mac Nóis
375 ra-adnacht."
53. "Dáil de for Níell nGlúndub glanfus roí Rúadra, ririss flaith for-
busach Lini. Láechbuillech Locha Lébind. Loiscfid Cúalaind co fo dí.
Drongach Clári, cathach Crúachan, cétudach Coba, mórbuillech Bairchi.
Breóach Sléibi Cailggi frisna gaibther. Cath Oirggne, cath Codail (.i.
380 Grellaig Eilti for Níell ría Fland). Cath Tráchta Eóthaile[103] for Connachta
dia fich fuil Feirniu.[104] Cot n-úallai Albba (.i. Máel Mairi a máthair,
ingen Chináeda maic Alpín ríg Albban), artt láechda Liphi, riríss noíl
Lochæ Léibind die mbia fé innund fé ille. In lúan ós Martartaig bias
bróen cróu ós Tailtin (.i. cath Átha Clíath in ro marbad Níell).
385 –Teóra blíadnai co leith namá–   doda-cich noda-íbæ
–.l. blíadnae a áes huili– i nDruim Chailli rucad. Hi Cenandus ro adnacht
Níall –.iii. blíadnai dóu i rígi Ailig.–"
54. "Dáil de for crissalach (.i. reis i fingail) Codail, Dond a ainm (.i. Máel
Febail ingen[105] Flaind maic Conaing máthair *eius*). Caínbruth breóach
390 brissfes catha crúaidai, croithfes indnu for Tailtin. Togach Temrach.
Timgair gíallæ co Daball. Is hé firfes cath Febla for fini, for anfine.
Cath Cúaland. Imed toraid 'na ré. Grían na fírinde (.i. Ioseph comarba
Pátraic nó céili [Dé]). Cuínfider húas Cúal[n]giubeinn domnach etir dí
challaind –.xxu. blíadnai.–"
395 **55.** "Dáil de for cass find Colla, Congal Cerna (.i. Lígach a máthair,
ingen Flaind) –Firfid .x. mblíadnae– flaith in chon bic, bertfaid mór

---

101 Rawl. – brecaid etaig.
102 Rawl. – ndóine.
103 Rawl. – trathca eolthaile.
104 Rawl. – *cath* codail (.i. grellaig eilti *for* niell ria fland) dia fich fuil feirniu *cath*
     trathca eolthaile *for connacht*a; see note to ll. 379-80.
105 Rawl. – ingin.

ó Laignib, milliud a baíguil, nín-toiméla leth a saíguil.
Láech a Cernu, má du-phé,[106] biat brónaig a foglaide.[107]
Fer find, for-accai rígi, biat úati a chomdíni,
hi Mainistir ro adnacht Congalach."   400
56. "Dáil for Domnall mac dá leithi (.i. a lleth tes ₇ túaid dind Érinn) .i.
Domnall dalta Athbach (.i. túath Athbach ra n-alt[108] .i. Uí Erthuile). Eó
find fessach, foránach Cnogbai, cétudach Assail, ollbuidnech Uisnig.
Firfid cath [i m]Brí hÉli (.i. for Carrach Calma). Bandmaidm Lettrech
Ainge (.i. cath Cilli Móna) hi tóethsat .iii.l. gilla im Fíngin Corad. 405
Cath Sléibi Cúa fo dí ₇ matan Grophtini.
Tessbaid etha (.i. gorta) di Maig Cuind
          .ui. blíadnai imluim (.i. tercai).
Do-fóeth, cid álaind a lii, in lúan hi Carnd Furbaidi
(.i. Furbaidi Mend Macha ro adnacht ann nó forbba na ndaíne co n- 410
adnacal and) –.xxiiii. blíadnai– –.l.u. blíadnai a áes.–"
57. "Dáil de for sroiphtinid Macha (.i. teni dar Macha 'na ré .i. Machairi)
.i. Máel Sechlainn (.i. mac Dúnflatha ingine Muirchertaig), míad ngárcc.
Mórdrech dúr dechrass ar thuru Temrach. Tolcach Étair, losctech Liphi.
Fessach Cúaland, graiphnech Crúachan. Cridi nathrach, firfid cath fri 415
Cláire (.i. cath Cairn Fordroma),[109] cath Iroriss, cath [i] Moistin. Brían
regnat hic. Mórmatan Átha (.i. matan Midi). Marb di óul meda. Crúas íar
ngail, domnach hi Teilchinaib
  –.xxx.ui. blíadnai namá–
    hi rígi huli da-méla (.i. ruc Brían ó .xx. himach rígi nÉrend[110])." 420
58. "Dáil de for clíabchless (nó clíabach .i. clíab fota mór occai) Clóitige
.i. Flaithbertach firfes cath Locha Bricrend, breccfus ár im Chnámchailli.
Clóifid firu ó Ess Rúaid (Cenél Conaill), riríss roí Locha Lébind. Bebais
éc átbai hi táilcentaig –.xui. blíadnai namá.–"
59. "Dáil de for ossgamain nAssail, Murchad, núall Gaídel ngúr, gríanbili 425
find, fer trén datta, dálbúadach Étair. Úargalach Midlúachra (.i. Slige),
loisctech Lini. Firfid cath Lúachmaigi. Gébaid forbais Locha Léin (.i.
dar Críst bid marb Brían and). Línfaid Caisil co slúagaib. Sínfid firu for
Tarbgnu –.xx. blíadnae namá.–"

---

106 Rawl. – ma duphí.
107 Rawl. – foghlaidé.
108 Rawl. – ro nalth.
109 Rawl. – firfid *cath* fri cláriu *cath* iroriss (.i. *cath* cairn fordroma); see note to l. 415-6.
110 Rawl. – herind.

430 **60.** "Dáil de for Óengus [n]Óenaig Fánatt, coscrach rii. Firfid (.i. Óengus)
in cath tess amni. Firfid cath hi Maig Cruind (.i. sondchad Cairnd Aisi .i.
Sléibe Fúait) tria chin dá dá mac comdáni (.i. Cumasscach ₇ Li[...] [...]),
dia mbie ben cen chéili, dia mbiat fir thregtaig thuill.
Níbu adass máthair [m]bóid   cath hi Cenindass con-sóid.
435 Corr lóegbili (.i. Óengus) cétaín i nAllmaig Liphi. At-béla[111] Óengus,
firfidir a n-ár (.i. ó Laignib .i. ár) –.xxii. blíadnai namá.–"
    61. "Dáil de forsin tarbainech (nó Murchad) a Ailiuch. Con-rainnfi a
ainm fri muir .i. Muiredach mórbuidnech. Is hé scérus foilgi fri Laigniu.
Cath [i m]Brí Léith, brisfid for Bréfnechau. Cath Selca, cath Móna
440 Tuircc. Íarnóin Airbrech íar sein hi tóethsat trí Muredaig. Do-fuitt di
daigir (.i. teine gelán) día máirt hi Telenmaig –.xui. blíadnai nó .xxx. nó
.xiii.– *Sic exemplaria uariantur.*"
    62. "Dáil de for dondainech nDabaill .i. Áed Engach (.i. én, fíachach .i.
en, uisci nó *quod uerius est* .i. labar), dia tuicébat bárca for Ess Rúaid.
445 Lín maíni n-ingnad 'na ré. Firfid cath hi tóethsat na dá Dúnlang .i. cath
Maisten (.i. for Laigniu). Táilcend gignid 'na ré .i. Tipraiti, tor síthaigfes
co uru hÉrenn. Bid sí íar cáin chrésien. Is hé a lecht, canair dóu (.i. do
Áed), madan i n-úachtur Ocha –.xui. blíadnai.–"
    63. "Dáil de for ossnadach [n]Uisnig .i. Cerball (nó Cairell), caur c[r]úaid,
450 críchach Banda, buidnech Brea. Brisfid cath Locha Dá Cháech,
        lá íar méthrúd Beruhai.[112]   Mórchath Sláni selus taí.
Tuicébat dí ingen[113] tes Bréphni. Brisfid cath Cloan[a], clóifid turcu im
Luimnech. Loiscfid Tesgabair (.i. Osraigi) –.xu. blíadnai namá– Do-tuit hi
Fidga íar sein di bir ois fo thalmain."
455 **64.** "Dáil de for íartróg nAilig (.i. ní geib rí aili Temraig ass) .i. Fergal
foltgarb. Cúanaig Bregmaige. Firfid cath Sléibi. Slúaga fri roí Roth. Riris
gíallu Cairnd Lugdach. Firfid cath mór Midi. Brogfaid Cnámchailli.
Túaruscbáil[114] tened loiscess toirthiu. Síth mbecc, olcc mór.
    Do-tuit (.i. Fergal) la bé n-aidche n-án,   oc Findcharnd tic a brécdál
460 –.xuii. blíadnai.– Comflaithius for hÉrinn íar sein. –Trí noí mblíadnai–
.i. co tí Fland."

---

111 Rawl. –Atmbela.
112 Rawl. – mberuhai.
113 Rawl. – din i*n*gen.
114 Rawl. – Trua*rusc*baíl.

65. "Dáil de for Fland Cinuch, tigflaith hÉrenn, cinid do ṡíl Chuind
dóu, is cuit Chuind gaibess. Tóla n-echtrand 'na ré (.i. Gaill loingsi Inbir
Domnand), imed cech toraid. Lín catha ṅgarc firfidi. Crúach mór im
Chnámchailli. Aurscartad n-echtrand. Síth find –teóra mblíadnai .l.– fo- 465
génat[115] dúili Dé. Bid sain a delb cech ráithi.
    Roithfid Fál (.i. cloch) find fo thrí.   Teóra gríana. Trí samlaithi.
    Ainim créssin ciṅges ar chel   tintan for hÉrinn in-dech.
Nóifidir tegdaisi táilcend fria cimbal nguth ina ré. Regaid éc aitti íar sein
di chretair chréissin hi Temuir." Finet.   470

---

115 Rawl. – foṅgenat.

TRANSLATION OF *BAILE IN SCÁIL*

The beginning of 'The Phantom's Frenzy' here, according to the version of the Old Book of Dub dá Leithe, i.e. Successor of Patrick

1. One day after the fall of the kings when Conn was in Tara, he ascended the royal rampart of Tara early in the morning before sunrise and his three druids in front of him, i.e. Máel, Bloc and Bluicne, the poets Eochaid, Corb and Cessarnn and Conn himself. Because he used to set forth every day with that number so that the men of the *síd* or the *Fomoiri* would not attack Ireland without being detected.

2. On his arrival on the rampart from which he usually used to watch, he found a stone there under his feet. He leapt on the stone then and stamped on it and the stone cried out under his feet so that it was heard throughout all of Tara and the plain of Brega.

3. And then Conn asked the poet, what the stone had cried out, and what its name was, and from where it had come, and to where it would go and why it had come to Tara. Then the poet said to him that he would not tell him for fifty-three days. Then, when that reckoning was complete, Conn asked the poet again, and he had been meditating until his 'keys of poesy' revealed it to him.

4. "Fál (i.e. under a rock, i.e. a rock under a king) indeed", said the poet, "is the name of the stone and the Island of Fál is its place of origin and it was placed in Tara of the land of Fál. It [will] remain forever in the land of Tailtiu, that is the land in which there will be a games-assembly for your descendants as long as there may be sovereignty in Tara. And on the last day of the week of the assembly of Tailtiu, the lord whom it will not accept is doomed within that year. Then Fál cried out under your feet", said the poet, "and prophesied; the amount of roars it gave is the number of kings of your seed that will be over Ireland forever". "Relate them to me then", said Conn. "I am not the one destined to tell you", said the druid.

5. While they were there then, they noticed a great fog around them and they did not know where they were going because of the intensity of the darkness that descended on them. They heard the sound of a horseman coming towards them. "Great is our woe", said Conn, "if this fog should bring us into unknown lands". Then the rider threw three casts at them and the last cast came at them more quickly than the first. "It is to wound a king", said the poet, "for whoever casts at Conn in Tara". The rider ceased casting and he welcomed Conn and he called him to his house.

6. They went then until they came into a plain where there was a golden tree and a house under a ridge-pole of white-gold, thirty feet its size. Then they went into the house and they saw a young girl in a crystal chair with a golden crown on her head wearing a cloak edged with gold. There was a vat of silver with four golden corners in front of her, full of red ale, a ladle of gold [resting] on its handle. There was a golden cup in front of her. And they saw the phantom himself in the house, waiting for them on his throne. And his distinction was great, as was indeed fitting, for there was never found in Tara a man of his size or his handsomeness, on account of the beauty of his form and his appearance and because of his wondrousness.

7. He addressed them then and said: "I am not a phantom and I am not a sprite and it is from my renown I have come to you after death and I am of the seed of Adam and my name is Lug son of Ethniu son of Smreth son of Tigernmar son of Fáelu son of Etheor son of Iríal son of Érimón son of Míl of Spain. And it is for this I have come, to relate to you the duration of your lordship and that of every lord who will descend from you in Tara forever."

8. And the girl who was in the house awaiting them was the Sovereignty of Ireland and she gave a meal to Conn, i.e. an ox rib and a boar rib. The ox rib was twenty-four feet long and eight feet between its tip and the ground. The boar rib was twelve feet long and five feet between its tip and the ground.

9. Then when the girl went to dispense [the ale] she said to them: "to whom shall the cup of red ale be given?", and the phantom answered her then for he then named every lord, one after another, from the time of Conn onwards. It was difficult then for Cessarnn, the poet, to memorise that incantation all at once so he cut it in ogam on four staves of yew, each stave twenty-four feet long with eight ridges. They went then into the shadow of the phantom and the fort and the house were no longer visible. However, the vat and the vessel and the cup and the staves were left with Conn. And from that is derived 'The Dream and the Adventure and the Journey of Conn Cétchathach' and 'The Phantom's Frenzy'.

10. "Upon whom shall this golden cup of red ale be bestowed and who shall drink it?", said the girl. "That is not difficult. Bestow some of it", said the phantom, "on Conn Cétchathach, he will wage them, one hundred warlike battles: the battle of Brí Éile, the battle of Ache, the battle of Macha, the battle of Dubaiche, the battle of Olarba, the battle of Dam Derg, the battle of Renna, the battle on Selg, the battle of Cenn Tíre, the battle of Gaibthine, the battle of Étar, the battle of Ibar, the battle of Druimm nDub, the battle of Móenmag, the battle in Scaleda, the battle of Mibthine, the battle of Ross, the battle of Tortu, the battle of Grían, the battle of Mag Muí, the battle on the Camas, the battle on the Búas against kindred and strangers,

the battle in Drummat thrice,

the seven battles of Mag Line,

the battle in Fremainn, the battle in Máel, the two evening battles of Mide, the battle of Da Dule which they will wage and the great slaughter in Clochar. Twenty-two battles in Arb, four battles in Cláire – will he not fight them? It will be certain, he will wage the seven battles of Cúailgne along with the three bloody morning battles of Femen, the battle at Goll, the battle at Ergoll and the black night[-battle] of Immar.

Forannán the king will die,

the princes of Aidne will fall

Mane mac Bríathraig will die and Ailill Olgné, Conchobor besides, Fergus, Óengus Dubaigi

In an encounter around Tipraite,

though the journey may be half as strong,

it is he who will be born in combat,

the body of troops around him.

Woe to Conn Cétchathach

after the destruction by fire over every plain

He will be slain after going round every promontory

on a Tuesday in Túath Imrois.

One hundred years only,

he who shall approach it is he who shall drink it."

11. "Upon whom shall this golden cup of red ale be bestowed," said the girl? "That is not difficult. Bestow some of it on Art Óenfer," said the phantom, "a great fear-rousing man who will wage eighty battles: the battle of Slíab mBetha, the battle of Slíab Cúa, the battle of Maistiu, the battle of Móen, the battle of Drúag, the battle of Tortíne, the battle of Irlúachair

The battle of Coidlim, the battle of Loch Daim

in which the warriors will fall

It will be a well-known story in every house,
    the battle that will be fought in Collamair,
the battle of Druimm [Fi]unnglaissi, the battle of Áth Dairi Duib, the
battle of Senchúa, the two battles of Liffey, the battle of Dorcha, the
battle of Druimm nDígais, the battle of Sláine, the battle of Roigne,
the battle of Argatros in which many [will] die, two battles in Line, the
battle of Aidne, the battle of Lethet Lachtmuige, two evening battles
in Saimne, the battle of Finnmag, the battle in Fremainn, the morning
battle of Inis Dornglaisi.
    The battle in Brí Chobthaig Coíl,
        many [will] lament him, nobles [will] lament him.
    Woe to Fothad who [will] die
        and to Óengus mac Domnaill.
    This morning [battle] of Mag Mucrama
        in which many dead will fall.
    It will be sad for Art mac Cuinn,
        the crime of the sons of Ailill Aulom.
    On a long Thursday on the western side of a meadow
        they [will be] defeated by Lugaid's cavalcade.
    Twenty years only,
        he who shall approach it is he who shall drink it."

12. "Upon whom shall this golden cup of ale be bestowed?", said the
girl. "That is not difficult. Bestow some of it on Lugaid Mac Con," said
the phantom, "though he is not of the race of Conn, you will visit [him].
    Twenty-five years only,
        he who shall approach it is he who shall drink it."
His expedition to the land of the Orkneys or of Alba. He will defeat the
people of the Orkneys in twenty-seven battles. He will wage the battle
of Tuithme with three hostile attacks on Umall.
    On a Sunday in Áth Í
        he [will] die by a 'tooth of poison'."

13. "Upon whom shall it be bestowed?", said the girl. "Bestow some
of it on the great judge, on Cormac úa Cuinn.
    Sixty years only,
        he who shall approach it is he who shall drink it."
Kindred and strangers will be exalted. Great peace as far as the sea in
his reign.
    Three times he will be king of Tara
        in which will die many phantoms, i.e. *síd*-dwellers.

He will be taken overseas by Máelchenn one winter's night south of Benn Bairchi. Champion of Mide who will fight the battle of Granard, the battle in *Eó*, the battle in Eth, the battle in Cenn Dairi, the battle of Sruthair, the battle of Cúailgne, the battle of Áth Beth, the battle of Áth Dumai,

> the battle of Cúil Chaichir thrice,
>> the *advantages* will not be small.

Proud fall of splendid Assal
> without Cormac in his royal assembly,
three battles in Dubad.
> The morning battle of scorched Daire,
the battle of Lúachair beyond Mag Slecht,
> the battle of Eillne, the battle of Mag Techt,
the insulting of Cormac thrice,
> the son of the intimidator will be sorry.

After that, the escape of the king of Tara,
> great lamenting in Móenmag.

The expedition of Cormac over the ocean,
> three years, hear it far away.

Cormac will come after that to Munster,
> to his morning battle of judgement,
the battle of Bérre, the battle of Loch Léin,
> the battle around Limerick, the battle around Grían,
their great bands of troops will be extensive,
> [they will move] towards Tara over the plain of Fál.

He will bind the hostages of the Goídil on account of his red-anger of fury, he will wage the battle of Clasach. A great slaughter over Muiresc, bloodshed of the doomed,
> the Ulaid [will] pay heed to him,
> Eochaid Tóebfota will die,
the battle of Slabre, the battle of Ard Cam,
> it will not be favourable to the people of Munster.

The slaying of the princesses, it will be news, it will be a legal precedent for a long time.
> He will be the one with the power of lordships
>> over Aidne of the cattle-tribute.

A great incursion of Ireland by Cormac
> against Fergus, high-king of the Ulaid.

Fergus and Énna will die
 on account of which there will be a sad gloomy host.
A Tuesday battle in Crinna as long as the world will be,
 in which the hosts of Ireland shall give a roar.
Warriors bands who will wage battles, Cormac will win the battle.
Three years after that to the battle of Crinna Fregabuil. Fair Cormac will die, dead on a Tuesday beside Cleitech, the Goídil will lament [him]."

14. "Upon whom shall this golden cup (i.e. the kingship of the Irish) of red ale be bestowed?", said the girl.

"Bestow some of it on a man of many deeds,
 on Cairpre Liphechair, a man whom an abundance [will] bless.
Thirty battles in his reign.
He will be sixty years [in kingship].
The battle of Ireland to the sea,
 a battle that will be fought on the Liffey plain.
A Tuesday battle on the Liffey plain that [will be] in store,
 the royal-champion will die there."

15. "Bestow some of it on Fíachu Sroiphtine. The morning battle of Mide by him, two battles in Mag Rátha.

Twenty-five years his reign
 until the seeking of the cattle-tribute.
The death of Fothad mac Crúaid
 will be great news in every territory.
Three years then without decline,
 in Cnámros there will be royal-slaughter.
The Wednesday battle of Cnámros, it will be an evil battle
 in which will fall Fíachu Sroiphtine."

16. "Bestow some of it on Muiredach Tírech. Forty years in lordship,

the battle in Mórmag, he will give battle
 against the Ulaid, against [Dál n]Araide.
In the battle on the bank of the Daball,
 Muiredach Tírech will die."

17. "Bestow some of it on Echu Mugmedón, tall-sided one of Tara, military leader of Tlachtga, champion of Feimen, protector of Móenmag, sturdy champion of Liffey, invader of Torrach.

Twenty-five years only,
 he who shall approach it is he who shall drink it.

The slaying of Glúnfinn, great will be the slaughter.
The killing of Conchobar, the slaying of Mac Cécht.
The stability of Ireland under Echu throughout his reign, he will be the pick of good persons. From him will derive forever the stock of princes.
In Dub Commair during his reign
there will be a basis for kin-slaying.
The three Collas will complete the slaughter
in which will fall Echu Mugmedón."
18. "Bestow some of it on Níall Noígíallach, i.e. five hostages of Ireland and a hostage [each] from Alba, from the British, the Saxons and the Franks. Champions will be celebrated, plains will be increased, hostages will be bound, battles will be fought, hosts will be attacked, lords will be exalted. Níall will exact hostages three times,
sovereignty will choose him
because he will be a good king.
In the battle of Muirned in Forad Lúain,
it is there the hosts will fall.
The triumphant evening battle of Dún Cúair,
the fall of Aurthuile to the north of it.
Twenty-seven years only,
he who shall approach it is he who shall drink it.
A warrior of many exploits [will] fall then at Druimm nAlban, Níall will die,
it will be the cause of great sorrow
in Ardmóin on a Saturday."
19. "Bestow some of it on Colla Óss (i.e. Úais),
four years only,
he who shall approach it is he who shall drink it,
He will relinquish great sovereignty, glorious news,
for committing a kin-slaying."
20. "Bestow some of it on Ailill Molt mac Nathí maic Fíachrach. A proud man, a man lamented by a multitude. Twenty years only.
Many battles in his sovereignty
because he will be a good king.
Protector of Tara, disturber of Tailtiu, the battle of Áth Tálmaige. Champion of Séile, distinguished one of Aiche, the battle of Ráth Crúachan. A stride upon Sabralla, a stride upon the Alps. The destruction of the tower. A stride upon Eolarcca, the battle of Strathclyde, the slaughter of Geinned. A stride across the English Channel to the Alps. They will

walk the plain of Ireland, a swift course, foreigners will wound them. Ailill [will win] seven *battles* against the men of Ireland on a Friday in the Alps. Many will die violently, it will be sad for the men of Ireland, death at the hands of foreigners [will be] in store for many."

21. "Bestow some of it on Lóegaire, a man of many exploits, many lands and many languages will exalt [him]. Thirty years only. A swift expedition, a cleric will come (i.e. Patrick), a man of high rank who will make God known. He will kindle a great flame which will cover Ireland to the sea. Lóegaire will die (a king surrounded by crosiers) on the bank of the Caisse, the clerics [will] overwhelm a great keen warrior."

22. "Bestow some of it on Túathal Máelgarb (i.e. mac Cormaic maic Coirpri maic Néill), twenty years, the battle of Lúachair Ailbi, the battle of Detnae, the fall of Ardgal, the battle of Lége, the battle of Druimm nArbelaig, the battle of Bregonn. The binding of the hostages of the Goídil. After that it will be news in every plain, the only-begotten one will die, Túathal at Grellach Eilti. Máelmór will be killed in revenge for him in Túath Imrois."

23. "Bestow some of it on Lugaid mac Lóegairi, twenty-six [years] till his death during a circuit around Ireland on account of his rejection of Patrick in Escir Forchai."

24. "Bestow some of it on Muirchertach Mac Erca (i.e. the daughter of Loarnn). A victorious warlike king lamented by a multitude,

He will subdue Ireland, [both] men and women
because he will be the heir to Tara.
The battle of Áth Sigi after that
which will flood fighting-men to Ireland.
The victorious cutter gives battle
to the Laigin on a Tuesday.

much death, Muirchertach will die on a Tuesday in Cleitech."

25. "Bestow some of it on Ainmire, he will summon hostages of every plain across the country though not east of Trim, he will die on account of a mighty blaze, battles will be waged. Four years only."

26. "Bestow some of it on Báetán and Echu, four years."

27. "Bestow some of it on Díarmait (i.e. mac Fergusa Cerrbeóil), champion of Tailtiu, the prophesied one of Tara.

Prosperity in his reign
for he will be a good king.

Seven years after that to the day, a keen battle gained over Díarmait of Dreimne.

The host will approach from the north,
 they will complete the rout to Athlone.
The triumph will be secured.
 On the Friday in Ráith Becc,
  the fall of Díarmait [will] occur,
twenty years."

28. "Bestow some of it on Fergus and Domnall, the two sons of Muirchertach Mac Erca, i.e. Brandub mac Echach killed [them], two years in joint sovereignty."

29. "Bestow some of it on Áed Úaridnach mac Domnaill who will increase sovereignty, he will subdue Ireland. An aggressive spoil-laden lord. He will effect the sieges of Ireland. A year after that Ailill mac Domangairt [will] fall. There will be a deed in the plain of Tara.

 The Laigin will slay their (poetic) companies,
  their true tribes will die.
 His reign will be fierce and triumphant
  until the day of treachery.
 On the Tuesday in southern Liffey,
  the king will die there.
Eight years only."

30. "Bestow some of it on Áed Sláine. A great peace, lord of the Goídil. He will reward the people of Fúat Líamna well.

 Áed Sláine will fall then
  after a number of battles in his reign.
 Eight years only.
 He who shall approach it is he who shall drink it,
i.e. ale of battle, a 'vision-drink' as it was said."

31. "Bestow some of it on Áed Ollán. Eight years, he who shall approach it is he who shall drink it, champion of the plain of Fál, he will rule over the Liffey plain. He will bind the hostages of the Goídil. Many dead, much mortality. Great misfortune, the Goídil will lament him."

32. "Bestow some of it on Domnall Menn Ulad, nineteen years only. A warrior of many exploits

 who will wage two battles in Mag Roth.
 The royalty will fall there on a Tuesday.
And the blood-red morning battle of the Cruithne. He will wage the battle of Dún Cethirn with the battle of Ráith beyond Macha. He will proceed on his way then, great misfortune, the king [will] die."

33. "Bestow some of it on Suibne Menn, a warrior of many exploits, he will be eight years in lordship, he will bind the hostages of every high place. The king will wage the battle of Dathe.

He will fall there, it will not be a lie,
Colmán Mór mac Díarmata."

34. "Bestow some of it on Blathmac mac Áeda (i.e. Sláine), it is he who shall drink it. Five years for his certain sovereignty."

35. "Bestow some of it on the timid one (i.e. his blushing at the expelling of Mo Chuta), on Díarmait Daithi, in the first battle of Senchúa, the battle of Ross Corcu Búain, the battle of Ossory, the battle of Éile, the battle of Slíab between the two Inda. He will wage the seven battles of Aidne with the afternoon battle of Selg. The red morning battles of the Cruithne [will be] in store for him, it will be memorable valour north of the Cuib. Then the plague over Ireland in which there will be the sorrows of the host."

36. "Bestow some of it on Fínnachta, i.e. mac Dúnchada maic Áeda Sláine, he will stir up a quarrel with great Munster. He will wage the battle of Cúil Choíláin, sorrow beside Cithamair, a great man who [will] die in a famous kin-slaying on a Friday at [the] Dollad. His rule will be short, Áed (i.e. mac Dlúthaig) will not be king afterwards. Twenty years only."

37. "Bestow some of it on Sechnussach mac Blathmaic, he who shall approach it for one year, he will die of a tumour in the Imlech above the Boyne."

38. "Bestow some of it on Cenn Fáelad, seven years in lordship. The battle in the plain of Tara then, Cenn Fáelad will die in the Sunday-battle of Cúil Choíláin."

39. "Bestow some of it on Loingsech (i.e. mac Óengussa maic Domnaill), martial champion over Fálmag, custodian of Liffey. Troop-leader of Béirre.

He will fall at [the] white stones
at the hands of the emblem-wearing warrior bands.
He will go northwards waging war
the king of Ess Rúaid will be defeated,
i.e. by Cellach of Loch Cimbi.
On a Saturday he will die
between the two Uinnsiu [rivers] of Corann
(i.e. the battle of Corann).
Eleven years only."

40. "Bestow some of it on fiery Fogartach and on Congal mac Fergusa

Fánat. Fourteen years only. The two of them [will] fall on the Monday before Samain, one at the start of the day, the other at its end. They were buried in Clonard, as Pátríne said."

41. "Bestow some of it on the cock (on a Friday in the battle of Allen), on Fergal, spear-breaker of Ireland, armed one of Line, warrior of Áe.

Fergal will die by the Laigin at the end of his reign,
　　in the battle of Allen,
There will be great slaughter in the battle,
　　which will flood armies to Ireland,
in which will fall a host of wealthy kings
　　around the most wonderful cock.

Twelve [years], Fergal was buried in Durrow. Whence it was said:

Before his wounding in the battle-field,
　　firmly he used to instigate battles of champions,
today on (the plain of) Durrow
　　seeing Fergal is not a reality."

42. "Bestow some of it on Flaithbertach, the time which will be, he will wage the battle of Druimm Corcáin to the north of Tara, Cináed úa Conaing (an end under ground). The Goídil will lament him. Flaithbertach will be king for twenty-six years. He will die of a tumour at a monastery, i.e. in Armagh, on pilgrimage, the cleric [will] die at the burial place of the kings."

43. "Bestow some of it on Áed Allán (i.e. Altan the name of the place where he was fostered). Áed, high-king for ten years. He will wage a victorious battle, he will seize the *gein* of the battle of Sáiltíre, the two battles on the same day will be of concern for him, the battle of Áth Dá Charna, the battle of Áth Medóin. He will defeat Cenél Conaill. He will complete slaughters. Royal-lamentation of the Ulaid when Áed will defeat Áed (i.e. [Áed] Rón mac Béicce Bairche).

The Áed of carnage (i.e. the battle of Fochairt), perfection laid low,
　　half his name in the big sea (i.e. [rón] a seal).
He will attack the plain of the Laigin
　　it will be a famous hosting throughout the world.

On Tuesday in the north of Liffey, in revenge for the battle of Allen in which every renowned person will die, he will cause the misfortune of Uchbad. He will drive the Goídil to the sea, both Connacht-men and Munster-men. The battle of Kells,

a battle in Eochinn, he will attain it
　　in which lords will die.

There will be great sorrow in every house,
    after the battle in Seredmag.
There will be slaying among kings
    all around the corpse of Áed.
The king from Srúb mBrain will die
    on the shore of Loch Sailchitain.
Áed Allán was buried in Clonmacnoise."

44. "Bestow some of it on Domnall mac Murchada, battalions will be routed before him (i.e. the battle of Seredmag), men will be celebrated on a Thursday. He will die in Brega. Death of a tumour in a monastic house at Tailtiu, i.e. in Imlech Fía. Twenty years."

45. "Bestow some of it on Níall Frossach, many battles in his reign. They will not be waged against him,
    he will die of a bloody tumour.
    He will be brought to lands over the sea,
i.e. to Iona. Seven years only, i.e. Donnchad ousted him from his kingdom."

46. "Bestow some of it on Donnchad. The sovereignty of powerful Donnchad will come, the protector of the Island of the Irish, whenever he will be born.

The hosts will accompany him
    from the north around Carn Fíachach.
Ravens will drink gushes of blood
    on the edge of Loch Luglochta.
He will subdue Brega in mighty battles. He will wage the great battle of eastern Fúat.
He will have an abundance of [severed] heads (i.e. heads)
    on the morning in Forcalad,
Donn Midi will win the battle
    in which Congalach [will] perish.
Donn Midi will win the battle of Srúbair over kindred and strangers where he will slay Canán *who will take an open mouth*. A cleric will be killed, a sinful deed, from which Fíachra (i.e. mac Cathail) [will] die.

In front of him men [will] lie scattered,
    after coming from Laigille,
from within Tailtiu, a champion of battle
            (i.e. the battle of Carn maic Cáirthinn),
    will gain a victory in the North (i.e. over Áed Ingor),

he will stir up a quarrel with heads of wretches
    on a Sunday around Clóenloch.
There will be many dead
    at the battle of Étan Tairb
On guard (i.e. Áed Muinderg) in Brecc Fánat in which there [will be] a king, severe battle for Donn in the south, good fortune for the scald-crow. The nobleman whose name is Cellach will be his coeval; everybody will know him as far as the plain from the centre of red Liffey – sixteen years will be the period of the lord of Midi.
From the time that he will go as far as the sea,
    the true story of the slaying of Follaman (i.e. mac Con Congalt).
An entitlement of thirty years only
    till the end of Donnchad's kingship.
There will be lamenting in every plain
    at the start of the cold spring.
Donn Midi will die of a tumour
    on a Tuesday at a monastery,
i.e. in Clonard."

47. "Bestow some of it on Áed Ingor, on the champion, twenty-three years in lordship.
He is the victorious, harsh, triumphant Áed
    who will gain a victory.
Beware of the two victories on Clóitech.
    He will destroy men though kings will not fall.
He will perform bloody exploits twice,
    against whom the hosts of Mide will fall,
i.e. Fínnachta. Grievous bloody slaughters, he will commit them.
The harsh lord of Cerna will die
    it will be after victory when he will cease to be.
Fierce trials of valour of horsemen. He will destroy a monastery, i.e. the sanctuary of Armagh. Strongly warlike one of Cenél Conaill. Bloody fierce one of the plain of Tara. Host-attacker of Cláire. Custodian of Liffey.
Hosts that will come from Srúb mBrain
    in the month after a cold winter.
On account of him, ravens will drink blood
    on skins at Derclúachair (i.e. Druimm Ríg).
The host that will come to the left,
    the rear of their battalion to Tlachtga

Fair Áed hacking bodies,
    will rout before him south-westwards.
It is when he will turn the chariot breast to the left
    that Fínnachta will die.
Áed was buried in Armagh. Áed Ordnide was a son of Dúnflaith
daughter of Flaithbertach mac Loingsich. He died at Áth Dá Ferta in
Conaille because of a conflict with Máel Canaig."

48. "Bestow some of it on Conchobor mac Donnchada, he will drive
the Goídil as far as the sea. The son of a woman of the Connachta. Fair
flame of the land of Bregmag. Fourteen [years]. On coming to Tara,
showers of prosperity in his reign. Tidings of the coming of the Norse.

    On a Friday, multitudes [will] lament him,
        the death of Conchobor [will be] nigh,
he was buried in Clonard."

49. "Bestow some of it on Níall Caille who will spurn it (i.e. Tara).
He will wage the battle of Crúachu (i.e. the battle of Leth Cam), the
battle of Derry on the Norsemen. Níall in the sea, Níall in wounding,
Níall in flagration. Disturber (i.e. of Ireland). Thirteen years. Níall was
buried in Armagh after drowning in the Calann, i.e. in Linn Néill."

50. "Bestow some of it on Máel Sechnaill. No-one will know the
secrets in a heart. Three malicious lords [will] fall by the severity of his
anger. He will make a burial-mound of kin-slaying at Clúain. [It will
be] swiftly fought against foreigners (i.e. the Norsemen), destruction
of hosts of Forach. An evening battle in the south (as far as Munster),
a circuit over Ireland *concerning which* poems will be read (i.e. the
poem of Pátríne). On a Tuesday, the kingship of Ross, he [will] die of a
tumour in the battle-field of Ross (i.e. Aróc daughter of the king of Fir
Chúl, the mother of Máel Sechnaill). Sixteen years, he was buried in
Clonmacnoise."

51. "Bestow some of it on the slender pious one (i.e. who became a
cleric), on Áed Olach (i.e. [Áed] Finnlíath son of Donnchad's daughter,
Gormlaith, and Níall Caille). Warrior of Liffey, bloody one of Clóitech.
Horseman of Crúachu. He will wage the battle of Lettir Daigri (i.e.
the battle of Cell Úa nDaigri) a short time before his fall (i.e. one year
before his fall, i.e. before death). A great darkness [will] close in on a
Wednesday in early winter. Sixteen years. Áed died in Ráith Adomnæ
and was buried in Armagh."

52. "Bestow some of it on the lying stammerer, Flann Sinna, who
will wreak kin-slaying on his kinsmen. Many signs [will] come in his

reign, i.e. a messenger from heaven (i.e. a pilgrim from Rome) who will proclaim the slaughter of the Goídil at Dublin (i.e. of the pilgrim). *Slender death* the reputation for the king of Crúachu, i.e. for Áed mac Conchobuir who was killed in the battle. The seven sorrows of Tara (i.e. seven bad years). He will lay siege to a monastery (i.e. Armagh) with foriegners (i.e. Norsemen, i.e. the sons of Ímar). He will defeat the men of Bréifne. He will wage with fame the battle of Grellach Eilti (won by his son Óengus) and will win the battle of Mag nAilbi (with the Laigin). The enticement of jealousy in his reign. Hairs in heads, unfavourable judgement of people in his reign. Peaceful wealthy ruler (i.e. Flann), his own family will revolt against him (i.e. his seven sons). A death of wretched authority on a holy believer. The Sunday battle at [Lough] Ennell at the end of the autumn in which he [will] vanquish them. Thirty-seven years. Flann, daughter of Dúngal king of Osraige, was his mother. He died in his seventy-sixth year and was buried in Clonmacnoise."

53. "Bestow some of it on Níall Glúndub who will complete the rout of Rúadair, he will subdue the victorious lord of Line. Heroic warrior of Loch Lébinn. He will burn Cúalu twice. One attended by the companies of Cláire, warlike one of Crúachu, chief of Cuib, great warrior of Bairche. Fiery one of Slíab Cailggi who [will] not be opposed. The battle of Orgain, the battle of Codal (i.e. of Grellach Eilti where Flann will defeat Níall). The battle of Trácht Eóthaile where the Connachta will be defeated from which blood [will] flow in the Ferne. *Alba raised him* (i.e. Máel Maire his mother, the daughter of Cináed mac Alpin, king of Alba), the heroic bear of Liffey, he will bind the oath of Loch Lébinn from where there will be death on both sides. On the Monday over Martartech [from which] there will be a shower of blood over Tailtiu (i.e. the battle of Dublin in which Níall died).

Three and a half years only,
he who shall approach it is he who shall drink it.

Fifty years his complete age, he was born in Druimm Caille. Níall was buried in Kells. He was three years in the kingship of Ailech."

54. "Bestow some of it on the dirty-belted one of Codal (i.e. he will hasten into kin-slaying), Donn his name (i.e. Máel Febail daughter of Flann mac Conaing his mother). Fair flaming valorous one who will win harsh battles, who will brandish spears over Tailtiu. Chosen one of Tara. He [will] summon hostages as far as the Daball. It is he who will wage the battle of Febail against family and strangers. The battle of Cúalu. An abundance of produce in his reign. The sun of righteousness (i.e.

Ioseph abbot of Armagh or culdee). He will be lamented over the peak of Cúailnge on a Sunday between two calends. Twenty-five years."

55. "Bestow some of it on the curly fair-haired one of Colla, Congal[ach] Cerna (i.e. Lígach, the daughter of Flann, was his mother). He will provide ten years, the reign of the little hound, he will make a great number quake

from the Laigin, the ruining of his surprise attack,
    he will not live out half his time.
A warrior from Cerna, if he takes revenge,
    those who plunder him will be sorry.
A fair man, he [will] oversee kingship,
    his coevals will be few,
Congalach was buried in Monasterboice."

56. "Bestow [some of it] on Domnall, descendant of two sides (i.e. the southern half and northern half of Ireland), i.e. Domnall foster-son of Athba (i.e. the people of Athba fostered him, i.e. the Uí Erthuile). Fair knowing leader, aggressive one of Cnogba, chief of Assal, great leader of Uisnech. He will wage a battle in Brí Éile (i.e. upon Carrach Calma). The defeat of Lettir Ainge (i.e. the battle of Cell Móna) in which will fall one hundred and fifty youths around Fíngin Corad.

The battle of Slíab Cúa twice
    and the morning[-battle] of Grophtine.
Loss of corn from Mag Cuinn (i.e. famine),
    six years of great poverty (i.e. of scarcity)
He will die, though his beauty may be splendid,
    on a Monday in Carn Furbaidi.

(i.e. Furbaide Menn Macha was buried there, or the smiting of the people with a grave there). Twenty-four years [in kingship], fifty-five years his age."

57. "Bestow some of it on the lightning [one] of Macha (i.e. a fire over Macha in his reign, i.e. Machaire), i.e. Máel Sechnaill (i.e. son of Dúnflaith daughter of Muirchertach), honour of kings. Resolute broad-faced one who [will] become furious with anger before the hosts of Tara. Strong one of Howth, burner of Liffey. Knowledgeable one of Cúalu, horseman of Crúachu. Heart of a dragon, he will wage a battle against Cláire (i.e. the battle of Carn Fordroma), the battle of Iroros, the battle in Maistiu. Brian reigns at this point. The great morning[-battle] of Áth (i.e. the morning[-battle] of Mide). Dead from a drink of mead. Bravery after valour, on a Sunday in Telchinn.

Thirty-six years only
    he will spend in complete sovereignty (i.e. Brian obtained the
        kingship of Ireland from the twentieth [year] onwards)."
58. "Bestow some of it on the basket-feat [performer] (or the basketed-one, i.e. he [wiil] have a big long basket) of Clóitech, i.e. Flaithbertach who will wage the battle of Loch Bricrenn, who will scatter slaughter around Cnámchaill. He will vanquish men from Ess Rúaid (Cenél Conaill), he will win the battle of Loch Lébinn. He will die of a tumour in a monastery. Sixteen years only."
59. "Bestow some of it on the fawn of Assal, Murchad, acclaimed by the keen Goídil, great fair hero, strong noble man, battle-victor of Howth. The stern valiant one of (Slige) Midlúachra, the burner of Line. He will wage the battle of Lúachmag. He will lay siege to Loch Léin (i.e. in violation of Christ, Brian will die there). He will fill Cashel with hosts. He will spread men over Tarbgna. Twenty years only."
60. "Bestow some of it on Óengus of Óenach Fánat, victorious the king. He (i.e. Óengus) will wage the battle in the south then. He will wage a battle in Mag Cruinn (i.e. the stave-battler of Carn Aisi, i.e. of Slíab Fúait) through his love for his two fearless sons (i.e. Cummascach and Li [...]), from which there will be a woman without a spouse and pierced and wounded men.
    It [will] not be suitable for a tender mother
        the battle in Kells that he [will] incite.
Peculiar darling hero (i.e. Óengus) on a Wednesday in the further plain of Liffey. Óengus will die, the slaughter will be committed (i.e. by the Laigin). Twenty-two years only."
61. "Bestow some of it on the bull-faced one (or Murchad) from Ailech. He will share his name with the sea, i.e. Muiredach of many troops. It is he who will deprive the Laigin of [their] valuables. He will defeat the Bréifne in the battle of Brí Léith. The battle of Selca, the battle of Móin Tuirc. The evening battle of Airbre then in which three Muiredachs will die. He [will] die from a flash (i.e. of lightning) on a Tuesday in Telenmag. Sixteen years or thirty or thirteen. Thus the exemplars differ."
62. "Bestow some of it on the brown-faced one of Daball, i.e. Áed Engach (i.e. *én*, raven-like, i.e. *en*, water or more truly, i.e. talkative) for whom they will lift ships over Ess Rúaid. A complement of wonderful treasures in his reign. He will wage a battle in which the two Dúnlangs will fall, i.e. the battle of Maistiu (in which the Laigin will be defeated).

A cleric will be born in his reign, i.e. Tipraite, a hero who will spread peace to the ends of Ireland. Ireland will be according to the law of the believers. This is the grave foretold for him (i.e. for Áed), in a morning battle in the upper part of Ocha. Sixteen years."

63. "Bestow some of it on the complaining one of Uisnech, i.e. Cerball (or Cairell), stern warrior, many-territoried one of the Bann, leader of the troops of Brea. He will win the battle of Loch Dá Cháech,
on a day along the heavy forest of the Barrow.
The great battle of Sláine which will destroy silence.
They will carry off two girls to the south of Bréifne. He will win the battle of Clúain, he will vanquish chieftains around Limerick. He will burn Desgabar (i.e. Ossory). Fifteen years only. He [will] die then in Fidga from a deer antler embedded in the ground."

64. "Bestow some of it on the black-wretch of Ailech (i.e. no other king [will] get Tara from it), i.e. rough-haired Fergal. *Those attended by the troops of Bregmag*. He will wage the battle of Slíab. A host facing the battle-field of Roth. He will bind the hostages of Carn Lugdach. He will wage the great battle of Mide. He will advance on Cnámchaill. Account of a fire that [will] burn the crops. Little peace, great misfortune.
He (i.e. Fergal) [will be] killed by a fiery woman of the night,
at Finncharn his deceitful encounter [will] come.
Seventeen years. Joint sovereignty of Ireland then. Twenty-seven years, i.e. until Flann."

65. "Bestow some of it on Flann Cinuch, last ruler of Ireland, though not of the race of Conn, it is Conn's share that he [will] take. An invasion of foreigners in his reign (i.e. the Norse invasion of Inber Domnann by sea), an abundance of every crop. They will wage a number of champions' battles. Great slaughter around Cnámchaill. The driving out of the foreigners. Blessed peace, fifty-three years, they will be subject to God's Creation. His appearance will be different every season.
He will set bright Fál (i.e. stone) in motion thrice.
Three suns. Three summer days.
The soul of the believer who [will] die
[...] over Ireland which he [will] avenge.
Monasteries will be celebrated through the sound of bells in his reign. Death will proceed then from the relic of the believer in Tara." FINET.

NOTES

Title. *Incipit di Baile in Scáil inso ar slicht senlibuir Duib dá Leithi .i.*
comarpa Pátraic Dub dá Leithe (†1064) was appointed *fer léiginn*
of Armagh in 1046 and was Abbot of Armagh from 1049-60. As
Kelleher (1971, 117n.) points out, his book is 'cited in AU at 629
[recte 630], 963, 1004, and 1021'.
  Rawl. reads *hsenlibuir* here. The transposition of the mark of
lenition, *h*, and *s* is repeated in §7 (*de hsíl*). This is also a feature of
the orthography of *Cáin Adomnáin*; e.g., *do hsóerath* (Meyer (1905)
6 §11). For further examples, see *SnaG* III, §2.7.
1, §1. *dona rígaib* The loss of the dat. plu. ending of the definite article,
here with the preposition *do*, is quite common in late O.Ir. Ó Máille
(1910, §139) notes that it is already evident in the Milan Glosses
(e.g. Ml. 54ᵇ25 *honaigabalaib*; cf. Sg. 212ᵃ13 *forsna huilib*, Sg. 217ᵃ4
ocnafothaircthib) and points out that the last example of the dat. plu.
ending of the definite article in *AU* occurs s.a. 891 [recte 892: *isnaib*
caillibh]. For further examples of this development, see *SnaG* III,
§7.5.
3, §1. *in filid* The nom. plu. def. art. has been reduced from *ind* to *in* here
(see notes to ll. 9 & 300 for similar examples). The reading in Rawl.
is *in fil-*, which could be taken as a nom. sg. referring to Cessarnn
alone but this reading has not been adopted for two reasons: (a) the
motivation for having Eochaid and Corbb with Conn would then be
obscure; (b) in Harl. the reading (*et a trii filid .i. ethain corb cesarn*)
explicitly refers to all three as poets. Conversely, however, from §3
onwards, Conn is left dealing with Cessarnn alone.
  The names of Conn Cétchatach's *filid* are not mentioned in
Cath Maige Léna or *Oided Chuind Cétchathaig* but one of them,
Cessarnn, is mentioned in *Airne Fíngein* (Vendryes, 1953, §13)
where he is called *in druí i Temraig*. The final verse praising Conn in
Airne Fíngein is attributed to one *Eochaid Écius* 'Eochaid the poet',
though his relationship to Conn is not given. This reference helps to
fix the balance of probability in favour of *Eochaid* as the poet's name
(rather than *Ethain* in Harl.).
5, §1. For an account of the *Fomoiri*, see *EIHM* 523-5; Mac Cana (1975,
94-7) and Gray (1983, 132).
6ff. In the opening section (§§1-9) u-quality is marked quite consist-

ently, viz. *chiund*, l. 6; *toísiuch*, l. 27; *ciund*, l. 35; *Chunn*, l. 45. This may be contrasted with non-marking on *mullach*, l. 32; *cind*, l. 44.

7, §2. *géisis an chloch* For the 'crying' of the stone, cf. Introduction **5.4.**

7-8, §2. *co closs fon Temraig hule ₇ fo Bregmag* Here the prep. *fo* is followed by the acc. – in Harl. it is followed by the dat. Use of the dat. after *fo* with *ro-cluinethar* is more usual, e.g. *co clos fosnaib tuathaib uili, TBCL* 878.

9, §3. *din filid* – the article has been reduced here from *dind* to *din* (see notes to ll. 3 & 300 for similar examples).

12, §3. *ind árim* Note the use of the dat. sg. for the nom. sg. with the correct O.Ir. form of the definite article.

12-13, §3. *ro buí-side icc scrútan co n-écetar a eochra éccsi dóu* This phrasing is paralleled in *Tochmarc Étaíne* (*IT* i, 129, §18): *foillsighthir do triana eochraib écsi ocus triana oghumm*. See further, McManus (1991, 157e).

14, §2. *fo ail .i. ail fo ríg* This phrase is discussed in the Introduction **5.3.**

15, §4. *hi tairiss* Here the deponent vb *do-airissedar* has lost its deponent ending. For more on this development, see *SnaG* III, §12.4 and *EIV* VIII, §5.1; XII, §6.4.1.

16, §4. *iss ed tír* Note the correct use of the neut. pron. *ed*. In Harl. the neut. has been lost and the fem. pron. *í* is used instead – *is i an tir*.

17, §4. *a llá ndédenach* Note the correct use of neut. art. and nasalisation after neut. noun. In Harl. this use of the neut. has been lost – *la deginach*.

17, §4. For more on *óenach Tailten*, see Binchy (1958, 115-27).

18, §4. *flaith ná faigbi* This might also be translated as 'the lord who will not attain [it]' (i.e. the sovereignty). See further, Ó Broin (1996, 64).

19, §4. *a llín ngémind* The correct use of neut. art. and nasalisation after neut. noun in Rawl. has been lost in Harl. – *an lin gairm*.

23 & 26, §5. *dus-fánic* The Class A pron. 3rd plu. is used in the relative clause in these examples instead of Class C. The simplification of the infix. pron. is well documented for the Mid.Ir. period (cf. Strachan (1904, 162ff.) and *SnaG* III, §10.6) .

27, §5. *toísiuch* (Rawl. *quam in tossiuch* / Harl. *inas torchor toísech*) Rawl. *tossiuch* seems to be a mistake for *toisiuch* – a very easy mistake to make because of the similarity in MS of *is* and *ss*. Rawl. utilises the dat. sg. of *toísech* which is usual for the object of the comparative in O.Ir. [-(i)u + dat.]. Harl. preserves the O.Ir. relative form of the subst. vb. to express the object of the comparative with a following noun in the nom.

27, §5. *"Is do guin ríg", ol in file, "cip hé díbercess Conn hi Temair."* A similar injunction against casting in Tailtiu is to be found in *MD* iv, 154.125.

27, §5. *cip hé* A full analysis of this construction is to be found in Bergin (1934-38, 208-11).

30, §6. *assa mag* The correct use of the neut. art. (with Rawl. *assa* for *issa*) has been lost in Harl. – *isin mag nalaind.*

31, §6. *issa tech* Note the correct use of the neut. art. in Rawl.

34, §6. *airideog di ór ara bélaib* (Rawl. *airideog nech di ór ara belaib*). Over the 'n' of *nech* in Rawl. is written the symbol for *nó*, which may be interpreted as *nó ech* and taken as an incorporated gloss (*airideog (nó ech),* i.e. *airideog nó airidech*), thus giving an alternate spelling. Thurneysen (1936, 220n.) makes a similar suggestion. Against this interpretation, however, *airdeog* (§12) and *airedeog* (§14) are elsewhere written for *air(i)dech.* Harl. reads *copan di ór for a beolai.* See further, Thurneysen (1912, 70-2).

35, §6. *a scál* The correct use of neut. art. in Rawl. has been lost in Harl. – *in scal.*

37-40, §§6-7. Parts of these lines are illegible in Rawl. due to blackening of the MS. The Harl. readings have been adopted where possible.

39, §7. *is [dom' uirdercus dúib]* This reading has been restored from Harl. *Dom'* is here taken to represent the prep. *de, di* plus poss. adj. 1st sg. The confusion in Harl. between *de* and *do* is evident in §4 – Harl. has *dot* where Rawl. has *ditt.*

39, §7. *is de síl* Rawl. reads *is de hsil.* See note to the 'Title' above.

42-3, §7. *Et is dó do-deochad-sa co n-écius duit-siu sáegal do flatha* This is closely paralleled by the following phrasing in *In Tenga Bithnua* (Stokes, 1905i, 104 §14): *IS do dodeochadsa, or Pilip, far ndocumsi co n-ecius duib a scel-sa.*

48, §9. *tibérthar* Rawl. reads *tiberthæ* (the sec. fut. pass. sg. form) here.

50-2, §9. *Ba trom íarum la Cesarnd filid a ndíchetal sin do thabairt fri oínhúair co n-ecmaing tre ogum hi cetheóra flescæ iphair* For more on this incident and the technical vocabulary associated with the 'writing' of *ogam,* see McManus (1991, 156-63, §§8.10-12) and Ní Chatháin (1996, 215-6). A similar passage connected with the writing of ogam is found in *Tochmarc Étaíne* (*IT* i, 129, §18):

Ba trom im*orro* laissin druid dicheilt Etáiniu fair fri re bl*iadna*, co n-dernui iarsin ɪɪɪɪ flescca ib*ir* ocus scrípuidh oghumm inntib, ocus foillsighthir do triana eochraib écsi ocus triana oghumm, i. Etain do bith i sith Breg Leth iarna breth do Midir inn.

For another parallel with *Tochmarc Étaíne*, see note to 11. 12-13. Carey (1996, 191n.) believes that the Rawl. text 'is extensively interpolated at this point in the tale'. He is referring here to the recording of the prophecy in *ogam* on the staves of yew which goes unmentioned in Harl. It is hard to decide whether the material on *ogam* is an omission by the scribe of Harl. or an insertion by the Rawl. scribe – linguistically, there seem be no obvious criteria to date the varying sections to different periods of the language.

54-5, §9. There is some inconsistency in the use of the def. art. in these lines. Rawl. has *a scail / ind dabach / in airdech*. Harl. preserves better readings – *an scail / in dubach / and airech*.

54, §9. The Rawl. spelling *a dtech* (with marking of eclipsis after the neuter article) is probably a late orthographic feature. However, it could also be an early attempt at a 'phonetic' spelling similar to those discussed by Breatnach (1990).

56, §9. *argraige* This is a poorly attested word, perhaps a by-form of the more commonly attested *targraig* (Harl. reads *targraide*). This fluctuation is also evident in *Táin Bó Cúailnge* where *TBC*[1] 1710 reads *tarrgraige* while *TBCL* 1828 reads *arrgraige*. The only other example listed in *DIL* is from a medieval Irish glossary (*Ériu* 13, 63 §20) and seems to be drawn directly from *BS* though there it is treated as a fem. word (iā-stem?): *argraidhe .i. turus, ut est argraidhe Chuinn Chédchathaigh*.

58-9, §10. *nodas-íbai* This development of the by-form *das* for 3rd sg. f. and 3rd plu. infix. prons is a ninth-century development. See *GOI* §415.

59, §10. Here for the first time is the phrase 'Dáil de for X' which is used to introduce every king listed in *BS*. Translating this phrase as 'Pour some of it on X' would seem to suggest the image of an anointing ritual, but this translation would not answer the question posed explicitly at the start of §§10-14 and implicitly for the remainder of the text – 'Upon whom shall this golden cup of red ale be bestowed?'

60, §10. *firfidius* Note here the presence of a suffix. pron. 3rd plu. As Breatnach (1977, 107) has demonstrated, suffixed pronouns 'disappeared completely as meaningful pronouns by the end of the OIr. period'.

64, §10. *cath for Caimsi* This has tentatively been translated 'the battle on the Camas', with Camas taken to refer to the river of that name in co. Derry. However, I have no other example of Caimsi as the dat. sg. form of Camas. Perhaps, it refers to an otherwise unknown place (or river?), Caimse.

68-9, §10. There appears to be a corrupt transmission of verse here. Perhaps the original read:

> *canis firfea? Bid demin,   deora dergmaitni Femin.*
> 'Will he not fight them? It will be certain,
>   the tears of the bloody morning battle of Femen'.

69, §10. *-firfe* is O.Ir. fut. 2nd sg. conj. of *feraid*. For 3rd sg. one would expect *-firfea*. However, it has been translated as 3rd sg. (with loss of final 'a') to make better sense of the sentence. On l. 98, however, *do-aidlibe* is taken as O.Ir. fut. 2nd sg. and not as fut. 3rd sg. (with loss of final 'a') because the translation does not require it.

70, §10. *Immair* This could also be the gen. sg. of *ár* ('slaughter') with the intensive prefix *imm-*; *dubadaig immáir* would then translate as 'the black night of great slaughter'. Yet another possible interpretation as *dubadaig im Máir* would translate as 'the black night around Már'.

72, §10 / 259, §40. *da-fóeth / da-thuittet* These may be taken as either two examples of the use of (meaningless?) infix. prons with the verb *do-tuit* or, more probably, *da* may be interpreted as an orthographic variant of *do* with the lenition on *-thuittet* taken as an example of main clause lenition which is common in Mid.Ir. (see *SnaG* III, §11.1).

73, §10. Óengus's epithet could be taken as (i) *dubaige* 'dejection, mourning' or (ii) a reference to the placename *Dubaiche* mentioned in l. 61.

74, §10. *cith lethchomnart a n-ude* (Harl. *cet leth comnart a nuidhe*) The translation of this line poses problems of sense. The syntax seems relatively straightforward; the translation seems less so. Perhaps *cith* should be taken as the noun *cith* 'shower' used in its vaguer sense meaning 'trial, hardship, battle' and *uide* in one of its extended meanings 'death' or 'a fixed period or time'. None of these options would seem to improve the translation, however.

75, §10. Rawl. *is he gignetar a glé* could be translated as 'it is he who will derive from brightness/combat'. The difficulty of this line is reflected by the use of a variation in Harl. Here the scribe writes: *is e gidniter ac dluigi* which translates as 'it is he who will be born splitting/sundering'; *dluigi* is also closer to full rhyme with *suide* though *rinn / airdrinn* rhymes are prevalent in this section of poetry.

77, §10. This line may contain an etymological 'play on words' on the placename *Túath Imrois*, i.e. *géntair íar timchiul cach rois*.

78, §10. *cóic fichit* The sources have no common length of reign for Conn. Emending to *cóic ar fichit*, for example, might be attractive except that it would ruin the syllable count. Harl. gives a reign of fifty years (as does *AI* p. 35, §256).

78, §10. This line contains the first example of the gen. plu. of *blíadain* 'year', generally abbreviated in Rawl. The only time that the gen. plu. form is written out in full is in l. 293 where the Mid.Ir. form is used. Because the O.Ir. nom. plu. inflection of *blíadain* is found written out in full in l. 95 (cf. l. 235 *blíadnæ* and l. 272 *blíadna*, however), it has been decided to expand all abbreviated forms of this word according to classical O.Ir. usage.

78, §10. This is the first occurrence of the phrase *doda-cich noda-íba*, translated as 'he who shall approach it is he who shall drink it'. *DIL* translates it as 'he who shall attain it shall drink it'. The logic of the motif of the drink of sovereignty, however, dictates that the drink should be partaken of first before the kingship may be attained.

80-1, §11. *fer cétgretha* This could also be translated as 'a man of great knowledge' with the ordinal num. *cét* having its allied meaning 'primary, great' and taking *gretha* as the gen. sg. of *grith* 'knowledge'.

90, §11. *cóintit coím* has been switched with *cóintit ile* to give rhyme between *Coíl* and *coím*. For the form of the suff. pron. *–it* and its reflex in the later language, see Breatnach (1977, 104-7) and *SnaG* III, §12.18. Breatnach (1977, 104) notes that 'it is difficult to find instances where the *–it* functions unambiguously as a pronoun'. Therefore, it is possible that this line should be translated 'many lament, nobles lament'. See further possible example on l. 343.

92, §11. The demonstr. pron. *so* goes with the preceeding phrase and is separated from it to highlight the metre and rhyme in the couplet. This editorial treatment is by no means satisfactory.

92-3, §11. *Matan Maigi Mucramai ... cin mac nAililla Auluim* A slightly different version of these lines is to be found in *Cath Maige Mucrama* (O Daly, 1975, ll. 377-81).

93, §11. *Ba dirsan do Art mac Cuind / cin mac nAililla Auluim* The crime of Ailill Aulom's sons concerns the dispute between them (Cormac Cass, Eógan Már and Cían) and his fosterson, Lugaid Mac Con, over the possession of the Otherworld musician, Fer Fí, and the yew tree in which he was sitting (see Dillon, 1943-6). Ailill Aulom is said to have had 19 sons (*CGH* 147b41), among them is listed Eochaid Tóebḟota (see 1. 124).

102, §12. *da-n-aidli* (Rawl. – *donaidli*; Harl. – *dianaitbi*) This form is restored in the text from the Rawl. reading and is taken as pres. ind. 3rd sg. plus infix. pron. 3rd sg. m. Class A of *do-aidlea* 'comes to, visits, attacks'. The restoration is necessary to make sense of the text (lit. 'a "tooth of poision" [will] come to *him*') as well as accounting for the presence of the nasalisation in the MS.

102, §12. The *fíacail fidbai* is associated with Ailill Aulom (see *CA* no. 41), who uses his 'tooth of poison' in *Scéla Moṡauluim* (O Daly, 1975, 82 §12) to wound Mac Con.

107, §13. *Bid rii Temrach co fo thrii / ara-mbebat ilṡíabrai .i. síthaigi* This is paralleled in *Geneamuin Chormaic* (Hull, 1952, 83.65-6) where the text reads: *Bid ri Temrach co bo tri. Con·bebabat siabra* ... 'Three times he will be king of Tara. Phantoms will die ...'. The tradition that Cormac's reign was interrupted on a number of occasions is further alluded to in §13. For further detail, see Ó Cathasaigh (1977, 87-92).

109, §13. *cath i nEuo* may be for *cath i nÉba* as in Tírechán (Bieler, 1979; 158 §46.3) where *Euoe* is the form used for *Éba*. Against this interpretation, however, in *AFM, ATig.* (inc. Dublin fragment) and *AU* (see Appendix 2) the form in the dat. is *Eu* (nom. *Eó* 'yew-tree'?) and the battle is said to have occured in Mag nAí, of which *Éba* (now Magherow, co. Sligo) did not form part.

110-11, §13. *cath Cúal[n]gi, cath Átha Beth, cath Átha Dumai* In *AFM, ATig.* (inc. Dublin fragment) and *AU* these battles are given as *Cath Slige Cuailnge, Cath Atha Bethech* and *Cath Ratha Dumai*. See Appendix 2.

112, §13. *nípat becca ind lúadri*. What may be another attestation of the noun (cited in *DIL* s.v. *lúaidri*) occurs in in *ZCP* 6, 257, §6. Here, in one of the prophecies associated with Colum Cille, is the line: *Atach ind so atroithich Colum Cille co m-máthair nĪsu ar ind lúaidri rorat do Colum Cille. Nach aon dia tiberthá in brothc[h]án sa* ... 'This is a beseeching that Colum Cille made to the mother of Christ concerning the *l.* she gave to Colum Cille. To whomever you would give this pottage ...'.

If this is another example of the same word, then it may be an io-stem, m. *lúa(i)dre*, with regular nom. plu. in our text (*lúadri*) and a dat. sg. form *lúaidri* in *ZCP* 6 (for standard O.Ir. *lúaidriu*). 'Advantage, benefit' might be an appropriate rendering of *lúa(i)dre* in both sentences and this has informed my translation here. The suggestion in *DIL* that the *lúaidri* in *ZCP* 6 may be identified with *brothchán* 'pottage, soup' is obviously a possibility but, due to a lack of context, it is not necessary to interpret it this way.

It must be noted, however, that there is a further problem with the interpretation of this line as the form of the adj., *becca*, is originally nom. plu. f. (not m.). This form spreads at the expense of the nom. plu. m. (O.Ir. *bicc*) and is well established in *Saltair na Rann* at the end of the tenth century (see *SnaG* III, §6.5).

115, §13. *cath na Lúachrai all Maig Slecht, / cath Eillne* In *AU, ATig.* (inc. Dublin fragment) and *AFM* this is written as *cath Allamaig secht catha Elne*. See Appendix 2.

117, §13. *gubadán* could also represent *co badún* 'to a fortified enclosure'.

118, §13. The restoration of *Réin* is based on *ATig.* (*RC* 17, 13) which contains the sentence: 'Loingeas mór Cormuic m*aic* Airt tar magh rein fri re teora mbli*adan*'.

121, §13. *budni* This is an unusual nom. plu. form of *buiden* which I have no parallels for elsewhere.

122, §13. My treatment of this line is not altogether satisfactory. Rawl reads: *ar nena gíalla gaidel. aradercc duirri dremna* which quite possibly represents a corrupt transmission of verse. Perhaps it should be read as:

> *Ar-nena gíalla Gaídel   ara dercc duirri dremain.*
> He will bind the hostages of the Goídil
>   on account of his redness of furious anger.

However, I have treated this section as prose and restored to *ara derccduirr dremna* (6 syllables). Perhaps *aradercc* is a form of the vb *ar-derca* 'looks' or of the vb *ar-dérg(a)* 'proposes, intends'.

123, §13. *cráudórtad troch* could also be translated as 'fatal bloodshed'.

124, §13. *ar-túaset Ulaid occa, / do-fóeth hEchaid Tóebḟoda* This piece of information is paralleled in *CGH* 330b20. It seems, however, that *BS* may be stating here that the Ulaid (under Fergus Dubdétach) fought this battle against Eochaid Tóebḟota on Cormac's advice. This is not the tradition in *LL* where the text relates that Fergus became 'king of Ireland' afterwards before falling in the battle of Crinna in Brega at the hands of Tadc mac Céin and Cormac úa Cuinn. His death by the hand of Cormac is recorded in ll. 128-30:

> Tóla hÉrend la Cormac   *fri Fergus, ardrí Ulad.*
> Do-fóeth Fergus sceo Énda   *dia mbia slúag dérach dubach.*
> Máirt hi Crinda céin ṁbess bith   *hi foíchret slúaig hÉrend grith.*

> A great incursion of Ireland by Cormac
>   against Fergus, high-king of the Ulaid.
> Fergus and Énna will die
>   on account of which there will be a sad gloomy host.
> A Tuesday battle in Crinna as long as the world will be,
>   in which the hosts of Ireland shall give a roar.

This claim in *LL* that Fergus Dubdétach of the Ulaid was 'king of Ireland' is to be found in other places (e.g. Dobbs (1921), *Baile Chuind*), but no part of this claim is aired in *BS*.

125, §13. *cath Ardda Caim* The translation Ard Cam has been preferred to Aird Cham as (i) there are other examples of this nom. (see *HDGP* s.n.); (ii) *arda* is occasionally used as the gen. of *ard* (see *HDGP* 34-5); (iii) one would expect *cath Ardda Caime* (which would spoil both rhyme and syllable count) if Aird Cham were intended.

127, §13 & 142, §15. For information on the *bóraime*, see Ó Buachalla (1961).

127, §13. *DIL* does not treat *Aidni* as a placename but enters it under *aigne* 'advocate, lawyer'. It is possible that *hAidni* is a misreading of *naidm* (this is the reading preserved in Harl.). Perhaps the original read *for nadmaim na Bórime* or *for naidm inna Bórime* 'over the exacting of the cattle tribute'.

128, §13. This interpretation of *tóla* as 'incursion' is further strengthened if *longass Chormaic dar Mag [Réin]* on l. 118 is translated as 'the expulsion of Cormac across the ocean'. See l. 463 for another use of *tóla*.

128, §13. The term *ardrí* is only utilised twice in *BS*; here, where Fergus Dubdétach is referred to as *ardrí Ulad* and on l. 276 with reference to Áed Allán mac Fergaile.

132, §13. *Fregabuil* could also be treated as *fre gabuil* and translated as 'against a branch (of the family)' or, alternatively, it could be taken as *fre Gabuil* and translated as 'alongside Gabal'.

136, §14. There seems to be corrupt transmission of the second part of this couplet which is hypermetrical. Perhaps *Liphechair* should be omitted.

137, §14. Rawl. '.c.' is expanded to *catha* here (as at in ll. 220 & 464). The classical O.Ir. form of the gen. plu. was *cathae* (later *catha*), Mid.Ir. *cath*. The restoration to *catha* is supported by l. 81, where the gen. plu. form remains uniquely unabbreviated in Rawl.

139, §14. Cairpre Liphechair is referred to here as *in rígniä*. This can simply be translated as 'royal-champion'. However, *nia* can also have the meaning 'sister's son'. The sister's son had an important legally-bound role in medieval Irish society, which has been discussed in depth by Ó Cathasaigh (1986) and Jaski (1999). Possibly the use of the word *nia* here may refer to Cairpre Liphechair's role as a sister's son. His epithet and his importance (to the Leinstermen) in many texts derive from his being fostered by both his paternal and his maternal kindred [for the importance of the *máithre*, see Kelly (1988, 14-15)]. This importance is to be seen in *Esnada Tige Buchet* and the other Leinster stories found in MS Rawlinson B. 502 (pointed out to me by Michael Byrnes). Many different words are used for champion in *BS* (e.g. *ársid*, *clí*, *dúbartach*) but this is the only use of the word *niä* (which is disyllabic here) in the text.

139, §14. *bebaid and in rígniä* This is followed in Harl. by the following information that is not in Rawl.:

> *Tri maic coirpri lifechair .i. eochaid 7 eochu doimlén 7 fiachu raibtine la laighne. A torcratar a cath tuam ruis la bresal mbélach mac fiachach baicetha maic catháir .l. ar tri milib an lion do laignib dotuit ann a fritghuin.*

This material from Harl. was probably not in the exemplar as information of this nature is not given anywhere else in *BS*. It is also unlikely that the careful scribe of Rawl. would leave out a piece of the text this long. If this is the case, why did the scribe of Harl. feel that this information was worth adding? *ATig.* (*RC* 17, 28) relates that the three sons of Coirpre Lifechair did fall by Bresal Bélach (along with 9,000 of his people) and that the name of the battle was *cath Cnámrois*. Here *ATig.* also states that Dub Comair was Fíachu Sroiphtine's druid and that this is why the battle is also called *cath Dub Chomair*. The same information is also given in *The Book of Lecan* (601.45 – 602.8), i.e. that Dubcombair was Fíachu

77

Sroiphtine's druid.

145, §15. *bid gand glé.* A preposed adj. is utilised here to allow for the required rhyme.

149ff., §§17 & 18. Large sections of these paragraphs have been borrowed directly into the narrative of *Echtra mac nEchdach Mugmedóin* and have been closely scrutinised by Clodagh Ní Dhubhnaigh (Downey) in her Ph.D. thesis (2001, 283-9). She informs me that they agree most closely with the rhetorical sections as presented in Harl., rather than Rawl. In a later section of the tale some of the kennings from *BS* are utilised (cf. Introduction **4.3**(d) & **6.2**) with one of versions explicitly acknowledging *BS* as the source: *amail at-fét in Scál Baile* (Ní Dhubhnaigh, 2001, 262). As these borrowings are from §§59, 62 & 64, they must have come from a copy of the text in which the final paragraphs were present (possibly a complete version of Harl.?). Some of these correspondences may be seen by examining the versions in O'Grady (1892, i, 326-30; at 327) and Stokes (1903, 190-203; at 192) – all the textual evidence, however, is presented in Ní Dhubhnaigh's thesis. She has now published an in-depth analysis of the relationship between these two texts (Downey, 2004, 80-91).

154, §17. *bid forggu maithe* could also be translated as 'there will be the choice of good deeds'. Alternatively, this line may be read as *bid forggu maith é* 'he will be a good choice'. However, this would mean the use of an indep. pron. with the copula, a development traditionally dated to the Mid.Ir. period (see *SnaG* III, §12.193). This usage is present, however, in ll. 161 & 172.

154, §17. There could be a corrupt transmission of verse here, with the original reading possibly along the following lines:

Forus ṅHér[e]nd (fo Echaig) fria ré, [Echu], bid forggu maithe.
The stability of Ireland throughout his reign
Echu, he will be the pick of good persons.

154, §17. *Is húad gignedar* This shows the use of the relative form of the verb where one would normally expect an independent clause. For further examples of this usage, see *GOI* §506.

156, §17. *I nDub Chombair* Harl. reads *a nuib conchobair* here which is incorrect. It must be noted, however, that this place is more often associated with Fíachu Sroiphtine who is said to have fallen in battle there, not with Echu Mugmedón which is what both of our MSS have. *The Book of Lecan* (602.19 ff.) gives another reading where it is said of Fíachu Sroiphtine: *co [...]dorchair i cath dub chomair* *i cnamros la macaib echu doimnell .i. colla uais 7 colla da chrich 7 colla mend*, which is what we have in two short lines under Echu Mugmedón (§17). It looks as if these two lines may be misplaced in our text. See above, note to 1. 139.

156-7, §18. The 'basis for kin-slaying' in these lines is the fact that the three Collas of tradition (noted above) were nephews of Echu Mugmedón so his death at their hands is properly described as a *fingal*.

158-9, §18. *Dáil de Níall Noígíallach .i. cóic géill hÉrend 7 gíall Albun 7 Bretan 7 Saxan 7 Franc* According to F.J. Byrne (1969, 19), Níall Noígíallach's surname probably refers to the nine *túatha* of the Airgíalla who gave their hostages to him when they 'transferred their allegiance from the Ulidain overlords to Niall' (cf. *EIHM* 233). The tradition in *CA* (no. 118) is that the five Irish hostages came one from each *cóiced* and that the other four hostages came from *Alba*.

159, §18. *mórfaitir maigi* could also be translated as 'territories will be increased'.

161, §18. There is a corrupt transmission of verse here as indicated by the incorrect syllable count.

162, §18. *A cath Muirned hi Forath Lúain* Perhaps Rawl. *muirnedh* should be emended to *muirnech* 'tumultuous' and *hi* deleted (to restore the correct syllable count)? The line could then be read as *A cath muirnech for Áth Lúain*, 'in a tumultuous battle at Athlone'.

163, §18. The emendation to *Au[r]thuli* goes against both MSS (Rawl. *tathaimm nauthuli*; Harl. *totaim nothaili*) but I have no other examples of a personal name Authuile, whereas Aurthuile is a relatively common name (cf. *CGH* p. 514).

This is not the only occasion where significant shared readings in Rawl. and Harl. may point towards a common exemplar. Other examples include:

173, §20. *cath Átha Tálmaig[e]* (Rawl. *Tálmaig*; Harl. *talmaigh*);

178, §20. *at-ethfat* (Rawl. *athet*; Harl. *atheat*);

179, §20. *toitimm* (Rawl. *thoitimm*; Harl. *thoitim*);

191, §23. *i nEscir Forchai* (traditionally *Achad Forchai*; see *HDGP* s.n. *Achadh Farcha*);

198, §25. *timgéra* (this univerbated form is present in both MSS).

233, §33. *Díarmato* (old gen. sg. of Díarmait attested in both

MSS).

240, §35. *túath in Cuib* (use of def. art. is found in both MSS).

165, §18. *gríb thuile glond* This phrase is found in another form in the text – *fer ilair glond*, ll. 136 & 180).

165, §18. There may be a corrupt transmission of verse here, with the original possibly reading:

Íar sen gríb[a] tuile glond, do-fóeth Níall ar Druimm nAlban.

166, §18. *Arddmóin* has not been identified. Instead of this placename, Harl. reads *iarnoin*.

169, §19. The reading in Harl. has been adopted here as it makes clearer sense and seems to be another excerpt from the metrical source. The reading in Rawl. (*scairfaid fri arddscél do denam na fingali*) seems corrupt by comparison. A possible translation would be: 'he will bring himself into disrepute by committing a kin-slaying'.

169, §19. *scairfaid* The verb *scaraid* usually has an ē-fut. in Mid.Ir. (this is present in l. 438. *scérus*) but the earlier f-fut. (cf. *nosscairiub* Ml. 43ᵃ23) is attested here. However, as Kim McCone points out (*EIV* 221) 'on the evidence of compound forms such as *con:scéra* 'he will destroy' (Wb. 26a8), *eter:scértar* 'they will be separated' (Wb. 8b3) the *f*-fut. of Ml. might be the innovatory form'. Here, however, is another early example to add to the evidence of Ml. The same progression (from an original f-fut. to ē-fut.) is also evident in *Lebar Aicle* where *ō scarfat* (*CIH* 1628.27) is replaced by *ō scērait* (*CIH* 1209.1).

170ff., §§20-1. These paragraphs are in this order in Rawl. – the correct chronological order (i.e. Lóegaire mac Néill before Ailill Molt) is given in Harl.

170ff., §20. Much of §20 has been re-used in *YBL* where it serves as an addendum to *Suidigud Tellaig na Cruachna*. There, however, the material is pressed into the service of Nathí mac Fíachrach instead of his son, Ailill Molt. The text from *YBL* (without the additional material based on *BS* §20) is printed by Ó Concheanainn (1975, 149-57). The addendum to *Suidigud Tellaig na Cruachna* is printed here from the text given in Bănăţeanu (1930, 183-4):

Nat*h*i m*a*c Fiachra*ch* gabais flait*h* n-Er*end* i *n*-diaid Neill Fo*r*ranac*h* ge[i]n uallach fear. Teora bl*iadn*a fichead do hi flait*h*. Cat*h*a ili i*n*a flaith. Cucilcid Temro, meascbadach Taillten rofich cat*h* At*h*a Talmaigi, dubartach Seilli, cat*h*-boadaig Achae rofich mor-cat*h* Rat*h*a Cruach*an* ⁊ cat*h* Maigi n-Ailbe, cat*h*a ili *in*

Albai*n*, cat*h* Maigi Circi*n*, cat*h* Srat*h*a Cluat*h*a, foirtbe Gemet*h*, foirtbe Mairrech.

Luid Nat*h*i iarsi*n* co f*e*raib*h* Eri*n*d ⁊ Alban dar m*uir* Ic*h*t doc*h*um Let*h*a co*m*bai oc sleb Elpae do digail Neill, fobith ba o f*ar*c*h*aib asan dunud fochres i*n* tsaeiged dianebelt Niall. Ba cai*n* rem n-Er*e*nd hi tirib Leat*h*a me*m*datar *secht* cat*h*a re n-Gaidelaib hi tirib Frang*c* f*or* cet*h*ir belrae. Ba dirsan iarsi*n* do Gaidelaib isi*n*d ai*n*didi*n* ar Alpi. Fersait gle mair. Is and fert*h*a an ar isi*n* mor cat*h* la hec*h*tranda. Batir dian ar roga f*r*is nim im medo*n* m-betho moir doroc*h*air i*n* airi*n*ach i*n* mor cat*h*a Nat*h*i oc sleb Elpa.

Ailill Molt m*a*c Nat*h*i, ba flait*h* techtaide. Ferais cat*h* Gabra Lifi, *cath* Co*n*deri, *cath* Ci*n*d Delcae. T*r*i *secht* mbliadan do hi flaith. Fear treoroc*h* rogob giallu h-Eri*n*d ⁊ Alban. Rofich *cath* f*or* Ilat*h*aib ⁊ *cath* in Uachtur Colle. Ba mor fingal do Lugaig; docer leis i*n* dor(...) .i. Ail*ill* Molt, m*a*c Dat*h*i.

As may be observed from the above three paragraphs, the bulk of para. 1 is taken directly from *BS* §20. Para. 2 is a paraphrase of the remaining material in *BS* §20 while the only tie between para. 3 and *BS* §20 is that both are concerned with Ailill Molt. Because of the close similarities between Rawl. and Harl. at this point, it is impossible to determine which of the MSS is closer to the text in *YBL*.

171, §20. The form *adcuínti* (cf. *atcuínti*, l. 193) is problematic. It has been treated tentatively here, following *DIL*, as an inflected form of *accaíned* 'lamentation'. It would be preferable to treat both examples as 3rd plu. pres. ind. rel. of a simple verb *accaínid* (< *ad-caíni*) translating the phrase in l. 171 as 'a man whom multitudes lament' and the example in l. 193 as 'a victorious warlike king whom multitudes lament'. This proposal has not been adopted, however, as *ad-caíni* is treated as a compound verb throughout *BS* (ll. 133, 225, 272).

173, §20. *cath Átha Tálmaig[e]* See note to l. 163.

177, §20. *.uii. mbél fri firu Góedel* It is very hard to make any sense of the phrase *.uii. mbél* in this context (the reading is *mbel* in both MSS). Perhaps it should be read as *.uii. mbéli* (or *mbéla*) and translated as 'seven axes'. It might also be emended to *.uii. mbella* 'seven battles', though the contexts within which Latin is utilised in *BS* would not support this interpretation. However, this could have influenced the relevant passage in *YBL* (quoted above), which reads: *memdatar secht catha re n-Gaidelaib*.

One factor militating against any emendation which would

increase the syllable count of this line is the fact that it may be half of a rhyming couplet. Thus, an emendation to *mbéli* or *mbella* would render the line hypermetrical.

178, §20. *at-ethfat* The restoration of the fut. 3rd plu. of *at-etha* 'gets, obtains' is the only emendation (against both MSS) that suggests itself here (see note to l. 163). Alternatively, the pres. ind. 3rd plu. (*at-ethat*) could be restored as the ind. frequently has the force of a fut. (see *DIL* s.v. *at-etha*); this is also a common feature of other verbs in *BS*. It is possible that we have a corrupt transmission of verse here:

> *i n-oín dídin ar Elpai.*   *Bit ili athet martrai.*

179, §20. *toitimm* See note to l. 163.

181, §21. Though *fer gráid* 'ecclesiastic' would seem to be a better rendering here, it must be noted that the adj. *móir* (it is written thus in both MSS) is in the gen. and, therefore, agrees with *gráid* and not with *fer* which is nom. Thus, one is obliged to translate *fer gráid móir* as 'a man of great rank' instead of 'a great cleric'.

183, §21. *flaith him bachla* This phrase is also in *Bethu Phátraic* (Mulchrone, 1939, l. 350) as is the phrase *ticfat tailcind* which is glossed *.i. Baili Cuinn dixit* in the Egerton 93 MS version of the text.

186, §22. The use of the gen. *Ardgail* (for classical O.Ir. *Ardgaile*) is also attested in *AU* 837.2. For more on the treatment of names ending in *–gal*, see Ó Máille (1910, §153) and Lloyd-Jones (1947, 85-6).

188, §22. *óenguine* The reference to Túathal Máelgarb as the 'only-begotten one' is unclear. It may be a reference to the fact that none of his descendants became king of Tara (see *NHI* 9, 127). The interdiction concerning Túathal's descendants is also reported in *Bethu Phátraic* (Mulchrone, 1939, ll. 952-66). *Óenguine*, however, is most probably a reference to only-child status, an inference which cannot be checked against *CGH* as Túathal is conspicuous by his absence from those genealogies. In *Baile Chuind* (Murphy, 1952, 146), he is referred to under the kenning *óengarb* 'uniquely rough one'.

Perhaps the text should be emended to *bebaid óenguin namá* 'he will die of a single wound'. However, if this is the surviving half of a poetic couplet, as seems likely (rhyming with *doda-cich noda-íba*), then this emendation would render the line one syllable short.

191, §23. *i nEscir Forchai* This may be an alternative form of Achad Forchai (cf. Mulchrone, 1939, ll. 628-31), the placename traditionally associated with his death. See note to l. 163.

193, §24. *atcuínti* For discussion of this form, see the note to l. 171.

194, §24. *DIL* (s.v. *fo-naisc*) suggests that *fir* and *mná* are used here for O.Ir. dat. sg. *fiur* and *mnaí*. However, I take both forms as nom. (plu.), a usage employed 'where a noun stands in no precise syntactical relationship' (*GOI* §247).

195, §24. *Cath Átha Sigi íar sen / línfus co hÉrinn airbiu* Here the word-order seems to have been changed around to facilitate rhyme (*airbiu : Laigniu*), with *airbiu* as acc. plu. of *airbe* 'phalanx, serried rank (of fighting-men)'. It might be preferable to take it as a prepositionless dat. (for *i n-airbiu* 'in a phalanx') except for the parallel sentence in l. 265: *biaid ár mór isin chath / línfus co hÉirinn airbriu,* where *airbriu* is taken to be the acc. plu. of *arbar* 'host, army'. The word-order also seems to have been changed in this line to facilitate (imperfect) rhyme (*airbriu : amru*).

196, §24. Although unsatisfactory, *cáirb* is here taken as an alternative nom. sg. form of *cerb* 'cutter'. The only other possibility seems to be to treat it as the dat. sg. of *carb* 'ship', a late-attested loan-word from Old Norse *karfi*, which does not appear to make much sense in the context. Muirchertach's death is also the subject of a Middle-Irish tale (Nic Dhonnchadha, 1964, ll. 918-9), in which the older name for Áth Sige is given as Áth Cirb; it is possible (though doubtful) that this information lies behind some of the confusion here.

198, §25. *timgéra* Both MSS preserve the univerbated fut. form of the verb *do-imgair*. See note to l. 163.

199, §25. *ar daig rúaid* The emendation to *rúaid* (MSS read *ruad* and *ruád*) is to allow for agreement between dat. sg. adj. and dat. sg. fem. noun, *daig* 'blaze'. It would be possible to interpret *ar daig* as *ar dáig* 'on account of, because' if one took *rúad* as a substantive (possibly a name?). However, one would then expect the gen. after *ar dáig*.

200, §26. *Echaig* is the regular acc. form of Echu. The king who jointly reigned with Báetán, however, is more commonly known as Eochaid mac Domnaill. Echu (Eochu) and Eochaid are frequently confused (cf. *CGH* pp. 613, 616). Alternatively, one could see this as an example of the tendency (pronounced in Mid.Ir.) of lenited *d* and lenited *g* to fall together, especially when palatal (see *SnaG* III, §3.18). There is another example of this on the next line, where nom. sg. *tairngertaig* is written for *tairngertaid*.

204, §27. Thurneysen (1936, 226) reads *Dreimin* instead of *Dreimni* though Rawl. clearly has *dreimni* and Harl. *dremne*. The epithet seems to be attached to his name because of the famous defeat he suffered at the battle of Cúl Dreimne. Thurneysen assumed a corrupt transmission of poetry here. Perhaps the original read something like:

Día .uii. mblíadnae íar sein   cath fáebrach for Dreimin

with Díarmait's name not listed until the last line of the poetry, i.e. *díth Díarmata* (l. 207).

207, §27. *Ind aín díten hi Ráith Bic / díth Díarmata imma-ric* Díarmait's death at Ráith Becc is also noted in *ATig.* (*RC* 17, 146).

214, §29. *Iurait Laigin a ndáma* Carney (1989, 53) takes this line to refer to the persecution of poets in Leinster around the year 600. Cf. *AI* s.a. 600.

218, §29. *con-bibsat a fírdála* Although *con-bibsat* is entered in *DIL* s.v. *con-beba*, perhaps it would be better to take the form as the fut. 3rd plu. of *con-boing* and *fírdála* as the acc. plu. of a compound based on *dál* 'assembly', and to translate the sentence as 'they will violate their true assemblies'.

218, §30. This use of *caín* is described as follows in *GOI* §384: 'certain adjectives when used adverbially, are prefixed to the verb like prepositions; but the verb is apparently never attached to them in enclisis. Examples: *caín·rognatha* "well have they been done" ...'.

219, §30. *Fúata Líamna* seems like the gen. of a placename. The second word is uncontroversial, i.e. it is the gen. of the placename *Líamain* (near Dublin). The form *Fúata*, however, is more problematical. *Fúat* (gen. *Fúait*) is a common placename element, perhaps with the meaning 'waste land' (see *Ainm* 7 (1996-7) 169-70) – examples include Cenn Fúait, Druim Fúait and Slíab Fúait although it is not clear whether this element may be connected to *fúata* here (see *DIL* s.v.). Some connection is apparent in *MD* iv, 264: *Fuat ben tSláine, a qua nominatur Slíab Fúait 7 Inis Fúata*, 'Fúat the wife of Sláine, from whom is named Slíab Fúait and Inis Fúata'. Perhaps *Fúat* could be treated either as an o-stem, (gen. *Fúait*) or as a u-stem (gen. *Fúata*).

222, §30. Both MSS have p̣ here, the regular abbreviation for *pro* or *per*. I have expanded it to *potio* 'drink'. Perhaps, it should be expanded to *poculum*, however, which is glossed *eredig* in Ml. 55ᶜ1.

224, §31. *gébaid for Liphemaig* can also be translated as 'he will attack the Liffey plain'.

84

226, §32. I am not aware of any other example of the epithet *Mend Ulad* used for Domnall mac Áedo maic Ainmerech. It is unclear to me what exactly this epithet is supposed to mean in the context of a Cenél nEógain king who defeated Congal Cáech, over-king of Ulaid, in the battle of Mag Roth (AD 637).

228, §32. Both MSS omit *do* before *tóeth*, presumably to keep the syllable count at seven.

229-30, §32. *cath Rátha al Machi* The translation of this phrase as 'the battle of Ráith beyond Macha' is far from certain. Perhaps one should follow the MSS and treat the final three words as a placename, *Ráith Almachi* (or *Almoichi*). The forms *Machai* and *Mache* are attested as acc. / dat. sg. forms of *Macha*, however (see *DIL* s.v.). Alternatively, *almachi / almoichi* could be the gen. sg. of a compound of *múich* 'sadness'.

233, §33. This couplet contains the oldest spelling of *gáu* 'falsehood' and preserves the old gen. sg. of *Díarmait* in rhyming position (*Díarmato*). See note to l. 163.

235, §34. *derbḟlaith* 'certain sovereignty'. Note, however, that *derb* can also be translated as a 'vessel for dispensing liquids, pail' and could, together with *(f)laith*, give the same play on words as *derg(f)laith*.

236-7, §35. *Dáil de forsin rúanaid (.i. a ruidiud ig gabáil láma Mo Chuta), for Díarmait Daithi* Even though translating *rúanaid* as 'a strong man, champion' would accord well with the use of epithets and kennings in *BS,* it seems better to translate *rúanaid* as 'timid (one)' because of the addition of the gloss showing Díarmait as blushing at the expelling of Mo Chuta. According to *AU*, this expulsion took place in 636. His expulsion from Rahan is the subject of a story titled *Indarba Mochuda a rRaithin*; see Plummer (1922 i, 300-11; ii, 291-302, esp. i, 304 §17).

CA (no. 134) gives three different reasons why Díarmait mac Áeda Sláine was known as Díarmait Rúanaid: (i) after a plant *ruán* which makes a face go red; (ii) because he was a *roféinnidh* 'a great champion'; (iii) because he would not help his brothers expel Mo Chuta whence he was known as *rúanaid (.i. rí[g]da)* 'royal'.

I have not come across the epithet *Daithi* ('of swiftness'?) elsewhere with regard to Díarmait mac Áeda Sláine.

238, §35. *Inda* This could be for *inde* 'paddock' or perhaps a form of *indes* 'a milking place, enclosure'. It cannot be *ind* (o,n.) 'summit, edge (of a territory)' unless the phrase be emended to *da n-ind*. It is taken here as a placename, possibly referring to Inde Mór and Inde Becc in co. Kildare.

240, §35. I have no other examples of the placename *Cuib* used with the def. art. It is generally attested in the gen., e.g. *Mag Coba, Uí Echach Coba.* Perhaps the line should be read *bid crúas cuimnech túath i Cuib* and translated as 'it will be memorable valour of [the] peoples in Cuib'. See note to l. 163.

242, §36. *Fínnachta*'s usual epithet, *fledach*, is not mentioned here.

243, §36. *Firfid cath Cúile Coíláin, scíss hi tóeb Chithamra* This line could also be translated as 'the battle of Cúil Choíláin will pour down sorrow beside Cithamair'.

244, §36. *fingail* An example of a prepositionless dative. See notes to ll. 292 & 381.

252, §39. *Do-tóeth ic lecaib finnaib* This line might contain a placename (in the dat. plu.). Cf. *Bethu Phátraic* (Mulchrone, 1939, ll. 1567-9): *Luid sair du Licc Find, baile dorónai Pátraic croiss isin cloich os Chill Móir Óchtair Múade aníar, acht Lía na Manac[h a] ainm indiu.*

252, §39. *fo minnaib* See the parallel phrase in *ÄID* ii, 22 §1: *dofeid fíana fo mindaib* which Meyer translates as 'er führt Kriegerscharen unter Kronen' ('he leads warrior-bands under crowns') which he suggests may be an an allusion to winning the kingship.

However, in both *BS* and *ÄID* it would appear that this phrase may refer to the practice of *díbergaig* wearing *signa diabolica* (Sharpe, 1979, 83). Though Sharpe argues that 'we do not hear of *fíana* wearing *signa diabolica* or the like' (1979, 86), McCone (1986ii) has assembled an impressive body of evidence to show that 'in older sources, however, there is no such attempt at consistent differentiation, whether implicit or explicit, between *díberg* and *fíannas* or their respective practitioners' (p. 4). The material cited above could point us in the same direction. As Mac Cana (1987, 97) succintly expresses it: 'when the *fiana* were good, they were very, very good, but when they were bad, they were *díbergaig* – more or less'.

Two further options present themselves. Firstly, one could translate *fo minnaib* as 'under oaths' and take it to refer to the *votum mali* also associated with *díbergaig* (Sharpe, 1979, 83-4). Secondly, perhaps one could take the *minn* to refer to the banners of the *fían*, which are well known to us from later sources (Meek, 1986) though I have no other example to hand of *minn* used in this sense.

255, §39. Rawl. *cichiss ar chel* / Harl. *cichis ar cel* Following McCone (1986i, 32-3), the Rawl. reading, which shows lenition on *cel*, has been preserved here. Lenition is also marked in Rawl. on the same phrase in l. 468.

255, §39. Rawl. *etir da corand uinnsen* / Harl. *itir 2 corann uindsen* While this phrase may be translated as 'between the two weirs of [the] Uinnsiu', the translation makes little sense in this context. It seems better to take *corand* (recte *coraind*) as a preposed gen. and translate as 'between the two Uinnsiu [rivers] of Corann'. The Ushnagh r. in Sligo has many tributaries to which this phrase might be applied. The phrase *teora Uinnsin* 'the three Ushnaghs' is attested, for example, in *AFM* i, 32 and elsewhere (see *OnomG* s.n. *uinsend* for further details).

259, §40. *Da-thuittet* See note to l. 72.

260-1, §40 / 353, §50. *ut Pátríni dixit* / *dúan Pátríni* It is stated in *DIL* s.v. *patrene* that this is 'prob. a proper name used as a generic term' for a class of bard. Examples of both follow. Generic term: *Auraicept na nÉces* (Calder, 1917, 1928): *Trefocul in so amal rocumsat na baird 7 na patreni* 'This is *trefocul* as the bards and the *patreni* have devised it' (cf. *ACL* 3, iv, 293). Proper name: In Meyer (1909, 51) there is the following footnote: 'According to a note by Michael O'Clery in the Brussels MS. 5057-59, fo. 36, Pátríne is identical with Máelpátraic presbyter Cluana, who died A.D. 1028'. This note is just below the heading 'Patriní cecinit' and above the poem beginning *Hi ccathraigh in toirnidhe* ('In the monastic settlement of the ordained-one'?), edited by B. O'Looney in Petrie (1872, 76-8). This poem was re-edited by J.G. O'Keefe in *Irish Texts* iv, 44-6 (Fraser et al., 1931-3) under the title 'The kings buried in Clonmacnois'.

There are two marginal notes on fo. 36r of Brussels MS 5057-59 which are reproduced in their entirety by O'Keefe (p. 44n.). He gives it as his opinion that 'the Latin hand is that of one of the 17th century Irish Franciscans, occuring frequently in their MSS.; probably Fr. John Colgan's'. Here follow the notes (from O'Keefe):

In the margin: Author videtur esse Malpatric presbyter Cluan qui obiit an. 1028. Mael-patric enim Latine (Latini *MS.*) dici potest Patricius, seu Patricianus.

And again at the end: Author qui hic Patrinus seu Patricius dicitur videtur esse Moel-patric presbyter Clánensis (sic) qui obiit an. 1028, sexto post mortem Malachiae regis, quia in hunc locus,

tempus et nomen conspirant: author enim ut ex textu colligitur
videtur deguisse Cluaniae et esse sinchronus Malachiae regis
Hiberniae, quem quasi recenter sepultum post alios commemorat.
Nomen etiam consentit Malpatric Latine didi potest Patricius vel
Patricianus. It would seem that a proper name is in question in both examples
occuring in *BS*.

262 / 266, §41. *cailech* 'cock' is here used as a laudatory nickname
for Fergal mac Máele Dúin. This terminology is paralleled in *Baile
Chuind* with the use of the phrase *Flaith Cailig* (see Murray, forth-
coming: i).

264ff., §41. This poetic material on the battle of Allen may be among the
oldest surviving records of that event. See Ó Riain (1978, xx).

265, §41. See note to l. 195.

266, §41. *amru* The historical comparative form is here utilised as a
superlative form, a process that was already underway in O.Ir. – see
SnaG III, §6.15.

272-3, §42 *écu atbai* (Rawl. *éc uatba*). Meyer (1918, 232) prints this
as *éc ūatba*. As Breatnach points out (Murray, 1999i, 186 n.6), the
employment of the plural of *éc* is the older usage.

272-4, §42. *Con-beba écu atbai fo tháilcentaig .i. i nArd Macha i n-
ailithre at-bath clericus i n-ailaid na ríg* This is confirmed by *AU*
765.2.

275, §43. *Dáil de for Áed [n]Aldén (.i. Altán noimen loci ubi nutritus est)*
The Latin gloss is paralleled exactly in Irish in *CA* (no. 122) where it
is given as one of the reasons for Áed's epithet:

> *Aedh Ollán .i. oll lán in mhara .i. lán rabarta ann intan
> rugadh. Nó Aedh Allán .i. Alltan ainm na haíti inar' hoiled é.
> Nó Aedh Allán .i. Aedh ildán .i. ildána dogníthi dó. is dé isberar
> ind agnómen.*

276-7, §43. *airdrí* See note to l. 128.

276-7, §43. There are problems of interpretation with this line, with
Rawl. reading: *firfid .c. coscrach gein .c. sáiltiri ara ngeba*. This has
been taken here as two separate clauses: *Firfid cath coscrach* and
gein catha Sáiltiri ara-ngéba. The first clause is easily translated,
the second is problematical. *Gein* may mean (i) 'birth' (perh. used
figuratively to mean 'origin'?); (ii) 'wound' (a by-form of *guin*?);
(iii) 'sword' (for regular nom. *gen*?). None of these meanings seems
to fit in this context, however.

Perhaps the line should be broken up as follows: *Firfid cath coscrach gein* and *cath Sáiltiri ara-ngéba* but there are two objections to this. Firstly, the problem of interpretation regarding *gein* remains; secondly, the verb *ar-gaib* 'seizes, captures' is not used elsewhere in the sense of seizing (i.e. winning?) a battle. A final alternative would be to read Rawl. *gein .c. sáiltiri ara ngeba* as *geinchath Sáiltiri ara-ngéba* 'he will seize the wounding battle of Sáiltíre', but the problem of interpreting *ar-gaib* as 'winning' would still remain and *DIL* has no other example of a compound *guinchath*.

For all these reasons, *gein* has been left untranslated in the text.

276-7, §43. The references to *cath Sáiltiri* and to the two battles on the same day are misplaced here. These events occured in 637 during the reign of Domnall mac Áeda (§32 of our text). The other battle on the same day is a reference to the battle of Mag Roth; cf. *AU* 637.1: *Bellum Roth ₇ bellum Sailtire in una die facta sunt.* It seems that the compiler of *BS* has reworked this material to name the two battles on the same day as those of Áth Dá Charna and Áth Medóin, two battles which are usually cited together (e.g. *LL* 23641-2).

277, §43. *na dá chath* The use of *na* as the dual article (instead of *in*) has many parallels elsewhere, e.g. Henderson (1899, 54 §45), Murray (2001iii, 22.20). See also l. 445.

278, §43. Confusion between the pret. and fut. forms of *maidid* occurs in various texts. Here the pret. 3rd sg. form (*memaid*) is used for the fut. 3rd sg., while the correct fut. 3rd sg. form is attested in the very next line (*memaiss*). Similarly, in Todd (1867, 90) the fut. 3rd sg. form is given as *mebaidh*. The fut. form is also used for the pret. in an example cited by Dillon (1953, l. 593): *mebais ríam forsna slógu* 'he defeated the hosts'. See note to l. 320.

278, §43. The meaning of *fálguba* is not entirely clear. It is a compound of *guba* 'mourning, lamenting' and *fál*, for which there are a number of possible translations (see *DIL* s.v. *fál*). The option preferred here is *fál* 'king' and the compound is translated 'royal-lamentation'.

278-80, §43. *Fálguba Ulad, memaiss for Áed (.i. Rón mac Béicci Bairche) re nÁed. Int Áed aurbaig (.i. cath Focharta)* This information is confirmed in *AU* 735.2 where the battle is given as occuring *in regionibus Muirtheimhne* but the placename (*Fochairt*) is not mentioned. However, the place is named in *CGH* 330d35: *Áed Rón is é* *orta i Fochaird.* For the political implications of this battle, see Byrne (1965, 49-50) and (1973, 117-9).

280, §43. *aurbaig* It may be preferable to take this as a later gen. form of *airbág* 'boast, battle' but I have no other examples of such a gen. form. Because of the doubt involved, I have left the word as written in the MS while taking it as the gen. sg. of *árbach* 'slaughter, carnage'.

280, §43. Rawl. *forma fan* has been emended to *formna i fán*, with elision leaving the syllable count the same. *Forma* could also be a preposed gen. (< *fora(i)m* 'course, hunting') but no obvious translation presents itself if this interpretation is followed.

282, §43. *gébaid grith* may also be translated as: (i) 'he will take a fit of frenzy' (ii) 'he will shout'; (iii) 'he will seize power'.

289, §43. *Do-fóeth in rí ó Srúb Brain / for brú Locha Sailchitain* Áed Allán's death on the shores of Loch Sailchitain is commemorated in a verse cited in *AU* 743.4 and *AFM* 738 (i, 338).

292, §44 / 302, §46. *Bregaib / borrchathaib* Examples of prepositionless datives. See notes to ll. 244 & 381.

292-3, §44. *Éc atbai hi Tailtentaigh .i. i nImliuch [Ḟ]ía* Meyer (1918, 233) emends Rawl. *tailtentaigh* to *táilcentaigh*. It has been shown, however, that *Tailtentaigh* is actually the correct reading, referring to a monastic house at Imlech Fía beside Tailtiu (Murray, 1999ii, 309). It is twice mentioned in *AU* (740.1 and 744.2) that Domnall entered clerical life.

295-6, §45. *bebaid éc atbui la fuil. / Bérthair hi tíre dar muir .i. co hÍ Coluim Chilli* His death in Iona is noted in *AU* 778.7.

300, §46. *in slúaig* The nom. plu. def. art. has been reduced from *int* to *in* here (see notes to ll. 3 & 9 for similar examples).

300, §46. The reading in Rawl. (*fíachrach*) has been emended to *Fíachach* as Carn Fíachach (in co. Westmeath) is the location of a battle fought by Donnchad mac Domnaill in *AU* 765.5.

301, §46. *Íbait fiäig lommæ cróu* This image is directly paralleled in *AFM* 866 (i, 506) where a quatrain about the battle of Cell Úa nDaigre has the line *blaisfit fiaich lomann cró* 'the ravens shall taste sups of blood'. The image is re-used in l. 332: *Is lais íbait fiäich fuil / for seichib ic Derclúachair (.i. Druim Ríg)*. In both examples, the syllable count guarantees that *fiäch* is disyllabic.

301, §46. *Loch Luglochtau* There is a reference in *FFÉ* ii, 120 to *seacht gcatha i Lughlachta ar Loch Lughdhach*. This would place Luglachta

90

at Loch Curran near Waterville, co. Kerry. This may explain the confusion between *fíachach / fíachrach* in l. 300 as *Carn Fíachrach* is near Ventry, co. Kerry. Loch Luglochta, however, more probably refers to the place called Luglochta Loga in *Tochmarc Emere* (van Hamel, 1933, 27 §17; 30 §25). The vowel ending *–au* (for *–a* [earlier *–o*?]) seems to have been inspired by a need to rhyme it with *cróu*.

302, §46. *Tróethbaid Brega borrchathaib* may also be translated as 'he will vanquish Brega with great battalions'. See *AU* 777.3, the note to l. 292 and Binchy (1958, 118).

303, §46. Rawl. *co nimniud* seems to be a miscopying of *co n-immud* (with *m* read as *ni*). As Meyer (1921, 150) pointed out, these lines are quoted in *AFM* 773 (i, 378):

> *I mBuile in Scáil atá an rannsa:*
> *Biaidh co nimbiud accan [accaín] an madan hi Forcaladh,*
> *Ria nDonnchadh Midhe meamhais cath init apail Conghalach.*

The following quatrain is in Buile-an-Scail:

> There will be increase of lamentation in the morning at Forcaladh;
> By Donnchadh of Meath the battle shall be won in which Congalach shall perish.

303-4, §46. *in maten hi Forcalad. / Ré nDond Midi memais cath / inidabbaill Congalach* This conflict is recorded in *AU* 778.1.

304ff., §46. *Dond Midi* This is a shortened form of Donnchad's name. He was known as Donnchad Midi mac Domnaill. It is also a play on words as *dond Midi* may also be translated as 'chief of Mide'.

305-6, §46. *Cath Srúbrach ara-sela Canán géba[s] mén, ré nDund Midi for fini, for anfine* The interpretation of this line is very problematical. The translation of *Cath Srúbrach ... ré nDund Midi for fini, for anfine* is straightforward but what exactly the middle section (Rawl. *arasela canangeba mén*) means is not clear. *Canán* (recte *Canan*?) has been taken here as a personal name, the object of the verb *ar-slig* 'smites, slays'. The interpretation of MS *geba mén* as *géba[s] mén* 'who will take an open mouth' is not put forward with any confidence.

306, §46. For other possible examples of *fíne* with the meaning 'sin', see Murray (2001ii, 304).

309, §46. *(.i. for Áed nIngor)* As Binchy (1958, 119) has pointed out, this is a gloss on *ruínfid riäm hi fochlæ* and not on *íar tuidecht ó Laigillib* where it appears in Rawl.

311, §46. *biat* This is the first of three examples (the other two are at ll. 398-9) where the form *biat* is used for the fut. 3rd plu. of the copula (for Classical O.Ir. *bit* [which is attested at ll. 121 & 178]). This spelling is also to be found, for example, in *LL* 18515: *Biat mathi do chland*.

312, §46. *Fomnais (.i. Áed Muinderg) i mBricc Fánat* This gloss is out of place here. The death of Áed Muinderg of the Cenél Conaill is recorded in *AU* 747.4. Perhaps the gloss should read *m. Áeda Muinderg* and be taken as referring to the hosting by Donnchad into the North (*AU* 779.10) in which he took hostages from Domnall, son of Áed Muinderg.

312-3, §46. The translation of this sentence is unsatisfactory, the whole line being fraught with difficulties.

313, §46. *rúed* Here 'e' is written for 'ai'. This is repeated on l. 323 (*búed*), and l. 324 (*mbúed*).

314, §46. *dá n-ocht [m]blíadnae* For this restoration, cf. Stokes (1905ii, 141 §22): *dá ñocht cét* and *LL* 14958: *da n-ocht ḿbliadan*.

314-5, §46. The Cellach in question is Cellach mac Dúnchada who was king of Laigin from 760-76 (the length of his reign is correctly noted here). Donnchad mac Domnaill probably reigned as king of Tara from 770-797; the length of his reign, however, is disputed (cf. Charles-Edwards (2000, 576-8); *BS* gives him a thirty-year reign). Donnchad was king of Mide for a number of years before becoming king of Tara (probably from 765 onwards).

314-5, §46. *bass ind amsir in duind Midi* This is an example of the double article, a phenomenon discussed at length by Ó Gealbháin (1991).

316-7, §46. *fírscél gona Follamain (.i. mac Con Congalt)* The slaying of Follaman mac Con Congalt is recorded in *AU* 766.2.

320, §46 & 423, §58. As with *maidid* (see note to l. 278), there is some confusion in *BS* between the pret. and fut. forms of *baïd* 'dies' [as previously noted by Thurneysen (1936, 214)]. The form *bebais* (formally the pret. 3rd sg. form) is taken to represent the fut. 3rd sg. form (regularly *bebaid*, as attested elsewhere in *BS*).

322, §47. The epithet more commonly associated with Áed is *Oirdnide* 'the anointed one'. *Ingor* as an epithet means 'the undutiful one'. Binchy (1958, 119) suggests that he may have been called this because of his revolt against the king of Tara, Donnchad mac Domnaill, who was titular head of the dynastic kindred.

322, §47. *a flaith* Lenition could be restored on *flaith* here and translated as 'his lordship'.

323 / 327, §47. *cernach crúaid / Cerna crúaid* There is a deliberate play on words here.

325-6, §47. *Fo-dercfa bandæ fo dii, / fris[a] tóethsat slúaig Midi .i. Fíndachta* This is a reference to the battle of Druimm Ríg (won by Áed Oirdnide mac Néill in *AU* 797.3) where the two sons of Domnall Midi, i.e. Fínnachta and Díarmait Odar, were slain along with Fínnachta mac Follamain.

332, §47. *íbait fiäich fuil* See note to l. 301.

334, §47. Lines 331-6 are all in *deibide*. Thus, Rawl. *Tlachtgé* has been emended to *Tlachtge* (: *clé*) because in *rinn / airdrinn* rhymes, 'an absolute final stressed long vowel may rhyme with its unstressed short form' (Murphy, 1961, 31).

336, §47. When the chariot was turned to the left, it was a challenge to combat. For example, see *TBC*[I] 1341-1: '*Dofil in carpat afrithisi 7 dorala clár clé frinn.' 'Ní fíach opaid,' ol Cú.* ('The chariot is coming again and has turned its left side to us.' 'That is a challenge which must be met,' said Cú Chulainn).

338-9, §47. *Ic Áth Dá Fertæ hi Conaillib at-bath per conflictionem Máel Canaig* The death of Áed Oirdnide and the part played by Máel Canaig therein are discussed by Kelleher (1971, 122-3).

341, §48. *Caínbreó bruigi Bregmaigi* This may refer to Conchobor's two invasions of Brega cited in *AU* 822.3.

342, §48. *cassra tocaid ina ré* Traditions concerning showers of prosperity are more commonly associated with Níall Frossach. See *AU* 764.15 and *CA* no. 124.

342, §48. *Túaruscbáil tíchtan geinti* The first report of Viking attacks in Ireland is in *AU* 795.3, during the reign of Donnchad Midi mac Domnaill. This line probably refers to the fact that 'during Conchobor's reign the Viking attacks, largely in abeyance in Áed Oirdnide's time, accelerated sharply' (Charles-Edwards, 2000, 557).

343, §48. *coínti[t] tuir* Similar forms of the verb with suff. pron. are attested on l. 90 (see note to this line).

347, §49. *Níell* This archaic spelling of the name is also attested in *Baile Chuind* (Murphy, 1952, 147).

347, §49. *Níell hi muir, Níell hi nguin, Níell hi tein* For the most recent discussion of the motif of threefold death, see Ó Cathasaigh (1994).

350 / 355, §50 & 413, §57. *Sechlainn* In Rawl. this is first written *Sechl-*

and then *Sech-* on two other occasions. These have all been expanded
to *Sechlainn*, the later metathesised form of *Sechnaill.*

350, §50. *Ní fiastar nech rúna a cridiu* Perhaps *a cridiu* should be
emended to *a chridi* and the line translated as 'No-one will know
the secrets of his heart'. There are examples elsewhere in Rawl. of
unstressed final *–e* being represented by *–iu* (cf. Introduction **7.1**).

352, §50. Rawl. *Dían fichta* One could possibly take *fichta* to represent
fíchda 'angry' and argue for the substantival use of this adj. here
(though no other adj. with the suffix *–da(e)* is treated similarly in
BS). The sentence would then translate 'swift anger against foreign-
ers'. The form could also be taken as the pret. pass. sg. form of the
verb *fichid* 'fights' (for classical O.Ir. *fechtae*). This remains unsatis-
factory, however, because one would expect a fut. (or perhaps pres.)
tense form. It seems best taken as a participle of *fichid.*

352, §50. *Díanfichta fri hechtranda (.i. Gaullu), slúagdórtad Forchai*
This encounter is noted in *AU* 848.4.

352-3, §50. *Fescur tess (.i. co Mumain)* This may refer to the invasion of
Munster by Máel Sechnaill as recorded in *AU* 858.4. The gloss *(.i. co
Mumain)* is misplaced in Rawl.

353, §50. *ata* How exactly the rel. form of the copula (whether it contains
a poss. pron. or not; cf. *GOI* §507c), is to be translated here is unclear
to me. Perhaps the original read *it a laídi légfaiter* 'they are his
poems which will be read'.

353, §50. *dúan Pátríni* See note to ll. 260-1.

357, §51. Though referred to as *Olach*, Áed's usual sobriquet (*Finnlíath*)
is given in a gloss. The epithet, *olach*, may translate as 'anointing
one' from *ola* 'oil'. This suggestion is strengthened by the fact that in
BS, Áed is said to have become a cleric. For another use of *olach* as
an epithet (*Díarmait Olach*), see van Hamel (1941, 90, §49).

361, §51. *hi cétaín chétgaimrid* The compound *cétgaimred* usually trans-
lates as 'early winter, the beginning of winter'. *DIL* (s.v. 1 *cét-*)
suggests, however, that in this case it may be best translated as
'November' as it is recorded in *AU* 879.1 and *AFM* 876 (i, 524) that
Áed mac Néill died on the 20th November.

363ff., §52. Practically all the references to the reign of Flann Sinna are
negative in *BS* – the same is true of *AU.*

364, §52. *fora bráithri* This has been translated 'upon his kinsmen' rather
than 'upon his brothers' as there is no evidence to show that Flann
Sinna had any brothers. This kin-slaying may refer to the events

recorded in *AU* 904.2 when Flann Sinna attacked his son, Donnchad, at Kells, where *alii multi decollati sunt circa oratorium*.

364-6, §52. *Tecait airdi ili 'na flaith .i. techt di nim (.i. ailithir ó Róim) dia foicertar ár ṅGoídel ic Duiblind (.i. ind ailithir). Bás cóel a clú do ríg Crúachan .i. Áed mac Conchabuir ro marbad isin chath* This battle is recorded in *AU* 888.5. It is worth noting that the exact name of the battle is not given in *AU* or in *BS* though it seems to be implied in *BS* that the battle occurred in Dublin. The glosses in *BS* referring to a pilgrim (from Rome) have an intriguing parallel in *AU* 888.5 where the H² interpolator refers to this battle as *cath ind Ailithir* 'the battle of the Pilgrim'. This may be a reference to either Lergus m. Cruinnéin (bishop of Cell Dara) or Donnchad m. Máele Dúin (superior of Cell Delca), both of whom were killed in the battle.

The many signs that come in his reign might also refer to (i) the solar eclipse recorded in *AU* 885.5; (ii) the 'fiery sky' recorded for the kalends of January in *AU* 890.1; (iii) the great windstorm on St Martin's feast in *AU* 892.2; (iv) the shower of blood which fell in Ard Cíannachta in *AU* 898.2.

365, §52. *ic Duiblind (.i. ind ailithir)* The examples cited in *DIL* (*ind ailithir*, *LL* 1013; acc. plu. *ailithriu*, *Ériu* 2, 194) along with *AU* 888.5 (gen. sg. *ind Ailithir*) point to *ailithir* as a mas. / neut. noun. Therefore, the gloss must either be gen. sg. 'of the pilgrim' (or perhaps nom. plu. 'the pilgrims').

365-6, §52. *Bás cóel a clú do ríg Crúachan* There are many problems of interpretation with this line. *Bás cóel* (Rawl. *bas cóel*) has been translated as 'slender death', perhaps with the implication that Áed was easily killed or that his death was a useless waste or that he suffered an inglorious death. No usage of *cóel* parallel to this has been found, however. *Bas cóel* could also be translated as 'slender palm / hand', perhaps with the implication that Áed lacked generosity, but once again no parallel usage has been uncovered. Perhaps *bas* should be taken as the fut. 3rd sg. rel. of the copula but how exactly this would translate here is unclear to me. *A clú* 'the fame / reputation' (with O.Ir. neut. art.) could also be emended to *a chlú* 'his fame / reputation'.

367-8, §52. *Firfid forbais for táilcentaig (.i. Ard Macha) co n-echtrandaib (.i. Gaill .i. maic Ímair)* This attack on Armagh with the Norsemen is recorded in *AU* 882.1 but it says nothing about the involvement of Ímar's sons.

368, §52. *Brisfid for Bréifnechu* This rout of the men of Bréifne is recorded in *AU* 910.1.

369, §52. *cath Grellaigi Eilti, cath Maigi Ailbi (.i. Óengus a mac ro bris ⁊ Laigin)* The gloss has been split in the translation as the first part refers to the battle in Grellach Eilti and the second part to the battle in Mag nAilbi.

370, §52. The translation of *brécach* as 'lying, deceitful' on l. 363 paves the way for the interpretation of *brécad étaig* as 'the enticing of jealousy'. *DIL* emends Rawl. *brecaid etaig* to *breccad étaig* and translates as 'plaid dress'.

370, §52. *Grúaca a cennaib* 'Hairs from / in heads'. This phrase may have some hidden meaning, i.e. '(like) hairs on heads', i.e. very common and very numerous. If so, the whole sentence would translate as 'the unfavourable judgement of people [will be] very common in his reign'.

370, §52. *glasmes* There is no suggested translation for this word in *DIL* (s.v. 2. *glas*). It is taken here as a compound of *glas* 'lock, fetter' used fig. as 'fettered, constrained' and *mes(s)* 'judgement'. Although this meaning goes well with the other unfavourable comments about Flann Sinna, this analysis is not completely satisfactory as it has been necessary to emend Rawl. by removing the nasalisation after *glasmes*, as there is no reason to posit neuter gender for a compound of *mes(s)* 'judgement'.

371, §52. *Síthflaith (.i. Fland) toiccthech* This is the only explicitly complimentary reference to Flann in the whole paragraph.

371-2, §52. *fris-tercha a chúaine féini friss (.i. a uii. maic)* The revolt of two of Flann's seven sons, Donnchad and Conchobor, is recorded in *AU* 915.3.

372, §52. *Bás duimrecht[a]* The word *duimrecht* is taken as a compound of *doimm* 'poor, wretched' and *recht* 'law, authority'. It is paralleled in formation (and meaning) by the compound *dubrecht* 'black law' (attested in *Thes.* ii, 357).

372, §52. *cád* This is still an o/ā-stem adj. here; it has not yet become an i-stem (*cáid*).

372, §52. *Domnach Aindin* The omission of the generic (i.e. *Loch*, before *Aindin*) is a common feature in medieval Irish sources and has been discussed by Baumgarten (1990, 119-22).

374, §52. Although noted here as 76, Flann's age at death is given as 68 in *AU* 916.1.

376-7, §53. *ririss flaith forbusach Lini* This victory over the lord of Line seems to refer to Níall's defeats of Loingsech úa Lethlabair, king of Dál nAraide, which are recorded in *AU* 914.3.

378, §53. *DIL* (s.v. *cétadach*) offers no explanation for *cétudach*. This word is taken here to be based on *cétad* '(chief) seat' and the adj. formed from this noun (using the suffix *–ach*) translates as 'seated', which is used substantivally as 'the seated one'. Since the word *cétad* also has the meaning 'chief seat', this substantive may also be translated as 'the one in the chief seat', i.e. 'the chief'. Substantival use of adjectives formed from nouns is a feature of *BS* (e.g. *armach* l. 263, *buidnech* l. 251, *cathach* l. 378).

379, §53. *Oirggne* This seems to be the gen. of a placename *Orgain*, rather than the gen. sg. of *orguin* 'murder, raiding, destruction'.

379-81, §53. Rawl. here reads: *cath codail (.i. grellaig eilti for niell ria fland) dia fich fuil feirniu cath trathca eolthaile for connachta.* The clause, *dia fich fuil feirniu*, seems to be misplaced and has been moved to clear up the onomatic confusion. The blood flowing in the Ferne (a river in barony of Tireragh, county Sligo) is most probably a reference to the battle of Trácht Eóthaile (also in barony of Tireragh).

380, §53. *Cath Tráchta Eóthaile for Connachta* This attack on the Connachta is described in *AU* 913.6, though the location of the battle is not given there.

381, §53. *Feirniu* An example of a prepositionless dative. See notes to ll. 244 & 292.

381, §53. *Cot n-úallai Albba* The translation of this phrase is unsatisfactory. *Albba* is in the nom. case here and the verb, *con-úala* 'goes up', seems to be used transitively with an infixed pronoun. For more detailed information on the verbal form, see Shaw (1962, 259-62).

382-3, §53. *ririss noíl Lochæ Léibind* cf. l. 423: *ririss roí Locha Lébind*.

383, §53. *fé innund fé ille* Lit.: 'death to one side and the other'. For this phrase, see Shaw (1947, 77-82).

388, §54. *crissalach* There may be another example of this compound in *Fled Bricrenn* (Henderson, 1899, 28; *LU* 8361-2): *at salaig úantaind athúanaind chrisalaig*.

392, §54. *Grían na fírinde* Lit.: 'the sun of righteousness'. This phrase is glossed .i. *Íssu Crist* in Stokes (1890, 28).

393, §54. *Dé* has been added after *céili* because the translation made no sense as the text stood. It seems that the glossator was implying that

Ioseph was either abbot of Armagh or a *céile Dé* at Armagh. In the notice of his death in *AU* 936.1, Ioseph is referred to as *princeps Aird Macha, episcopus ⁊ sapiens ⁊ ancorita.*

396, §55. *flaith in chon bic, bertfaid mór* It seems possible that this may be half of a couplet, with the second piece missing.

396, §55. *bertfaid mór* This could be a scribal miscopying of *bert– faid mór,* i.e. *bérthair faíd mór* 'a great cry will be brought forth' (which would negate the previous suggestion).

398, §55. *má du-phé* (Rawl. *madup hí*) This has been taken here as the pres. subj. 3rd sg. of the verb *do-fich* 'punishes, avenges'. That final *–é* (rather than *–í*) might have originally stood in the exemplar is suggested by the fact that the nom. plu. of *foglaid* is written *foghlaidé* in Rawl. (the nom. plu. is given as *foghlaidhe* in *IGT* [cf. *DIL* s.v. *foglaid*] although in O.Ir. one would expect a nom. plu. *foglaidi*).

The alternative is to analyse the words as *má duph-í,* the pres. subj. 3rd sg. of *do-icc* with the infix. pron. 2nd plu. Class A (with lenited 'p' for lenited 'b' as attested elsewhere in *BS,* e.g. *treiph,* l. 29). This would then mean that the expected O.Ir. nom. plu. form of *foglaid* could be restored. The first option has been preferred, however, because the use of a 2nd person form in this way in *BS* (outside of the introductory section, §§1-9) would be exceptional.

401, §56. This use of the definite article with *Ériu* (for the more usual *d'Érinn*) is attested elsewhere in O.Ir., e.g. *dond Érinn* (*Thes.* ii, 312.5).

402, §56. *ra n-alt* (Rawl. *ronalth*) This emendation is necessary as the nasalisation could only make sense as it stands in the MS if *túath Athbach* were treated as the object antecedent of a nasalising relative clause. For the gloss to make sense, however, *túath Athbach* must be taken as the subject antecedent.

403, §56. *cétudach* See note on l. 378.

404, §56. This could also have been emended to *cath Breg hÉli.* See note on l. 439.

412, §57. *sroiphtine* 'sulphurous fire, lightning'. This is also the sobriquet of Fíachu Sroiphtine, §15. For further discussion, see O'Rahilly (1942, 184-8).

415, §57. *nathair* (gen. *nathrach*) has been translated as 'dragon' here (rather than 'snake, serpent') to retain the fire imagery associated with Máel Sechnaill. There is a similar positive usage of *nathair* attested in Mac Cionnaith (1938, 224, no. 73 §8), where we find the phrase *nathair ionghuire a himill* 'guarding dragon of her border'. Both images are present in *TBC*[1] 1087 where Fergus is described as a warrior 'with the fierceness of a dragon, the venomous breath of a viper' (*co mbruth dracon co n-anáil n-athrach* [sic!]).

415-6, §57. Rawl. *firfid cath fri cláriu cath iroriss (.i. cath cairn fordroma)* The gloss is taken to be misplaced in the MS as the battle in Carn Fordroma was waged by Máel Sechnaill against Túadmumu in *AU* 990.3.

417-8, §57. *Crúas íar ngail, domnach hi Teilchinaib* could also be translated 'bravery after valour, a Sunday [battle] in Telchinn'.

421, §58. *clíabach* is also the name of some wild animal, perhaps 'a wild boar'. This phrase about the basket-trick brings to mind the modern ball-game *jai-alai*. This is said to be the fastest ball-game in the world and is played like handball but with the players using hand-held baskets to catch and throw the ball. This method of firing an implement would work equally well with a stone. Therefore, Flaithbertach's basket could be a weapon (a kind of sling) and he could have been renowned for his skill with this implement.

What militates against this is the interpretation offered by the phrase *clíabh clis* ('a feat basket') in Stokes (1908, §§47-48). Here, in the story of 'The Training of Cú Chulainn', Scáthach is said to have had a *clíabh clis* under her when she went to speak with the gods. It seems from the two references to it that the *clíabh clis* may have been some form of small mobile chariot.

423, §58. *ririss roí Locha Lébind* cf. 11. 382-3: *ririss noíl Lochæ Léibind.*

425, §59. *gríanbili* The first element of this compound could be the word for 'earth, land' (rather than 'sun'), referring to the king's essential relationship with his territory. The compound could then be translated as 'scion / hero of the land'.

426, §59. *Úargalach* This compound has been formed from words with opposite meanings – *úar* has the primary meaning 'cold' while *galach* has the primary meaning 'hot'.

428, §59. *Línfaid Caisil* The use of the form *Caisil* for the nom. / acc. (regularly *Caisel*) is attested, for example, in *SC* §391 and in *AU* 1102.11.

430-1, §60. Perhaps there is a corrupt transmission of poetry here with *coscrach* and *rii* reversed to give rhyme, i.e.

Dáil de for Óengus

[n]Óenaig Fánatt, coscrach rii.   Fírfid (.i. Óengus) in cath tess amni.

431, §60. *sondchad* The first element of this compound is taken to be *sond* 'stake, club, palisade'; the second element is presumably *cath* 'battle' (cf. *Donnchad < donn + cath*; *Murchad < muir + cath*). In these compounds, it seems preferable to translate the second element as 'battler' instead of 'battle', a meaning not otherwise attested for *cath*. There is another example (of *sonnchad*) in *AU* 929.4 which Mac Niocaill translates as 'palisade-like fighter'.

432, §60. *dá dá mac comdáni* Note the absence here of the dat. dual forms.

432, §60. *cin* is no longer treated as a dental stem here.

433, §60. There may be some corrupt (or partial) transmission of verse here.

dia mbië ben cen chéili,   dia mbiät fir thregtaig thuill

434, §60. The predicative adj. *adass* is followed by the acc.; this necessitates the restoration of nasalisation on *bóid*.

435, §60. The translation of *corr* as 'peculiar, odd' is unsatisfactory.

436, §60. There is a suggestion in *DIL* s.v. *ár* that it may originally have been neuter. This is backed up by the treatment of *ár* as neut. in l. 365 (*ár ṅGoídel*). Thus, *a n-ár* is translated as 'the slaughter' rather than 'their slaughter' (both being possible).

439, §61. This could also have been emended to *cath Breg Léith*. See note on l. 404.

440, §61. *DIL* s.v. *airbrech* cites *renóin airbrech* (from Plummer MS notes) for Rawl. *iar nóin airbrech*. This is a mis-reading.

443, §62. *Áed Engach* 'vociferous Áed'? See *Ériu* 12, 236-7. Ó Buachalla (1989, 229 n. 57) suggests that *engach* may mean 'truthful'.

443ff., §62. There are some textual parallels between *BS* §62 and *Baile Bricín* §57. For further details, see Murray (2002, 53-4).

444, §62. *bárc* has a secondary meaning 'stronghold' and *do-fócaib* also has the meaning 'raises', i.e. 'builds'. Thus, *dia tuicébat bárca for Ess Rúaid* could also be translated 'for whom they will build strongholds over Ess Rúaid'.

445, §62. *na dá Dúnlang* See note to l. 277.

446, §62. *gignid* The verb, which shows loss of deponent ending, may be contrasted with forms with deponent endings in ll. 75, 154 and 299. For a similar development with *gainithir*, see *Anecd*. ii, 8.23.

446, §62. I originally read Rawl. *tor sithaigfes* as *forsíthaigfes*, an otherwise unattested verb (though the verbal noun of such a verb, *forsídugud* 'pacifying, pacification', is cited in *DIL* s.v.). The correct reading, i.e. *tor síthaigfes* 'a hero who will spread peace', is the same as that in *BBr.* (see Murray, 2002, 54).

451, §63. *méthrúd* (Rawl. *methrud*) This has been taken here as a compound of *méth* 'fat, rich, fertile' and *rúd* (< *ro* + *fid*) 'forest' rather than as the dat. sg. of the more common noun *méthrad* (o,m.) 'fat, grease', which would lead to problems of interpretation.

451, §63. There is an alternative tentative suggestion in *DIL* that Rawl. *selustai* may be fut. 3rd sg. rel. of *slaidid* with suffix. pron. 3rd sg. m.

456, §64. *Cúanaig Bregmaige* The interpretation of this phrase is fraught with difficulties. The adj. *cúanach* may be translated 'full of packs (of wolves)' or 'attended by troops'. Used substantivally it could be translated as 'one attended by troops'. If this were used in the sing. (i.e. *cúanach Bregmaige*), it could be translated as 'one attended by the troops of Bregmag'. However, *cúanaig* is nom. plu. here (as it stands) so the phrase would translate as 'those attended by the troops of Bregmag', a peculiar translation in reference to one person (i.e. *Fergal foltgarb*).

Another option is to take *cúanach* as an adj. derived from *cúán* 'little dog' used substantivally in the above phrase to mean 'dog-like ones of Bregmag'. Alternatively one could take the preceding word to be part of the same sentence, i.e. *foltgarb cúanaig Bregmaige* and treat it as half a couplet, taking *cúanaig* as a preposed adj. This would then translate as 'the rough-haired one of Bregmag of the (wolf-)packs'. The final option is to read it as *cúan áig Bregmaige* and to translate as 'troop of battle of Bregmag'.

457-8, §64. *Brogfaid Cnámchailli. Túaruscbáil tened loiscess toirthiu* Perhaps these two sentences should be run together with *túaruscbáil* (for *fo thúaruscbáil*) taken as a conjunction showing the manner in which something occurred. The translation would then read 'he will advance on Cnámchaill like a fire that burns the crops'.

462, §65. *Fland Cinuch* 'Flann the voracious'.

465, §65. *fo-génat* (Rawl. *foṅgenat*) *dúili Dé* Keeping the MS reading, this line could be translated as 'God's Creation will serve us'. However, this type of use of a 1st plu. infix. pron. would be exceptional in *BS*.

468, §65. *ciṅges ar chel* See note to l. 255.

469, §65. *cimbal* is a preposed gen.

469, §65. *fria cimbal nguth* The same phrase (*fri cimbal [n]guth*) is used
in O'DG §357.

469-70, §65. *Regaid éc aitti íar sein di chretair chréissin hi Temuir* This
could also be translated 'He will die then by the power of the relic of
the believer in Tara'.

DIPLOMATIC EDITION FROM MS RAWL. B. 512

(fo. 101ra) Incip*it* di baile i*n* scail in so a*r* slicht hsenlib*uir* duibh da leithi .i. coa*r*pa pat*r*a*ic*

^{1.} Laa ro bui *con*d i temraich iar ndith do*n*a rigaib at*r*ara*cht* mati*n* moch fo*r* [...]aith na temrach ria t*ur*cb*áil* gr*é*ni ⁊ a t*r*i druid ríam .i. mæl ⁊ blouc ⁊ bluiccniu. Eoch*aid* ⁊ corbb ⁊ cessarnd in fil*id* ⁊ *con*d fadeissin. Fodeg at*r*aigedso*m* cach dia in lín si*n* arna ragabtais fir ṡithi u*e*l fomoiri fo*r* herin*n* cen airegudh. ²ln dua dia ndecad do g*r*es co fuair cloich and ara chiund foa chosaib. Fo*r*ling i*n* cloich iar*um* ⁊ salt*r*ais fuirri ⁊ geísis an cloch foa chosaib co closs fo*n* temraig hule ⁊ fo bregmagh.³⁺⁊ Is and si*n* ro íarfacht *con*d din ḟil*id*. Cidh ro geisi in cloch ⁊ cía ain*m*. ⁊ can doralad ⁊ cid no regad ⁊ cid f*r*isa táraill temr*aig*. IS and si*n* asp*er*t in file f*r*is ni sluindfed dóu co cen*n* .l. laithiu ⁊ treissi fair. In tan iar*um*¹ ba lan ind arim si*n* ro iarf*acht con*n a f*r*ithisi dond ḟil*id* ⁊ ro buiside icc scrutan *co* n*é*cetar a eochra eccsi dou. ⁴Fal (.i. fo ail .i. ail fo rig) em ol an fili a hainm na clocha ⁊ inis² f*á*il asa torlad ⁊ is i tem*r*aig tire fail foruirmed. Tir tailten hi tairiss hi co brath ⁊ iss ed tir i*n* sei*n* bas oenach cluchi dot claindsiu cei*n* bes flaithi*us* hi tem*r*aig. Oc*us* a lla ndedenach di secht*main* oenaich tailten flaith na faigbi is trú issi*n* blia*dain* si*n*. Ro gesi iar*um* fal fad chos-saibsiu ol in file ⁊ dorairngert a llin ngemind ro geisi is é lín r*í*gh bias ditt silsu fo*r* heri*nn* co brad. Attafeid da*m* amal sodain ol *con*n. Ni da*m* ro thocad a rad f*r*itt ol in drui. ⁵·A mbat*ar* and iar*um* co naccat*ar* ciaigh (**fo. 101rb**) moír impu *con*a fetatar cia dochotar ar meid i*n* dorcha d*us*fanic. Co cualatar trechan an marcaigh ara cend. Mor mai*r*cc du*n* fo*r con*d ma ru*n*fucca i*n* ceosa hi tiri anetargnaide. La sodain doleci i*n* marcagh t*r*i haurchuru fo*r*ru ⁊ is t*r*aidiu d*us*fanic int *er*chor dedenuch q*uam* in tossiuch. IS do gui*n* rig ol in ḟhile cip he dibercess *con*n hi temair. Anaid an marcag di*n* dibruc*ud* ⁊ f*er*aid failti f*r*i *con*n ⁊ *con*gart leis dia t*r*eiph. ⁶·Docotar iar*um* ass *con*darala assa mag ⁊ bile norda an*n* tech foa ochtaig findruine and .x. t*r*aigid .xx. a mét. Lotar iar*um* issa tech *co* n*a*ccat*ar* ingen maccthacht i cathair glanidi ⁊ barr órdhai fo*r*a mullach ⁊ b*r*at co srethaib di or impe dabach arcait co cethraib c*er*naib ordaib ara bélaib lán di dergflaith. escra oir ara óu airideog nech³ di ór ara belaib. Et *co*

---

1   Over the 'a' of iarum there is a mark (like ^) in the manuscript.
2   *inis* is written in superscript.
3   There is a mark of lenition over the 'n' of *nech*.

*n*accatar a scál fadeissin isin taig ara ciund i*n*na rígsudiu. Oc*us* ropu mór
a delgnaidhe ba dethbir so*n* ar ni f*r*ith hi temr*aig* riam fer a meti nach a
chaime ar aille a delba n[...] chrotha ₇ ara inganti. ⁷˙f*r*i[...]tisidi doib iar*um*
₇ as [...]. Nimda scálsa [...] aurdrach ₇ is f*or* [...] muccai iarmu [...]od ₇ is
d*e* hsil a[...] is he mo slon*n*ud [...] (**fo. 101va**) nen m*aic* smretha m*aic*
tigernmair m*aic* fælad m*aic* etheuir m*aic* iriail m*aic* erimo*in* m*aic* miled
espaine. Et is dó dodeochadsa *co n*ecius duitsiu sægal d*o* flatha ₇ cacha
flatha bias huait hi te*m*r*aig* co brad ⁸Et ba sii i*n*d ingen boi esin taigh ara
cind flaith her*enn* ₇ ba si dob*er*t dithait do chun*n* .i. dama*s*næ ₇ torcasnæ.
Cethair t*r*aigid fichet fott i*n* da*m*asnai ocht t*r*aigid et*er* a thuai*m* ₇ tal*main*.
Dá t*r*aigh deuc fott in torcasnai ₇ coic t*r*aigid et*er* a tuai*m* ₇ talmai*n*. ⁹˙In
tand di*diu* luid ind ingen do*n* daíl asb*er*t f*r*iu cia dia tibe*r*thæ ind airdech
cosi*n* dergf*h*laith ₇ f*r*isgart i*n* scál di iar*um*. O r*us* sluin*n*sidi iar*um* cach
flaith i ndegaid a*r*aile o ai*m*sir cuin*n* co brad. Ba t*r*om iar*um* la cesarnd
fil*id* a ndichetail si*n* do thabairt f*r*i oinhuai*r co n*ecmaing t*r*e oghu*m* hi
cetheora flescæ iphair cethir t*r*aigid fichet fott cacha flesci ₇ ocht
ndrui*m*ne cacha flesci. Lotar iar sein hi foscad a scail ₇ ni arrdraigestair a
ndu*n* nacha dtech. Foracbad im*m*urgu la co*n*n ind dabach ₇ i*n*t esc*r*a ₇ in
airdech ₇ na flescæi. Oc*us* is di sen atta aislingi ₇ echt*r*a ₇ argraige cuind
cetcath*aig* ₇ baile i*n* scáil. ¹⁰˙Cia f*or*sndailfider i*n*d airdech oirse cosi*n*
[...]lait ₇ cia nodas ibai ol in ingen. ni *anse*. Dail de ol in scál f*or co*nn
cetchadach chet chadræ firfidius cath b*r*eg (**fo. 101vb**) hele cath ache
cath machæ *cath* dubaichi *cath* olarba *cath* daim deirg *cath* rendai *cath*
f*or* seilg *cath* chinn tiriu *cath* gaibthi*n*e *cath* etair *cath* ibair *cath* d*r*oma
duib *cath* moi*n*maige *cath* hi scaleda *cath* mibthiniu *cath* roiss *cath*
tortan *cath* g*ré*ine *cath* magi muí *cath* f*or* caimsi *cath* f*or* buáis f*r*i fini f*r*i
anfine *cath* i ndru*m*mut co fo t*r*i secht catha maige linéi *cath* i fremaind
cath i máil da f́escur midhe *cath* da dule firfide ₇ t*r*omár hi clochur. Da
chath fichet i nairb cethri catha i clairiu canis firfe bidemi*n* firfid secht
catha cualgi la deora dermaitni fe*m*in *cath* f*or* gull *cath* f*or* ergull ₇
dubadaig i*m*mair dofoith f*or*annan i*n* rí dofoetsat rig*r*ad adni da foeth
mane m*ac*⁴ briathraigh ₇ ailill olgné *con*chobar chena fergu*s* oingu*s*
dubaigi a co*m*rac im tipraiti cith leth cho*m*nart a nude is he gignetar a glé
i*n* sluagad im suidé. Dirsan do chund chetcath*ach* iar nár thened tar cech
mag gentar iar timchiul cach rois dia máirt i tuaith imrois coíc f́ichit
blia*dn*ae na*m*má dodacich nodaíba. ¹¹˙Cia f*or*si*n*dáilfider i*n*d airidech

---

4   Or *mend*? See Thurneysen (1935) 221.14.

óirse ol ind ingen cosin dergflaith. Ni *anse*. Dail de f*or* art oenfer ol i*n* scal fer chétgretha .lxxx. catha firf*h*ess c*ath* sleibe betha c*ath* sleibe cua c*ath* moisten c*ath* móin c*ath* druáig c*ath* tortini c*ath* irluachra c*ath* coidlim c*ath* locha daim hi toethsat in duinechoin Bid scél nairdircc hi cech taig c*ath* ḟesair hi collobair c*ath* dro*m*ma (**fo. 102ra**) undglaissi c*ath* atha dairi duib c*ath* senchua. Da chath liphe cath dorcha cath dro*m*ma dígais c*ath* sláini c*ath* roigni c*ath* argatrois dia mbaat ili. Da cath i liniu c*ath* aidni c*ath* leithit lachmuige. Da f*h*escur hi saimniu c*ath* fin*n*maigi c*ath* i fremui*n*. madan i*n*si dor*n*dglaissi. In ca**t**h i *m*brí cobthaig coil. coíntit coím cointit ile. Dirsan do fothud ad baill ⁊ oeng*us* mac do*m*naill. Matan maigi muc*r*amai so hi toethsatt mairb ile. Ba dirsan do art m*ac* cuind cin m*ac*⁵ naililla auluim. Dia dardai*n* sír iar srath maidtir la echraid lugdach .xx. blia*dnae* na*m*ma dodacich nodaíba. ¹²Cia f*or*sindailfidher i*n*d airdeog óirsi cosind f*h*laith ol in ingeu*n*. Ni *anse*. Dail de f*or* lug*aid* m*ac* con ol in scál cini di sil chuind dóu doaidlibe .u. blia*dnai* .xx. na*m*ma dodacich nodaíba. A lo*n*gas co iath norc u*e*l alban. Arbrisf*h*i .iii. nói cath f*or* tuatha orcc. Firfid cath tuithmi la teora húarg*r*esu hu*m*ail. Dia do*m*naigh f*or* áth híí do*n*aidli fiacail fidbai. ¹³Cia f*or*sindailf*ider* ol ind i*n*gi*n*. Dail de f*or*sin mórbrethach f*or* corm*ac* ua cuind .lx. blia*dnae* na*m*ma dodacich nodaíba. Mórfuitir fine ⁊ anfine. Sith noll co ría*n* ina *r*e. Bid ríí te*m*rach co fo thríi ara *m*bebat ilsiabrai .i. sithaigi. A breith dar muir la mælcend i naidchi gaim tess beind bairchi. Dúbartach midhe dia f*h*essair c*ath* g*r*anairdd c*ath* i neuo c*ath* i neuth c*ath* i cind (**fo. 102rb**) dairi c*ath* sruthra c*ath* cualgi c*ath* atha beth c*ath* atha du*m*ai c*ath* cuiliu caichir fa thri nipat becca i*n*d luádrí. Tothaim di meís assail aín cen corm*ac* ina righdail c*ath* hi ndubad co fo thri. Matan dairi follscaide c*ath* na luac*r*ai allmaig slecht c*ath* eillne c*ath* maige te*cht* i*m*d*er*cad corm*ai*c fo thri bid mair128cc mac ind fubthairi. Elud rig temrach iar sein gubadan mor hi mæ*n*maig. Longass chormaic dar mag .iii. bliadnai cluinti cein. Ticfa iar sein co m*um*ain cormac f*r*ia matin fugail cath berri c*ath* locha lein c*ath* im lui*m*nech c*ath* im grein a mbudni ola bidh mair dochom the*m*rach da*r* mag fail. arnena gíalla gaidel. aradercc duirri dremna firfid c*ath* clasaig. Ar mor os muiriscc craudortad troch artuaset ulaid occa d*o*foeth hechaid toebfoda c*ath* slabræ c*ath* ardda caim do clai*n*d mu*m*an nipa moín. Orggain na rigingen bid scél bid f*h*assach naenre Bid oen di neort ha flathæ for haidni na borime. Tola herend la corm*ac* fri ferg*us*

---

5   This could be restored to *mac* or *maic*.

ard*r*i ul*ad* Dofoeth f*ergus* sceo enda dia *m*bia sluag dupuch. Mairt hi
c*r*inda ceín ṁbess bith hi foichret sluaig herend grith. Fianda firfhit
dubarta me*m*ais i*n* c*ath* ria corm*ac*. Teora bli*adnai* iar si*n* co c*ath* crind*æ*
fre gabuil. Bebaid (**fo. 102va**) corm*ac* caín marb dia mairt hi toeb cletig
adcoinfet goidil. [14.]Cia f*or*sindail*fider* ind airedeog oirsi (.i. regn*um* scot-
tor*um*) cosin derclaith ol i*nd* ingen. Dail f*or* fer iolair glond for coirp*r*i
liphechair fer noíbas tond .xxx. c*ath*a ina re. biaid .lx. bli*adnae*. Dubairt
her*enn* cota muir c*ath* fhessair i liphimaig. Mairt hi liphimaig arathá
bebaid and i*n* rignía. [15.]Dail de f*or* fiach*u* roiphtine. Matan midi la suide
da c*ath* hi maig ratha .xx.u. bli*adnai* a ré co saigid na boramai. Tothaim*m*
fothaid m*ai*c cruaíd bid scel mór hi cach tuaith. Teora bli*adnai* iar*um* cen
meth. hi cna*m*ross bied rígbath. Ceta*in* cnamroiss bid gand gle hi toeth
fiachu roiph*tine*. [16.]Dáil de f*or* muredagh tirech .xl. bli*adnae* hi flaith c*ath*
he mórmaigh firfid gle f*ri* hultu f*ri* araide. For brú dabaill hisin c*ath*
dof*æ*th murethach tirech. [17.]Dail de f*or* echaig mugmedóin toebfota te*m*ra
du*n*adach tlachtgai. dubartach feimi*n*. Costudach moenmaighi. Cruind
ársid liphi. Toichmech toirrchi .xx.u. bli*adnai* namá dodacich nodaíba
Gui*n* glui*n*find bid mór i*nt* echt. gui*n* co*n*chobair gui*n* m*ai*c cecht. Forus
ṅhernd fo echaig f*ri*a ré bid f*or*ggu maithe. IS huad gignedar co brath
bunad na flaithi. I ndub combair f*ri* ré bied fo(**fo. 102vb**)tha fingaile. Na
t*r*i colla glanfait ár hi toeth echu muigmedán [18.]Dail de f*or* niall nóigi-
all*ach* .i. cóic geill herend. ⁊ gíall albu*n* ⁊ breta*n* ⁊ saxan ⁊ franc. Nóitfitir
tuir mórf*h*aitir maigi nensitir geill fessait*ir* catha. Sesait*ir* sluaigh
Mórfaitir flathi fugeillfi níel fo thri Daṅgega flaith ar bidh hé i*n* ri maith.
A c*ath* muirnedh hi f*or* ath lúain. IS and dofoethsat in sluáigh. Fescur
coscrach dúi*n* cúai*r* tathai*m*m nauthuli f*ri*ss antuaith .xxuii. bli*adnai*
nama dodacich nodaíob*æ*. Dufhuit iar sen griba tuile gluind ar drui*m*m
nalba*n* dofoeth níall bid adbar mairg trui*m*m i *n*arddmói*n* die sathairnd.
[19.]Dail dé f*or* colla noss (.i. uais) .iiii. bli*adnai* nama dodacííg nodaíb
scairfaid f*ri* arddscél do denam na fi*n*gali. [20.]Dail dé f*or* ailill molt m*ac*
nathi m*ai*c fiachrach. fer uallach fer adcui*n*ti sochaidi .xx. bli*adnae*
nama. Catha ile na flaith ar bid he in rí maith. Cucligid temra. C*um*ascach
tailten c*ath* atha tálmaig. Dubartach séile nóitech aichi c*ath* ratha
cruachan. Ceím f*or* sabralla ceím f*or* elpa. Togal i*n* tuir. Ceím f*or*
eolarcca c*ath* sratha cluithi f*or*tbe ngeinnet. Ceím dar muir nicht docu*m*
nelpa. Cichsit herendmaig reim ndian atacu*m*bat echtraind .uii. mbel f*ri*
firu goedel f*or* ailill i *n*oin didin ar elpai. Bit ili athet martrai ba dirsun do
feraib herend is mor artha thoi (**fo. 103ra**) tim*m* la echtranda. [21.]Dail de
f*or* lóigairi fer ilair glond mórfait iltire nilbélras .xxx. bli*adnae* nama.

Tascur dían ticfa tailcend (.i. pat*raic*) fer graidh móir nóifidsi dia mór.
breó adandaba lin*fhus* herend cota muir. bebaid loigairi (flaith him
bachla) *for* bru chaissi mór caur cicharda dof*or*tat tailcind. ^{22.}Dáil de for
tuathal mælgarb (.i. m*ac* corm*aic* m*ai*c coirpri m*ai*c neill) .xx. (bl*iadnae*)
c*ath* lúachra ailbi c*ath* detnai totim nardgail c*ath* légi c*ath* dro*m*ma
a*r*belaig c*ath* bregoi*n*d. fo*r*naid*m* ngiall ngoidil. IAR sin bid scél hi cach
maig bebaid oengui*n*e namá tuathal oc grellaigh eilti. gentar mæl mór
dia digail hi tuaith imbroiss. ^{23.}Dail de f*or* lug*aid* m*ac* lóigairi .xxui. co
thotim dóu di chuáirt f*or* hérind t*r*iá diultad táilcind i *n*escir f*h*orchai.
^{24.}Dail de for muircertach mac ercci (.i. i*n*gen loairnd). ri cathach coscrach
atcui*n*ti sochaide fonen héri*n*d fir ₇ mná. Ar bid co*m*arbba temra cath
atha sigi iar sen linf*us* co heri*n*n airbiu. benaid dubart hi máirt in cáirb
coscrach co laigniu mór áttba bebaid muir*certach* éc atbai mairt cletig.
^{25.}Dáil de f*or* anmirig timgera giallu cach maigi íartír cinip a taír truim*m*
dofoeth ardaig ruád firfithir catha .iiii. bl*iadnai* namá. ^{26.}Dail de f*or*
baetán ₇ echaig .iiii. bl*iadnai*. ^{27.}Dáil de f*or* diarmait (.i. m*ac* f*er*gu*s*a
cerrbeoil) dubartach tailten tairngertaig temra. cen mair i*n*a f*h*laith ar bid
hé in ri maith. dia .uii. mbl*iadnae* iar sein c*ath* fæbrach f*or* diar*m*ait
dreimni. i*n* slóg dosia an*n*tuaith glanfait i*n* rói co ath lúai*n*. (**fo. 103rb**)
berthair a cathbuáid. i*n*d ai*n* diten hi raith bic. dith diar*m*ata i*m*maric
(.xx. bl*iadnae*). ^{28.}Dail de f*or* fergg*us* ₇ do*m*nall da m*a*c muircertaich
m*ai*c ai*n*mirech .i. brandub m*a*c echach ro marb di bl*iadain* hi co*m*f*l*aith.
^{29.}Dail de for aedh uáredach m*a*c do*m*naill. mórf*h*ass flaith fonen héri*n*d.
flaith fodbach f*or*anach. firfidh f*or*basa herend. bl*iadain* iar sei*n* dothuit
ail*ill* m*a*c do*m*angairt. bied gni*m* hi temairmaig. Iurait laigen a ndá*m*a
*con*bibsat a fírdála. bid gárgg bid coscrach a ré co llaithe tangnechta. In
máirt i *n*descurt liphi. IS an*n* atbela i*n* ríí .uiii. bl*iadnai* namá. ^{30.}Dail de
f*or* aedh slane. sith noll flaith goedel. caín ernfi f*h*ini fuáta liamna.
Dothóet ia*r* sei*n* aedh slán*e* iar lín c*ath*a na ré .uiii. mbl*iadnai* namá.
Dodacaich dodaíba .i. coirm c*ath* p*otio* so*m*pni ut dicébat. ^{31.}Dail de f*or*
aedh olldai*n* .uiii. mbl*iadnai* dodacaich nodaiba dubartach falmaigie
gebaid f*or* liphemaigh. arnena giallu goedil. mór marb mór átbai. mór ail
atcuinf*h*et goideil. ^{32.}Dail de f*or* do*m*n*all* me*n*d ulad nóií mbl*iadnai* déc
namá. Drauc ilair band firf*h*es da cath i maig roth. mairt is an*d* toeth i*n*d
rig*r*ad. Et dergmaten cruthni. firf*id* c*ath* dúi*n* cethe*r*nd. la c*ath* ratha
almachi. cichis iar*um* a réim mór ail atbath ind ríí. ^{33.}Dáil de for subni
me*n*d drauc ilair band bl*iadain* coa .uii. bías a f*l*aith fonena gia(**fo.
103va**)llu cach rois c*ath* dathe fir*fe*s in ríí IS and dothoet nipi gau colma*n*
mór m*a*c díarmato. ^{34.}Dail de f*or* blathm*a*c m*a*c æda (.i. slaine) is hé

nodaíba .u. bliadnæ ara derbflaith. ³⁵·Dail de forsin ruanaid (.i. a ruidiud
ig gabail lama mocuta) for diarmait daithi a cétcath senchua cath roiss
corcu búain cath ossraidi cath eile cath sléibi etir doinda. firfid .uii.
catha aidni la cath seilgi íar noín arataat immurgu dercmaitni cruithni
bid crúas cuimnech tuáth in cuib. IAR sen in mortlaid for herind i mbiat
múcna int slúaig. ³⁶·Dail de for finnachta .i. mac dunchada maic æda
sláni consaidfi fri mumain móir. firfid cath cuile cóiláin sciss hi toeb
cithamra fer mochtaidi adbaill fingail moír i naín dídin for dollud.
Duthain a recht nipa ri aed (.i. dluthaig) iarum .xx. bliadnae namá. ³⁷·Dail
de for sechnusach mac blaithmaic uno anno. dodacaich atbeba éc átbai
issind imbliuch os boaind. ³⁸·Dail de for cend fælad .uii. mbliadnai a
flaith. iar sen in cath hi temuirmaigh dotoeth cenn fælad i ndomnach
cuíli cóiláin. ³⁹·Dail de for loingsich (.i. mac oengusa maic domnaill)
siabraid for falmaig costudach liphi. Buidnech beirri. Dotoeth ic lecaib
finnaib lassna fianna fo minnaib. regaid a nimguin fa thuaith. memais for
rígh essa ruáidh .i. ría cellach locha cimbi. die sathairn cichiss ar chel etir
da corand uinnsen (.i. cath coraind) .xi. bliadnai namá. ⁴⁰·Dail de for
fogartach nán ₇ for (fo. 103vb) congal mac fergusæ fánat .xiiii. bliadnai
namá. Dathuittet a ndiis in lúan ria samuin. ind ala nai hi tosuch ind laí.
alaili inna deriud hi cluain irairdd sepulti sunt ut patrini dixit ⁴¹·Dail de
forsin cailech (.i. i nain didin a cath almaine) for fergal clethblugaid
herenn. armach lini. ársid ai. bebaid la laighniu iarna re. fergal hi cath
almaine. biaid ár mor isin cath linfhus co heirinn airbriu⁶ hi toéth ind
rigrad moínech immon cailech ass amru .xii. i ndermaigh ro adnacht
fergal. UNde dictum est. Rena fuiligud hi rói tailcc arbertad catha clí.
indiu for lár dermaigi aicsiu fergaili ní ní. ⁴²·Dail de for flaithbertach ind
re bias is lais firfidhir cath droma corcáin fri temraigh antuaid cinæd
ainm hua conaing (fin fo talmain) atcoinfed goidhil .xxui. bliadna bass ri
flaithbertach Conbeba éc uatba fo tailcentaig .i. i nard macha i nailithre
atbath clericus i nailaid na ríg. ⁴³·Dail de for æd alden (.i. altan noimen
loci ubi nutritus est) æd airdri .x. mbliadnae firfid cath coscrach gein
catha sáiltiri arangeba bidh ní dáu na da cath isind oenlóu cath atha da
charnda cath atha medóin memaid for cenel conaill. Glanfaid arú. falguba
ulad. Memaiss for æd (.i. ron mac beicci bairche) re næd. int æd. aurbaig
(.i. cath focharta) forma fan leth a anmæ hi muir (.i. ron) már. Do maigh
laigen gebaid grith bid sloged naurderc fon mbith an máirt hi tuaiscirt

---

6   Version in MS Harl. 5280 breaks off at this point.

liphi. Dighail *catha* almai*n*e i nebbela cach amra fir*fid* ail uchbad (**fo. 104ra**) gebaid goedhelu co muir etir *con*d is mu*m*ain *cath* ceni*n*dsa *cath* i neochi*n*d da ríí ara*m*bebat tigernai. bied mairc mór hi cach taigh iar si*n* *cath* a s*r*edmaig. Biaid ernbas i*m* rígu sain can im colai*n*d næda. dofoeth in ri o srub brai*n* *for* brú locha sailcitai*n*. hi cluai*n* m*ac* noiss ro adnacht æd aldán. ⁴⁴·Dail de *for* dom*n*all m*ac* murcadhæ roí*n*fitir catha (.i. cath sredmaigi) ria*m* noifitir fir i*n* darddáin. atbeba bregaib. éc atbai hi tailtentaigh .i. i *n*imliuch ia .xx. bliadan. ⁴⁵·Dail de *for* niall frosach catha ili na flaith níba f*r*iss firfithir bebaid éc atbui la fuil. berthair hi tire da*r* muir .i. co hí col*u*im cilli .uii. mblia*dnai* namá .i. dondchad expulsit eu*m* de regno suo. ⁴⁶·Dail de *for* don*n*cha*d*. Ticfa flaith dondcadæ t*r*iui*n* coicligid insi scott gignidir nach tai*n*. is lais doregat i*n* sluaig. Ti*m*chell cairnd fíachrach antuáith. Ibait fiaig lom*m*æ cróu *for* brú locha luglochtau. Troethbaid brega borrcathaib. Morc*ath* airthir fuáta fir*fes*. Bied *co* *n*im*n*iud acain (.i. cenn) i*n* maten hi *for*calad. Re ndond midi memais *cath* i*n*idabbaill *con*galach *cath* srubrach arasela canangeba mén re ndund midi *for* fini *for* anfine. Gentair táilcend gní*m* co fíni aramba fiachru (.i. m*ac* cathail). ara belaib sinit fir. iar tuidecht o laigillib (.i. *for* aed ningor). Di lár tailten ruanaid gle (.i. *cath* cairnd m*aic* cairthind) rui*n*fid riam hi fochlæ⁷ *con*saidhfe co cendaib troch. die dom*n*aich i*m* chloenloch. Cath (**fo. 104rb**) etain tairb biat ili mairb. Fomnais (.i. aed muind*er*g) i mbricc fanat i mbi ríí t*r*ess tinduind tessad bodbai. bid co*m*aimser do in dondf*her* *co* mag di lar liphi rúed rafiastar cach. Cellach ain*m* da nocht bli*adnai*. bass ind a*m*sir in duind midi. Ond huai*r* reg*u*s cota muir firscel gona follamain (.i. m*ac* con *con*galt). cert .xxx. bli*adnae* nama co cend rigi dondcada. biaid golgairi hi cech maigh hi tossach ind uarerraigh. IN dond mide bebais aitt die mairt fo tailcentaig .i. hi cluai*n* eraird. ⁴⁷·Dail de *for* æd ningor *for*sin gercc .xxiii. bli*adnai* a flaith. IS he int aed cernach cruaid. cosc*r*ach brisfess bued. fomnas da na mbued *for* clóitig. dofoirtbe firu ceni toithsad rig. fodercfa bandæ fo dii. f*r*is toethsat sluaig mide .i. findachta. Ruáid aír truim dosfoírtbi. Atbeba dond cerna crúaid. i*n* tan ainfes bid iar mbuaid. Citha garcc a gaile g*r*aphand. Dof*or*tbi tailcentaig .i. t*er*man*n* aird macha. Trenchathach ceniuil conaill. Dergtresach temarmaigi. Slogindredach clairi. Costadach liphi. Sluaig doregat o s*h*rúb brain isi*n* mís ia*r* núa*r*gaim. IS lais íbait fiaich fuil *for* seichib ic dercluachair (.i. druim rig). IN sluag doficfe f*r*i cle. cul a catha

---

7   Over the *æ* of *fochlæ*, 'v' is written.

fri tlachtgé. aedh findi cummha chnes. memais riam síardes. in tan sóifes
clár fri clé arambeba finachtæ. (**fo. 104va**) I Nard macha sepultus est
aedh. Mac dunflatha ingeni flaithbertaigh maic longsich aedh ordnidi IC
ath da fertæ hi conaillib atbath. per conflictionem mæl canaigh. [48.]Dail de
for conchabor mac donnchada gebaid góidelu cota muir mac mná
condacht. cáin bréo bruighi breghmaighi .xiiii. ar techta temuir cassra
tocaid ina ré. Tuaruscbáil tichtain geinti. INd oín diden cóinti tuir artha
étsecht conchobuir hi clúain iraird sepultus est. [49.]Dail de for niall cailli
doda nesfa (.i. temair). firfid cath cruachan (.i. cath leithi caim) cath
dairi chalcaig for geinti. Niell hi muir niell hi nguin niell hi tein.
Cumasscach (.i. herenn). teora bliadnai déc. I Nard macha ro adnacht
niell iarna bádud hi calaind .i. hi linde neill. [50.]Dail de for mæl sechlainn.
ni fiastar nech rúna a cridiu tuitet tri duind elgnæi la dubai a gossa. IS
leis firfidhir fert fingaile uc clóin. Dían fichta fri hechtranda (.i. gaullu).
Sluagdortad (.i. co mumain) forchái fescur tess cuaird for herinn. ata
laídi legfaitir (.i. duan patrini). die mairt ríghi roiss dofuit atbai i roi ruis
(.i. aróc ingen rig fer cul máthair mail sechlainn) .xui. bliadnai hi clúain
mac nois ro adnacht. [51.]Dail de forsin coel cresen (.i. cleirech dognid) for
oed olach (.i. finnliath mac gormlatha ingeni dondcada ₇ neill cailli).
Sluagadach liphi cruach clóitigi. Graiphnech cruachan. IS leis firfidir
cath leitrech daigri (.i. cath cilli ua ndaigræ) gair riana dith (.i. oen
bliadain rena dith .i. ria ec). iadaid dorcha mór hi cetain céthgaimrid
.xui. bliadnai i raith adomnæ atbath æd. I Nard macha ro adnachtt. (**fo.
104vb**) [52.]Dail de forsin mend mbrecach for fland sindæ. Firfes bróen
fingaile fora braithri. Tecait airdhi ili na flaith .i. techt di nim (.i. ailithir
o roím) dia foicertar ár ṅgoidel ic duiblind (.i. ind ailithir). bas cóel a clú
do rig cruachan .i. æd mac conchabuir ro marbad isin chath. Na .uii.
nduba temrach (.i. uii. anni mali). firfid forbais for tailcentaig (.i. ard
macha) co nechtrandaib (.i. gaill .i. maic imair). Brisfid for breifnechu.
firfid cath grellaighi eilti cath maigi ailbi (.i. oengus a mac ro bris ₇
laigin) co clu brecaid etaig na ré. Grúaca a cennaib glasmes ndóine na ré.
Sithflaith (.i. fland) toicctech fristercha a chuaine feini friss (.i. a uii.
maic). Bás duimrecht for cresion cád. Domnach aindin ardafich i nderiud
in fogmair .xxx.uii. bliadnai. Flann ingen dúngaili righ osraide máthair
eius .lxxui. etatis suæ anno moritur hi clúain mac nois raadnacht. [53.]Dail
de for niell nglundub glanfus roi ruadra ririss flaith forbusach lini. læch-
buillech locha lebind. loiscfid cualaind co fo dí. drongach clári. cathach
cruachan. cetudach coba. mórbuillech bairchi. breoach sleibhi cailggi
frisna gaibther cath oirggne cath codail (.i. grellaig eilti for niell ria

fland) dia fich fuil feirniu *cath* t*r*athca eolthaile *for connacht*a. Cotnuallai albba (.i. mael mairi a *máthai*r ingen cinæda m*aic* alpi*n* rig albban) artt læchda liphi ririss noil lochæ leibi*n*d. die mbia fe i*n*nund fe ille in luan os martartaig. Bias bróen cróu os tailti*n* (.i. *cath atha* cliath i*n* ro marbad niell). Teora bli*adnai* co leith na*m*á dodachich nodaíbæ .l. bli*adnae* a æs huili i *n*drui*m* chailli rucad. hi cena*n*d*us* ro adnacht niall .iii. bli*adnai* dóu i ríghi ailigh. ⁵⁴·Dail de *for* crissalach (.i. reisi fingail) (**fo. 105ra**) codail dond a ainm (.i. mæl febail ingin flaind m*aic con*aing m*áthai*r *eius*). Cáinbruth breoach b*r*issfes catha c*r*uaidai. Croithfes indnu *for* tailtin. Togach temrach. Timgair giallæ co daball IS he firfes *cath* febla *for* fini *for* anfine *cath* cualand. IMed toraidh na ré. Grian na firinde (.i. iosep c*omarba* p*átrai*c *nó* ceili). Cuínfider huas cúalgiubein*n* do*m*nach etir di cal*laind* .xxu. bli*adnai*. ⁵⁵·Dail de *for* cass find colla *con*gal cerna (.i. ligach a m*áthai*r *in*ge*n* flai*n*d). firfid .x. mbli*adnae* flaith in chon bic bertfaid mór o laignib milliud a baíguil ni*n*toiméla leth a ṡaiguil. Laech a cernu ma duphí bíat bronaig a foghlaidé. Fer find f*or*accai rígi bíath uati a cho*m*dini hi mainistir ro adnacht *con*gal*ach*. ⁵⁶·Dáil *for* do*m*nall m*ac* da leithi (.i. a ll*eth* tes ₇ tuaid dind er*inn*) .i. domnall dalta athbach (.i. tuath athbach ro nalth .i. ui ertuile) eo find fessach. f*or*anach cnogbai cetudach assail. Ollbuidnech uisnig. firfid *cath* bri heli (.i. *for* carrach calma) Bandmaid*m* lettrech ainge (.i. *cath* cilli mo*n*a) hi toethsath .iii.l. gilla im fingin corad *cath* sleibi cua fo dí ₇ matan grophtini Tessbaidh etha (.i. gorta) di maig cuind .ui. bli*adnai* imluim (.i. t*er*cai). Dofóeth cid alai*n*d a líí in luán hi carnd furbaidi (.i. furbaidi me*n*d macha ro adnacht an*n* *nó* f*or*bba na ndai*n*e co *n*adnacal and) .xxiiii. bli*adnai* .l.u. bli*adnai* a aes. ⁵⁷·Dáil de *for* sroiptinid macha (.i. teni da*r* macha na ré .i. machairi) .i. Mæl sech*lainn* (.i. m*ac* dunflatha i*n*ge*n*e muir*certaig*) miad ngárcc Mórdrech dúr dechrass ar thuru te*m*rach. Tolcach étair. Losctech liphi. Fessach cúaland graiphnech cruachan. Cridhi nathrach firfid *cath* f*r*i clár*i*u *cath* iroriss (.i. *cath* cairn fordroma) *cath* moistin. Brian regnat hic. Mormatan atha (.i. matan midhi). Marb di óul meda. Crúas iar ngail do*m*nach hi teilchi*n*aib .xxx.ui. bli*adnai* na*m*á hi rigi huli damela (.i. ruc b*r*ian o .xx. himach rigi heri*n*d). (**fo. 105rb**) ⁵⁸·Dail de *for* chliabchless (*nó* cliabach .i. cliab fota mór occai) clóitige .i. flaithb*er*tach firf*h*es *cath* locha bricrend. breccf*us* ár im cna*m*chailli. Clóifid firu o ess ruaid (cenel *con*aill). ririss roi locha lebind. Bebais éc átbai hi táilcentaigh .xui. bli*adnai* na*m*á. ⁵⁹·Dail de *for* ossga*m*ain nassail. murchad nuall gaidel ngúr. g*r*ianbili fi*n*d. fer trén datta. dálbúadach étair. Uargalach midlu-achra (.i. slige). Loisctech lini. firfid *cath* luáchmaighi. Gebaid forbais

KEVIN MURRAY

locha lein (.i. dar cr*íst* bid marb brian and). línfaid caisil co sluaghaib.
Sínfid firu f*or* tarbgnu .xx. bli*adnae* namá. [60.]Dail de f*or* oeng*us* oenaig
fh*á*natt coscrach r*íí*. firfid (.i. oeng*us*) in c*ath* tess amni. firfid c*ath* hi
maig cruind (.i. sondchad cairnd aisi .i. sleibe fuait) tria chin da da m*ac*
comdani (.i. c*um*asscach ₇ li[...] [...]) dia mbie ben cen ceili dia *m*biat fir
tregtaig thuill. Nibu adass mathair bóid c*ath* hi cenindass c*on*sóid. Corr
loegbili (.i. oeng*us*) cétáin i nallmaig liphi. Atmbela óeng*us*. firfidir a nar
(.i. o laig*nib* .i. ar) .xxii. bli*adnai* namá. [61.]Dáil de forsin tarbainech (*nó*
murchad) a ailiuch c*on*rain*nf*hi a ain*m* fri muir .i. muiredach morbuid-
nech. IS he scér*us* foilgi fri laigniu c*ath* brí leith brisfid for brefnechau
c*ath* selca c*ath* móna tuircc. IAR noín airbrech iar sein hi toethsat t*r*i
muredaigh. Dofuitt di daigir (.i. teine gelan) dia mairt hi telenmaig .xui.
bli*adnai* nó xxx nó xiii. Síc exemplaria uariant*ur*. [62.]Dail de f*or* dondai-
*n*ech ndabaill .i. aedh engach (.i. en fíachach .i. en uisci *nó* quod u*erius*
est .i. labar) dia tuicebat barca f*or* ess ruáidh. lín maini (**fo. 105va**)
ningnad na ré. firfid c*ath* hi toethsat na dá du*n*lang .i. c*ath* maisten (.i. f*or*
laigniu). Tailcend gignid na ré .i. tip*r*aiti tor sithaigfes co uru her*enn* Bid
sí iar cá*in* cresien. IS he a lecht canair dou (.i. do aed) Madan i *n*uacht*ur*
ocha .xui. bli*adnai*. [63.]Dail de f*or* ossnadach uisnig .i. c*er*ball (*nó* cairell)
caur cuáid crichach banda. Buidnech brea. Brisfid c*ath* locha da ch*æ*ch.
la iár methrud mberuhai. Mórc*ath* sláni sel*us*tai. Tuicebat din i*n*gen tes
brephni. Brisfid c*ath* cloan cloifid turchu im lui*m*nech. Loiscfid tesga-
bair (.i. osraigi) .xu. bli*adnai* namá. Dothuit hi fidga iar sei*n* di bir ois fo
talmain. [64.]Dail de f*or* iartróg nailig (.i. ni geib ri aili te*m*r*ai*g ass) .i.
fergal foltgarb. Cuanaig bregmaige. Firfid c*ath* sleibi. sluag f*r*i roi roth.
Riris giallu cairnd lugdach. Firf*id* c*ath* mór midi. brogfaid cná*m*cailli.
Truar*us*cbaíl tenedh loiscess toirthiu. Sith mbecc olcc mór. Dotuit (.i.
fergal) la bé naidche nán oc fi*n*dcarnd tic a brécdál .xuii. bli*adnai*.
Comflaithi*us* f*or* her*inn* iar sein. Trí nói mbli*adnai* .i. co ti fland. [65.]Dail
de f*or* fland cinuch tigf*h*laith her*enn* cinid do síl cui*n*d dou is cuit cuind
gaibess. Tola nechtrand na re (.i. gaill loingsi inb*ir* do*m*nand) imed cech
toraid. Lin c*atha* *ṅ*garc firfidi. Cruách mór im chna*m*chailli. Aurscartad
necht*r*and. Sith fi*n*d teora mbli*adnai* .l. fo*ṅ*genat dúili dé. bid sai*n* a delb
cech raithi. Roi(**fo. 105vb**)thfid fál (.i. cloch) find fo trí. Teóra griana. trí
samlaithi. ainim cressin ci*ṅ*ges ar chel tintan f*or* her*inn* i*n*dech. Noifidir
tegdaisi táilcend f*r*ia ci*m*bal nguth i*n*a re. Regaid éc aitti iar sein di
cretair creissin hi temuiR. FINet.

112

DIPLOMATIC EDITION FROM MS HARL. 5280

[1.](**fo. 71a**)[1] Laa ro boi cond i temr*aig* iar ndioth dona rig*aib* atr*acht* mat*in* moch f*or* ríraith na temr*ach* ria turcbail gr*éi*ne ⁊ a tri druith aroe*n* ris .i. maol bloc bluicne. et a trii fil*id* .i. ethain corb cesarn. Fodegh attr*ai*gesiom c*ach* dia in lion se*n* do airdecin a*r*na gabdaois fir side f*or* erind cen airiug*ud* dos*om* [2.]in dú dia ndéch*aid*s*om* do g*re*s co tarlaic cloich and foa cosaib ⁊ saltr*ai*s f*uir*ri. Ro ges an cloch fo cosaib co clos fo temr*aig* uili ⁊ fo bregaib. [3.]Is and si*n* ro iarf*acht* con*n* dia dr*uid*ib q*ui* ar*us*ges an cloch cia hai*n*m ⁊ ca*n* do ral*ad* ⁊ no rag*ad* ⁊ q*ui*d ro taraill temraigh. IS *ed* ro be*r*t an d*r*ai f*r*i con*n* ni slondad do co c*en*t .l. laithi ⁊ a tri. IN t*a*n ro cindiod an a*ir*iom si*n*. R*us*iarf*acht* con*n* don d*r*ai af*r*idhisi. [4.]Is an*n* adbe*r*t an d*r*ai. Fal an*n*aim na cloc*h*e. INis foail asatar*dad*. Tem*air* tiri fail i f*or*romadh. Tir taillt*en* a nai*r*isfe co brath et is i an tir sen b*us* oenach cluiche cen uhes f*l*aith*i*os a t*em*r*aig* ⁊ la degi*n*ach an aonaigh in f*l*aith nach*us* faigfi bid t*r*uú isan bli*a*d*ain* si*n*. Ro ges fal foat cosaibse annu ol in d*r*ai ⁊ dorairng*er*t an lin gai*r*m ro ges an c*l*och is *ed* lion rig bias dot siol co brath. Niba me nodsloindfe det ol i*n* d*r*ai. [5.]A mbat*ar* ier*um* co *n*acot*ar* ciuich moir immaquai*r*t con*n*a fedot*ar* q*ui*d docot*ar* ar med an dorchu d*us*nainecc *co* colat*ar* trethan i*n* ma*r*caigh ara na*m*us. Moar mai*r*c duin*n* ol con*n* dia*n*a ruccai a tir nainiuil. Ier si*n* dolleci a*n* ma*r*c*ach* t*r*i orchora cucai ⁊ is t*r*aide d*us*nainic i*n* torc*h*or degenach inas torch*or* toísech. IS do guin rig emh or in d*r*ai cibe dib*r*aici*us* con*n* a temr*aig*. Anaid iar sin a*n* ma*r*c*ach* din dib*r*accu*d* ⁊ tic cuca ⁊ f*er*ais failti f*r*i con*n* et *con*gart les dia treb [6.]d*us*cot*ar* iar*um*. C*on*d*us*rulai isi*n* mag nalai*n*d. C*o* *n*acat*ar* an righraith isin [maig] ⁊ bili orda i*n*a dor*us* ⁊ *co* *n*acat*ar* tech nal*ain*d nan*n* fo octæ findraine .x. t*r*aigid .xx. a fod. Lot*ar* iar*um* isin [tech] co nacat*ar* an i*n*gen m*ac*dacht*a* isi*n* toig ⁊ barr orda f*or*a mull*ach*. Dab*ach* airc*ait* co c*er*claib or*da* impe ⁊ si lan do d*er*glind escrai oir f*or*a ur. copan di ór f*or* a beolai. *Co* *n*acat*ar* an scal fodeisin isin tigh f*or*a cin*n* ina rigṡuide. Ni f*r*ith a temr*ai*ch ria*m* f*er* a mede nach a caoi*m*e a*r* aille a c*r*otha ar inganta a d*eu*luha. [7.]Prisg*ar*tsi*d*e doib ⁊ adbe*r*t f*r*iu nido*m* scalsa em ⁊ nido*m* urt*r*ach ⁊ domuird*er*cus duib iar mbas dodeochad*us* ⁊ is do ci*n*el adai*m* dau*m*. iss e mo slondad lug m*ac* et*h*lend m*ai*c tig*er*nmais. Is do dodechad*us* co *n*ecsi dedse saog*al* do f*l*ath*a*u fen ⁊ c*ech*

---

1 Scribal note at top of the folio – 'in dardai*n* iar *m*belltin*e*'.

113

flathai bias a tem*r*aich ⁸·₇ ba si an i*n*gen boi isi*n* tig fo*r*a ciond flaithi
er*enn* co p*r*ath. Ba si an i*n*gen dobe*r*t an diched do cond .i. da*m*asna ₇
torcasnai cet*r*i t*r*aig*i*d .xx. fod an damhasna. ocht t*r*aig*i*d iti*r* a tuai*m* ₇
tal*m*ain. ⁹·IN t*an* luid an i*n*gen don dail adbe*r*t f*r*iu. Cia da tibe*r*tar an
airdeochsa. Friscart an scal. o ro sluindside cach fl*aith* o cund co b*r*ath.
Lot*ar* a foscadh an (**fo. 71b**) scail co*n*a rathaicseta*r* an rath n*a*c an tec.
Fo*r*racb*ad* lia cond i*n* dub*ach* ₇ int esc*r*ai ordao ₇ and airech. IS de sin
at*tá* aisling an scail et egt*r*ai ₇ targ*r*aide cuind. ¹⁰·Cia fo*r*a ndailf*i*d*i*r an
airecsa cosan derglaith ól in i*n*gen. Dail de or in scal for cond cétchath-
ach .i. ced cathrai brisf*i*u*s* .l. bli*adnae* nama dodocaith nodoibhdhá. Firf*i*d
catha .i. cath breg c*ath* eli c*ath* aiche c*ath* machai c*ath* cind tiri .uíí. catha
i moighi line c*ath* quailgne .uíí. catha clai*r*i*n*e rl-. A com*r*ac am tib*r*aiti
cet l*eth* co*m*na*r*t a nuidhe. is e gidnit*er* ac dluigi. na slu*ag* bias la ssuide.
Dirsan do co*n*n cétchathach iar nar tened t*ar* [c]ech magh gonta*r* iar
timcell cech ruis dia a mai*r*t a tuaith emruis. ¹¹·Cia fo*r*sa dailfidir an
ai*r*ecsa cu*s*in dergf*l*aith or i*n* ingen. Dail de or in scal fo*r* art m*a*c qui*n*d
fe*r* t*r*i ngretha. Firf*i*d cath fidruis mat*an* mucraime ima toetsad mai*r*b ili.
Ba dirsan do a*r*t m*a*c qui*n*d cu m*a*ic ail*ell*a olui*m* Dia dardoín ficid cath
a taot*u*s la sil lugach .xxx. bl*iadnae* nama. in tan nodotibdáa. ¹²·Cia fo*r*a
ndailfidir in ai*r*ecsa cu*s*an de*r*claith. Dail de ol in sc*a*l fo*r* lug*a*id m*a*c
co*n* cinfid do sil cui*n*d doaidleba .u. bl*iadn*a .xx. nama. docaith nodoibdá.
A long*u*s co hiath nalp*an* fo*r*brisfi cet*r*i morcatha fo*r* tuata orca. Dia
domnaich fo*r*du*s*ri hi. di*a*naitbi fiac*ail* fidbi. ¹³·Dail de fo*r* a*n* moirb*r*eth-
ach fo*r* corm*a*c o cui*n*d t*r*i bli*a*dnai nama docait n*o*dodibdá. Sith noll co
ri*a*n ina re. Biaid t*r*i .xx. bli*adn*ae. B*i*d ri tem*r*ac co*m*ba t*r*i arambebad
siab*r*ai. Tuili tor*ad* ina re. Bid aon do nirt na flaithe. Fo*r*naidm mboraime
ner*enn* la corm*a*c fri f*er*g*u*s airdri nul*ad*. dotoed f*er*g*u*s sceo enda dia
mbia slu*ag* de*r*ach dub*ach* adcu*m*bec b*i*d mai*r*b dia mai*r*t i toaibh cletig.
¹⁴·Dail de fo*r* fer ila*r* nglon*n* fo*r* cairp*r*i lifech*air*. T*r*ica cath ina re. T*r*i
bli*adn*ai .xx. a fl*aith*ius. Diubairt er*enn* cota muir. cath fesa*r* a lifemuigh
i*n* mai*r*t a lifi ara*m*bebais a*n* rignía. T*r*i m*a*ic coirp*r*i lifech*air* .i. eoc*h*aid
₇ eoc*h*u doiml*é*n ₇ fiac*h*u raibt*i*ne la laighne. A torc*r*at*a*r a cath tuam ruis
la bres*a*l mb*é*l*ach* m*a*c fiac*h*ach baic*e*tha m*a*ic cath*aír* .l. a*r* t*r*i milib an
lio*n* do laig*n*ib dotuit an*n* a f*r*itghuin. ¹⁵·Dail de f*r*i fiac*h*u raibt*i*ne.
maidio*n* mide la saide ₇ da cath les .u. bli*adn*ai .xx. a re. oc saigid na
borui*m*e. ceta*i*n a cnam*r*os b*i*d gle a toeth fiac*h*u sroibt*i*ne. ¹⁶·D*ail* de fo*r*
muire*d*ach .xl. bl*iadnae* docaith nodoibhdha. Cath a mormuig firf*i*d gle.
f*r*i ullt*u* f*r*i haraide. for bru dabaill isa*n* cath dotaoth muire*d*ach tir*ech*.
¹⁷·D*ail* de fo*r* eoch*aid* muidm*eth*on. Toebfoda tem*r*ac dunadach femi*n*

fostad*ach* moe*n*maighi ai*r*midne a*r*mar airsid life .u. bli*adn*a docuith
nodoibdá. Guin glunm*air* b*id* mor an techt. gui*n* co*n*cob*air* guin m*aic*
c*acht* for*us* for eoch*aid* is uad gignit*ir* co b*r*at bunad na flatha a nuib
co*n*chob*air* f*r*ia ré biaid fotha la suide na t*r*i colla gla*n*fid a*r* an taoth
eoch*aid* [muig]medán. [18.]Cia f*or*sa ndailfid*er* ol in *ingen*. D*ail* de f*or*
niall .ix.g*iallach* noafidhir tuir morf*aid*er maigi indsaigfid*er* gell. Firfid*er*
catha. .Uíí. mbli*adnai* .xx. docaith totai*m* nothaili les antuaidh. Biet ile a
gluin*n* a*r* drui*m* nalpui*n*d. b*id* adbor mai*r*c t*r*uim a*m* ia*r*noin da sat*r*uind.
[19.]Dail de [...][2] .uii. mbli*adnai* docait nodoibhda. Scarf*aid* f*r*i ha*r*df*l*aith
scel ngle do den*um* na finghaile. [20.]D*ail* de f*or* laoigi*r*e f*er* ila*r* nglond ro
aichfi libthi 7 iltire .u. bli*adnai* a fla*ith* tascor dia*n*. (**fo. 72a**) ticf*a* tailc*ent*
.i. p*at*r*aic* fer g*r*aid moir noifidi*us* dia morbreo atandafa linf*us* eri*nn* cota
muir beb*aid* loigire f*or* bru caisi flait im bachla morcaur cichardha
dof*or*tat tailcend. [21.]Dail de f*or* ail*ill* mol*t* m*ac* nathi m*aic* fiac*r*ach. f*er*
nuall*ach* f*er* attcuinti sochuide .xx. bli*adnae* nama dodacich Cata iliu ina
fl*aith* ar bid he an ri maith cuiclidhi te*m*ra. cum*us*cach taillti*n* c*ath* atha
talmaigh. Diube*r*tach seli. noicech aici c*ath* rata c*r*uach*an*. ce*m* f*or*
sabruldai. ce*m* f*or* elpa. tog*al* an t*r*ui. ce*m* f*or* eolaorcau c*ath* sratha
cluaidi f*or*tuhi genne*th*. ce*m* dar moir nichd doc*um* nelpa. Cichsett ere*n-*
*n*maigh re*m* dia*n* atacumbat eachtr*aind*. uíí. mbel fri firu gaid*el* f*or* ail*ill*
and oin dhidi*n* ar elpa. Bit ili atheat mart*r*ai ba dirsan do f*er*uib ere*nn* is
mor arathá thoiti*m* la hectr*an*na. [22.]Dail de f*or* tuat*hal* moelg*ar*b .i. m*ac*
cor*maic* m*aic* coirp*r*i m*aic* nell .xx. bli*adnae* c*ath* luac*r*ai ailue c*ath*
detnai toiti*m* na*r*dgail c*ath* legi c*ath* dromma arbela*ig* c*ath* bregain*n*
f*or*naidm giall ngaid*el*. iar si*n* ba scel in cech moig. bebuid aonguine
nama tuat*hal* hoc grella*ig* elti gentoir moelmor dia dig*ail* hi tuaith imrois.
[23.]Dail de f*or* lug*aid* m*ac* loegiri .xxui. co toitim dou do qhuairt f*or* eri*nn*
tre diultad tailci*n*d inn escir forcha. [24.]D*ail* de f*or* muirce*r*tach m*ac* ercoi
i*d* *est* *ingen* loairn. Ri cath*ach* coscr*ac* attcuinti soch*aidi* fonen erind fir 7
mna. Ar bid comurbo te*m*rai c*ath* atha sidhi ier sin linf*us* co h*er*ind airbiu
benuid dubuirt hi mairt in cairb cosc*r*ach co llaigniu. mor atbai beab*aid*
m*uir*ce*r*tach ecc atbai mairt cletigh. [25.]D*ail* de f*or* ainm*ir*ig timgera gialla
gaid*el* cech moigi iartir cinip tair t*r*uim*m* dofoethsat a*r* daig ruad firfit*ir*
catha cet*r*i bli*adnai* nam*m*a. [26.]D*ail* de f*or* boetán 7 eoch*aid* .iiii. bli*adnai*
nama dod*acich* *n*otaíbha. [27.]D*ail* de f*or* diarm*ait* .i. mac fearcc*us*a

---

2   Manuscript is illegible here.

cerrb*eoil*. duba*r*tach tailltin. tairnge*r*taich tem*r*ai. cen ma*ir* ina fl*aith*. ar
bid he in ri maith dia .uíí. blia*dnae* iar sin ca*th* foebr*ach* f*or* diarmait
dre*m*ne in slo*g*h dosiá antuaith glanfaid in roi co hath luain. bertha*ir* a
cathbuaidh ind oi*n* diti*n* a rait bicc. dith diarmata i*m*marr*ic* .xx. bl*i*adnae
nama dodacich notaiobá. [28.]Dail de f*or* ferc*us* 7 dom*n*all *da* m*a*c muirce*r*-
taig m*aic* erca .i. bra*n*na*m* m*a*c ech*ach* ro ma*r*b dib liniub a comflaith.
[29.]Dail de f*or* oed uaridhn*ech* m*a*c dom*n*aill morf*us* fl*aith* fonen he*r*ind
flait fodbach forra*n*uch firf*id* for*b*assa he*r*end bliat*ain* iar sin dofuit. ail*ill*
m*a*c domanguirt. Biet gni*m* a temairmoig. iurait laig*in* a ndama co*n*bib-
sad a firdala. bid garg bud cosc*r*ach a ree co llaithi na tangnacté in mairt
hi *n*desc*ur*t lifi. Is ann atbeuhu ind ríí .uii. mblia*dnai* nama. [30.]D*ail* de f*or*
oett sslaine s̓it noll flait goidiul cain erni fini fuata lia*m*na dotoet iar si*n*
aod slá*n*i iar lin cath ina ré .uíí. mblia*dnai* nama doda*c*ich notaibhá .i.
coirm cata p[...] sompni ut dicebat. [31.]D*ail* de f*or* oed olldan .uíí. mbl*i*ad-
*n*ai dodacich *n*otaibha duba*r*tach falmoigi. gebaid f*or* lifimoigh arnenai
gialla gaidil mor marb mor atbai mor ail cainfit gaidhil. [32.]D*ail* de f*or*
dom*n*all mend ul*ad* .ix. mblia*dnai* .x. nama d*r*acc ilair band firf*ius da*
c*ath* a moig roth. mairt is ann toeth an rig*r*oth. 7 d*er*gmati*n* c*r*uithne firfid
cath dui*n*e cethirn lia c*ath* ratha almoichi cichis ioa*rum* a rem mo*r* ail
atbath inn rig. [33.]D*ail* de f*or* suib*n*e me*n*n d*r*acc ilair bann bliat*ain* coa
.uíí. bias i flaith fonena gialla gach rois c*ath* daithi fir*fess* in ríí. Is ann
dotoet niba gou. colm*án* mor m*a*c diarmottou. **(fo. 72b)** [34.]Dail f*or*
blathm*a*c m*a*c aoda slai*n*e iss e notaioba .u. blia*dnai* ara derbflaith. [35.]D*ail*
de f*or* in ruanaidh .i. hi ruidioth hoc gab*áil* lama mocutta diarmait daiti a
c*é*tcath senchua c*ath* rois corcoi buain c*ath* osruidi c*ath* eli c*ath* slebi it*ir*
da inda. fir*fid* .uíí. catha aithne la cath selgi iar lo nó noi*n* arataat d*er*g-
maitne cruichne bid cruais cuimn*ech* tuath in cuib. iar si*n* i*n* mortlaith f*or*
he*r*ind i *m*bíatt mucna ind tslu*aig*. [36.]D*ail* de f*or* find*ach*ta .i. m*a*c
dunch*a*da m*aic* aoda slai*n*e co*n*saidfie f*or* mumain moir. fir*fid* c*ath* culie
coilain scith i toib cithamr*a*e fer mocht*ai*ti atbaild fing*ail* moir ind oi*n*
didin f*or* doll*ud* duthoi*n* a recht niba ri aod iar*um* .i. m*a*c dluthaigh .xx.
bl*i*adnae. [37.]D*ail* de f*or* sechn*us*ach m*a*c blathmaic u*n*o anno. dotacaith
atbeuba ecc atbai isin imbliuch os boí*n*n. [38.]D*ail* de f*or* c*ent* foel*ad* .uíí.
mblia*dnai* i flait ia*r* sin an cath i te*m*uirmaigh dotoíth cend foel*ad* a
ndomnach cuili coelain. [39.]Dail de f*or* loings*ech* .i. m*a*c aongu*s*a m*aic*
dom*n*aill cobra for falmoigh cosdaduch lifi buignech berriu. ditoett hoc
lecuib finnaib. lasna fianaip fo minnuib ragaid a nimguin fo thu*aith*.
mebuid f*or* rig eassa ru*aid* .i. ria celluch locha cimbe. die sath*air*n cichis
ar cel itir 2 corann uindsen .i. fath cora*inn* u*n*sen aon blia*dain* .x. nama

dodacich nodaiobha. [40.]Dail de for fogartach nan ₇ for congal cind magair mac fergusa fanad cetri bliadnai .x. nama dotoit idna isin luan ier samain inddala nae hi tosach in laithi ₇ alaili ina deriod hi cluain iraird sepultus sunt. [41.]Dail de for in scal for feargal .i. a naoin dittin hi cath almaine clethblugaid erind. armach line airsid aí bebhaid la laigniu inna re. fergal hi cath almuiné biaid ár moar isin cath. linfus co herinn airpriu.

APPENDIX I

Order of kings as given in *NHI* 9, 189-94.	Accession	Death	Order of kings according to *BS* (with length of reign in years).
1. Niall Noígiallach	?	?453	§18 Niall Noígiallach, 27. §19 Colla Óss (.i. Úais), 4.
2. Lóeguire mac Néill	454/6	461-3	§21 Lóegaire, 30.
3. Coirpre mac Néill	fl. 485		
4. Ailill Molt mac Nath Í	?	482	§20 Ailill Molt mac Nathí maic Fíachrach, 20.
5. Lugaid mac Lóeguiri	?	507	§23 Lugaid mac Lóegairi, 26.
6. Muirchertach Mac Ercae	507	534/6	§24 Muirchertach Mac Erca.
7. Tuathal Máelgarb mac Coirpri	534/6	544	§22 Tuathal Máelgarb, 20.
8. Diarmait mac Cerbaill	544	564/5	§27 Diarmait (.i. mac Fergusa Cerrbéoil), 20.
9. Forggus mac Muirchertaig ⁊ Domnall Ilchelgach mac Muirchertaig	564/5	566	§28 Fergus ⁊ Domnall, dá mac Muirchertaich Maic Erca. 2.
10. Ainmere mac Sétnai	566	569	§25 Ainmire, 4.
11. Báetán mac Muirchertaig ⁊ Eochaid mac Domnaill	569	572	§26 Báetán ⁊ Echu, 4.
12. Báetán mac Ninnedo	572	586	
13. Áed mac Ainmerech	586	598	§31 Áed (Ollán), 8.
14. Áed Sláine mac Diarmato ⁊ Colmán Rímid mac Báetáin	598	604	§30 Áed Sláine, 8.
15. Áed Allán (*alias* Uaridnach) mac Domnaill	604	612	§29 Áed Úaridnech mac Domnaill, 8.
16. Máel Cobo mac Áedo	612	615	

No.	Name			§	
17.	Suibne Menn mac Fiachnai	615	628	§33	Suibne Menn, 7.
18.	Domnall mac Áedo	628	Jan. 642/3	§32	Domnall Menn Ulad, 19.
19.	Cellach mac Máele Cobo 7 Conall Cóel mac Máele Cobo	642/3	656/8 654		
20.	Diarmait mac Áedo Sláine 7 Blathmac mac Áedo Sláine	656/8	665/6	§34	Blathmac mac Áeda (.i. Sláine), 5.
				§35	Diarmait Daithi.
21.	Sechnussach mac Blathmaic	665/6	c. 1 Nov. 671	§37	Sechnussach mac Blathmaic, 1.
22.	Cenn Fáeled mac Blathmaic	671	675	§38	Cenn Fáelad, 7.
23.	Finsnechtae Fledach mac Dúnchado	675	695	§36	Finnachta .i. mac Dúnchada maic Áeda Sláine, 20.
24.	Loingsech mac Óengusso	695	12 July 704	§39	Loingsech (.i. mac Óengusa maic Domnaill), 11.
25.	Congal Cinn Magair mac Fergusso	704	710	§40	Fogartach 7 Congal mac Fergusa Fánat, 14.
26.	Fergal mac Máele Dúin	710	11 Dec. 722	§41	Fergal, 12.
27.	Fogartach mac Néill	722	724	§40	Fogartach 7 Congal mac Fergusa Fánat, 14.
28.	Cináed mac Írgalaig	724	728		
29.	Flaithbertach mac Loingsig	728	dep.734 d.765	§42	Flaithbertach, 26.
30.	Áed Allán mac Fergaile	734	743	§43	Áed Allán, 10.
31.	Domnall Midi mac Murchado	743	20 Nov. 763	§44	Domnall mac Murchada, 20.
32.	Niall Frossach mac Fergaile	763	abd.770 d.778	§45	Niall Frossach, 7.
33.	Donnchad Midi mac Domnaill	770	797	§46	Donnchad, 30.
34.	Áed Oirdnide mac Néill	797	819	§47	Áed Ingor, 23.
35.	Conchobor mac Donnchado	819	833	§48	Conchobor mac Donnchada, 14.

119

36. Niall Caille mac Áedo	833	846	§49	Níall Caille, 13.
37. Máel Sechnaill I mac Máele Ruanaid	846	27 Nov. 862	§50	Máel Sechnaill, 16.
38. Áed Findliath mac Néill	862/3	20 Nov. 879	§51	Áed Olach, 16.
39. Flann Sinna mac Máele Sechnaill	879	25 May 916	§52	Flann Sinna, 37.
40. Niall Glúndub mac Áeda	916	15 Sept. 919	§53	Niall Glúndub, 3.
41. Donnchad Donn mac Flainn	919	944	§54	Dond, 25.
42. Congalach Cnogba mac Maíl Mithig	944	956	§55	Congal[ach] Cerna, 10.
43. Domnall ua Néill	956	980	§56	Domnall, 24.
44. Máel Sechnaill II mac Domnaill	980	abd 1002 res. 1014 d 2 Sept 1022	§57	Máel Sechnaill, 36.
45. Brian Bóruma mac Cennétig	1002	23 Apr. 1014	§57	Brian, 20.

APPENDIX 2

Battles in the reign of Cormac úa Cuind

BS §13	AU 4177 a.m.	ATig. (RC 17, 13-17).	AFM 236	Dublin Fragment of ATig.
Cath Granairdd	Cath Granaird ria Cormac h. Cuind for Ultu	Cath Granaird ria Cormuc hua Cuind for Ulltaib	Cath Granaird ria cCorbmac ua cCuinn for Ultoibh	Cath Grainaird ria Cormac húa Cuind for Ultu
Cath i nEuo	Cath in Heu .i. hi Maig Aei Uair, .i. for Aed mc. Echach mc. Conaill rig Connacht	Cath Medha for Condachto	Cath in hEu hi Moigh Aei for Aedh, mac Eachdach, mic Conaill, rí Connacht	Cath in Heu .i. hi Maig Aei uair .i. for Aed mac Echach maic Conaill ríg Connacht
Cath i nEuth	Cath i nEth	Cath Anæith	Cath i nEth	Cath in-Eth
Cath i Cind Dairi	Cath Cind Daire	Cath Cind doire	Cath Cinn Daire	Cath Cind daire
Cath Sruthra	Cath Sruthra for Ultu	Cath Sritha for Ultu	Cath Srutha for Ultoibh	Cath Sruthra for Ultu
Cath Cúal[n]gi	Cath Slige Cuailnge	Cath Sligedh Cuailghne	Cath Slicche Cuailgne	Cath slige[d] Cuailnge
	AU 4178 a.m.		AFM 237	
Cath Átha Beth	Cath Atha Bethech	Cath Atha Beitheach	Cath Atha Beathaig	Cath atha bethach
Cath Átha Dumai	Cath Ratha Dumai	Cath Ratha duine	Cath Ratha Dumha	Cath Ratha dumae

	AU		AFM	
	AU 4179 a.m.		*AFM 238*	
Cath Cúiliu Caíchir fa thrí	Cath Cule Tochair fo thrí	Cath Chuile Tocuir fothri	Cath Chuile Tochair fo trí	Cath Cule tochair fothri
Cath hi nDubad co fo thrí	Tri catha i nDubadh	Tri catha a nDuibfíidh	Trí catha hi nDubadh	Tri catha i nDubadh
	AU 4180 a.m.		*AFM 239*	
Cath na Lúacrai all Maig Slecht	Cath Allamáig	Cath Allamuig	Cath Allamaigh	Cath Allamaig
Cath Eillne[1]	.uii. catha Elne	.uii. catha Eilline	Secht ccatha Elne	.uii. cath Elne
	AU 4181 a.m.		*AFM 240*	
Cath Maige Techt	Cath Maige Techt	Cath Muighe Techt	Cath Moighe Techt	Cath Maige Techt
	AU 4182 a.m.		*AFM 241*	
	(Ceithri catha for Mumain)	*(Ceithri catha for Mumain la Cormac)*	*(Attiad andso catha Chorbmaic for Mumhain an bhliadhainsi)*	*(Ceithri catha for Mumain)*
Cath Bérri	Cath Berri	Cath Berre	Cath Beirre	Cath Berri
Cath Locha Léin	Cath Locha Lein	Cath Locha Lein	Cath Locha Lén	Cath Locha Lein
Cath im Luimnech	Cath Luimnigh	Cath Luimnigh	Cath Luimnigh	Cath Luimnigh
Cath im Gréin	Cath Greine	Cath Grene	Cath Grene	Cath Greine
(For Mumain beos)	*(For Mumain beos)*	*(For Mumain beous)*		*(For Mumain beos)*

1   Text in Rawl. reads *.c. na luacrai allmaig slecht .c. eilhne*. If *slecht* was emended to *secht*, the information in *BS* would correspond more closely with the other sources.

Cath Clasaig / Ár mór ós Muiriscc	Cath Clasaigh / Cath Muirisc	Cath Clasaigh / Cath Muirisc	Cath Clasaigh / Cath Muirisc	Cath Clasaigh / Cath Muirisc
Ar-túaset Ulaid occa do-fóeth hEchaid Toebf ada	Cath Ferta hi torchair Eochu Toebf ota mc. Aililla Aulaim	Cath Ferta a torchair Eochaid Taebf ada mac Aililla Uluim	Cath Ferta hi torchoir Eochaidh Taobhfada	Cath Ferta hi torchair Eochu Toebf ota mac Aililla Aulaim
Cath Slabrae	Cath Samna hi torchair Cian mc. Aililla Aulaim		Cath Samhna hi torchair Cian, mac Ailealla Oluim	Cath Samna hi torchair Cian mac Ailella Aulaim
Cath Ardda Caim	Cath Arda Caim	Cath Aird caim	Cath Arda Caim	Cath Arda caim
Orggain na rígingen	Orgain na n-ingen isin Chloenfherta hi Temraigh	Orgain na n-ingen isin Claenferta a Temraig	Orgain na hingenraighe isin Claoinferta hi Tem-raigh	Orgain na n-íngen isin Chloenferta hi Temraigh
	AU 4189 a.m.		*AFM* 248	
	Cath oc Fochaird Muirtheimhne ria Cormac hua Cuinn	Bellum oc Fothaird Muirthemne	Cath hi Fochaird Muirthemhne	Cath oc Fochaird Muirthimhne ria Cormac hua cuinn
	AU 4201 a.m.		*AFM* 248	
Máirt hi Crinda	Cath Crinna Bregh ria Cormac hua Cuinn ... for Ultu	Cath Crinda Bregh ria Cormac ... for Ulltaib		Cath Crinna Bregh ria Cormac hua Cuinn ... for Ultu
	AU 4203 a.m.		*AFM* 262	
Cath Crínde Fregabuil	Cath Crinna Fregabail ria Cormac for Ultaib	Cath Crinna Frigabuil ria Cormac hua Cuind for Ulltaib	Cath Crionna Fregabhail ria cCorbmac for Ulltoibh	Cath Crinna Fregabail ria Cormac for Ultaib

APPENDIX 3

List of extant *baili* and their editions[1]

Baile Bercháin
Anderson, A.O., 'The Prophecy of Berchan', *ZCP* 18 (1930) 1-56.

Hudson, Benjamin T., *Prophecy of Berchán: Irish and Scottish High-kings of the Early Middle Ages* (Connecticut & London, 1996).

Baile Bicc maic Dé
Meyer, Kuno, 'Beg mac Dé Profetauit', *ZCP* 9 (1913) 169-71.

Thurneysen, Rudolf, 'Allerlei Irisches: 1. Bec mac Dé', *ZCP* 10 (1915) 421-2.

Zumbuhl, Mark, *Bec mac Dé and the Irish Traditions of Prophecy* (University of Glasgow, Unpublished M.Phil. Dissertation, 2000).

Baile Bricín
Meyer, Kuno, 'Baile Bricín', *ZCP* 9 (1913) 449-57.

Baile Chuind
Thurneysen, Rudolf, *Zu irischen Handschriften und Litteraturdenkmälern*, Abhandlungen der königlichen Gesellschaft der Wissenschaften zu Göttingen, Phil.-hist. Klasse, neue Folge, Band 14 (Berlin, 1913) 48-52.

Murphy, Gerard 'On the Dates of Two Sources Used in Thurneysen's Heldensage', *Ériu* 16 (1952) 145-56, at 145-51.

Baile Fursa[2]
Meyer, Kuno, 'Fursa Cráiptech Profetauit', *ZCP* 9 (1913) 168.

Baile Fíndachta
Meyer, Kuno, 'Baile Fíndachta ríg Condacht', *ZCP* 13 (1921) 25-7.

Baile Iarlaithi
Unpublished poem beginning, *Is dorcha indiu in laithi*, Leabhar Uí Mhaine fo. 63b.

Baile in Scáil
Meyer, Kuno, 'Baile in Scáil', *ZCP* 3 (1901) 457-66.

Meyer, Kuno, 'Das Ende von Baile in Scāil', *ZCP* 12 (1918) 232-8; corrigenda, *ZCP* 13 (1921) 150.

Pokorny, Julius 'Nachlass Kuno Meyer: Der Anfang von Baile in Scáil', *ZCP* 13 (1921) 371-82.

Thurneysen, Rudolf, 'Baile in Scāil', *ZCP* 20 (1935) 213-27.

---

1   There are two other *baili* listed in Tale List B (Mac Cana, 1980, 56) *Baile Cimbaith Fhátha* and *Baile Mochuta*, neither of which seems to be extant.

2   Flower (1926, 312) notes that this text is 'always (with the exception of the Book of Hy Many) found in association with' *Baile Bicc maic Dé*.

Baile Moga Ruith
Unpublished poem beginning, *Truagh an bhaethair, truagh don daimh*, British Library MS Egerton 92, fo. 9b.; TCD MS H.1.15 (no. 1289) p. 939.

Baile Moling
Story headed, *Incipit Baile Moling*, Yellow Book of Lecan, col. 340.

Baile Oisín
Unpublished poem beginning, *Fionn fairsing fial*, British Library Egerton 129, fo. 35 and Egerton 142, fo. 69; Maynooth M14, 94; Maynooth M69, 70; Maynooth C9(b), 64; Aberystwyth A7, 185; Cardiff C1, 129 [131].

Buile Shuibhne
O'Keefe, J.G., *Buile Shuibhne*, Irish Texts Society, vol. 12 (London, 1913; repr. 1996).
O'Keefe, J.G., *Buile Shuibhne*, MMIS 1 (Dublin, 1931).

Tucait Baile Mongáin
Meyer, Kuno, 'Tucait Baile Mongáin', *The Voyage of Bran Son of Febal*, Appendix 4 (London, 1895) 56-8.
Hull, Vernam, 'An Incomplete Version of the *Imram Brain* and Four Stories Concerning Mongan', *ZCP* 18 (1930) 409-19, at 419.
Mac Mathúna, Séamus, 'Tucait Baile Mongáin', *Immram Brain: Bran's Journey to the Land of the Women* (Tübingen, 1985) 478-9.

APPENDIX 4
Linguistic dating features in text
The definite article
Old Irish features

(i) Retention of neut. art.: *a llá* §4, *a llín* §4, *assa mag* §6, *a scál* §6, *a ndíchetal* §9, *a ndún* §9, *a tech* §9, *a n-ude* §10, *a cathbúaid* §27, *a clú* §52 (see note to 11. 365-6), *a lleth* §56, *a n-ár* §60 (see note to l. 436);

(ii) Retention of nom. plu. m. art.: *in duinechoin* §11, *ind lúadri* §13.

Developments

(i) Loss of neut. art.: *in lín* §1, *in scál* §§9-12, *int écht* §17 (if *écht* was orig. neut.), *ind ré* §42, *forsin tarbainech* §61;

(ii) Loss of nom. plu. m. art.: *Na trí Colla* §18 (this change was already present in the eighth century; cf. *natrirecte*, Wb. 29a16);

(iii) There are no examples in the text of the fully inflected form of the plu. (& fem. gen. sg.) article *inna* – only the monosyllabic form *na* is attested;

(iv) Loss of dat. plu. ending: *dona rígaib* §1;

(v) Presence of Mid. Ir. form of dual art.: *na dá chath* §43, *na dá Dúnlang* §62;

Orthographic

(vi) Reduced forms of the art.: *in* (O.Ir. *ind*) *f̉ilid* §1, *in* (O.Ir. *ind*) *ingen* §10, §12, *in slúaig* (O.Ir. *int s̉lúaig*) §18, §46, *in* (O.Ir. *ind*) *f̉ogmair* §52;

(vii) Use of later form of art., *an*: *an chloch* §2, *an fili* §4, *an marcach* §5, *an scáil* §9, *An máirt* §43.

The noun
Old Irish features

(i) Nasalisation marked after neut.: *bile n-órda* §6, *scél n-airdircc* §11, *Síth n-oll* §13, *fássach n-aenré* §13, *Forus ṅHér[e]nd* §17, *tathaimm nAu[r]thuli* §18, *scél nglé* §19, *fortbe nGeinned* §20, *réim ndían* §20, *totim nArdgail* §22, *Fornaidm ngíall* §22, *Síth n-oll* §30, *slóged n-aurderc* §43, *ár ṅGoídel* §52, *míad ngárcc* §57, *Síth mbecc* §64, *Tóla n-echtrand* §65, *Aurscartad n-echtrand* §65? (neut. is not certain).

(ii) Presence of hiatus: *rígniä* §14, *fiäig* §46, *Biëd* §46, *riäm* §46, *dië* §46 (twice), *fiäich* §47;

(iii) Use of prepositionless dat. (though this may be just stylistic): *ad-baill fingail móir* §36, *At-beba Bregaib* §44, *Tróethbaid Brega borrchathaib* §46, *dia fich fuil Feirniu* §53;

Orthographic

(iv) Early dat. sg. form of *ól* is attested, *di óul meda* §57;

(v) The nom. sg. form *togal* (vn. of *do-fich*) is attested in §20: it has not been replaced by the dat. sg. form *togail*;

126

(vi) Preservation of unstressed final vowels: (several exx. of *atbai* throughout text; a few inflected forms of *blíadain* are written out in full in Rawl. – *.iii. blíadnai* §13, *.u. blíadnæ* §34), *damasnai* §8, *torcasnai* §8, *fidbai* §12, *ilsíabrai* §13, *Dumai* §13, *Tlachtgai* §17, *Elpai* §20, *martrai* §20, *tigernai* §43, *dubai* §50, *Beruhai* §63.

Developments

(i) Nasalisation is not marked after original neut. noun: *Tothaim dímeis* §13, *Tóla hÉrend* §13, *Guin Glúinḟind* §17, *mór atbai* §24, *mór átbai* §31, *fírscél gona* §46, *Bás duimrecht[a]* §52, *Domnach Aindin* §52, *núall Gaídel* §59;[1]

(ii) §55 *nín-toiméla* – the infix. pron. (referring to *leth*) shows that it is being treated as mas. here (though it is treated as neut. in §56);

Orthographic

(iii) *láma* §35 is a late gen. sg. form (O.Ir. *láme*) attested in a gloss;

(iv) Dat. sg. form used for nom. sg.: *árim* §3, *breith* §13, *orggain* §13, *dígail* §43;

(v) *bruigi* §48 is a late gen. sg. form (in O.Ir. ending in *–o/–a*);

(vi) *Maíl*, the Mid. Ir. gen. form of *Máel*, is present in §50. This gen. (for earlier *Máele*) is first attested in the main hand in *AU* 912.4 (*m. Mail Morda*) and appears consistently thereafter;

(vii) Acc. plu. form of *bráthair* is given as *bráithri* in §52 (O.Ir. *bráithrea*);

(viii) *blíadan* §44 (written out in full in MS) is a Mid. Ir. gen. plu. form;

(ix) Change of O.Ir. initial *mr-* to *br-*: *bruigi* §48.

Possible archaic features

Orthographic

(i) *drauc* 'dragon' §§32-3 seems to represent the older spelling of this word (cf. *DIL* s.v. *draic*). It is also attested in *Immram Brain* (Mac Mathúna, 1985, §53) and in *ÄID* ii, 16.7, 18.4;

(ii) *slóged* §43 may be an archaic form (cf. Meyer (1910) 60, *slogeth*[2] and O Daly (1952) 181, §§23-5, *sloged / sluoged / sluoghed*);

(iii) Some of the forms of *día* 'day' attested in the text may be archaic. The forms in question are *die* §18, §39, §50 and *dië* §46 (twice). For a discussion of this issue, see Ó Cróinín (1981, 100-3);

(iv) The spelling *Níell* §49 (4 times) & §53 (thrice) may have some significance beyond scribal orthography. This spelling, which may be archaic, is also present in *BC* (Murphy, 1952, 146-7);

---

1 Unless *núall* is nom. plu. here.

2 Hull (1947) 891-2 would read the unstressed *-e* for *-a* in *slógeth* in Meyer's edition (1910) of 'Conall Corc and the Corco Luigde' as one of the significant factors pointing towards a date of composition before 750 (this feature is present in the O.Ir. glosses of the *prima manus* in Würzburg [*c.* 700] and not in the glosses written by the main glossators [*c.* 750]; e.g. Wb. 13d24, *roslogeth*: Ó Néill (2001) 237). Our example, if linguistically significant and not merely orthographic, would nevertheless not bear this weight of supposition.

(v)   The archaic form of *clúain* (*clóin*) is attested in §50;

(vi) Presence of an old gen. sg. in *–o* (guaranteed by rhyme), *Díarmato* §33 (though some examples of final *–o* are attested in *AU* from the tenth century, e.g. s.a. 912.3, 921.8 and 980.1; see Ó Máille [1910, §73]). However, this couplet also preserves the oldest spelling of *gáu* 'lie'.

The verb
Old Irish features

(i)   The f-fut. of *scaraid* is attested in §19 (see note to 1. 169);

(ii) Consistent retention of deponent flexion in deponent verbs in all but a few cases (see Glossary s.vv. *ardraigidir, gainithir, ro-cluinethar, ro-finnadar*).

Developments

(i)   The later ē-future of *scaraid* is present in §61 (see note to 1. 169);

(ii) Simple verbs from earlier compound verbs: *díbaircaid* §5 (< *do-bidci*);

(iii) Independent use of prototonic form: *ticfa* §13 §21 §46, *timgéra* §25, *tóeth* §32, *tecait* §52 (< *do-ecat*), *timgair* §54, *tuicébat* §63, *tic* §64;

(iv) Loss of deponent endings: *-tairiss* §4, *gignid* §62;

(v)   Replacement of subj. by fut.: *-toíthsat* §47;
      Orthographic

(vi) The Mid. Ir. variant of *ol* (*for*) is attested §5;

(vii) Change of O.Ir. initial *mr-* to *br-*: *brogfaid* §64.

The adjective
Old Irish features

(i)   Retention of dat. plu. form of adj.: *co cethraib cernaib órdaib* §6, *ic lecaib finnaib* §39;

(ii) The distinction between the mas. numeral *trí* and the fem. form *teóra* is preserved throughout (see Glossary s.v. *trí*);
      Orthographic

(iii) The early form of *mór* (*már*) is attested §43, and is guaranteed by rhyme (*:fán*);

(iv) The earlier form of *cáid* (i-adj.), i.e. *cád* (o/ā-adj.), is attested in §52.

Other
Old Irish features

(i)   The conjunction *sceo* is attested §13;

(ii) Presence of suffix. prons: *firfidius* §10, *coíntit* §11 (see note to l. 90).

Developments

(i)   *dus-fánic* (twice, §5) Use of 3rd plu. Class A infix. pron. instead of Class C in relative clause;
      Orthographic

(ii) Replacement of *dia* with *dá* §60 (cf. *SnaG* III, 3.24);

(iii) The falling together of lenited *d* and lenited *g*: *tairngertaig* §27.

GLOSSARY

1 a' poss. adj. 3rd sg. m. *his, its,* 2, 13, 36, etc.; 3rd sg. n. *its,* 31.

2 a n- poss. adj. 3rd plu. *their,* 121, 214, 334, etc.

3 a n- conj. (followed by nas. rel. clause) *when, while,* 22.

4 a prep. with dat. *out of, from,* 398, 437. With aff. pron. 3rd sg. n. ass, 30; 3rd sg. m., 455. With rel. part. asa, 15.

accaíned m. *act of complaining, lamentation.* gen. sg. adcuínti, 171; atcuínti, 193.

ád u,m.? *good luck, prosperity,* 313.

adaig, aidche iā,f. *night.* dat. sg. aidchi, 108. gen. sg. aidche, 459. In compound dubadaig *black night,* 70.

ad-anaig *buries, entombs.* perf. pass. sg. ro adnacht, 267, 290, 348, etc.; plus infix. pron. 3rd sg. m. Class A ra-adnacht, 375.

ad-annai *kindles, lights.* fut. 3rd sg. ad-andaba, 182.

adass predicative adj. followed by acc. *in accordance with, in keeping with,* 434.

adbar o,n. *cause, reason,* 166.

ad-caíni *bewails, laments.* fut. 3rd plu. ad-coínfet, 133; plus infix. pron. Class B 3rd sg. m. atcuínfet, 225; at-coínfed, 272.

ad-cí *sees.* pret. 3rd plu. co n-accatar, 22, 31, 35.

ad-cuimben *strikes, cuts, wounds.* fut. 3rd plu. plus infix. pron. 3rd plu. Class B ata-cumbat, 177.

ad-cumaing *cuts, strikes.* pres./pret. 3rd sg. -ecmaing, 52.

ad-fét, ind-fét *tells, relates.* impv. 2nd sg. with infix. pron. 3rd plu. Class B atta-féid, 20. pres. subj. 1st sg. co n-écius, 42. perf. 3rd plu. co n-écetar, 13.

adnacul o,n. (later m.) *grave, tomb, burial.* dat. sg., 411.

áes o,n. *age,* 386, 411.

aicenn *head* (poetically: of heads cut off in battle). gen. plu. acain, 303.

aicsiu n,f. *act of seeing,* 269.

1 ail i and k,f. *boulder, rock,* 14.

2 ail f. *misfortune* (esp. of death or wounding in a battle). acc. sg. 284. In compound mórail *great misfortune,* 225, 230.

ailad f. *tomb, burial-cairn.* dat. sg. ailaid, 274.

aile as adj. *other, second.* nom. sg. m. aili, 455.

ailid *rears, fosters.* perf. 3rd sg. plus infix. pron. 3rd sg. m. Class A ra n-alt, 402.

ailithir m.? *pilgrim,* 364. gen. sg., 365.

ailithre iā,f. *pilgrimage.* In phrase i n-ailithre *on pilgrimage,* 273.

áille iā,f. *beauty.* dat. sg., 37.

aimser ā,f. *time, period.* nom. sg. amsir, 314. dat. sg. aimsir, 50.

ainech o,n. *face.* In compound tarbainech *bull-faced one,* 437. In compound dondainech *brown-faced one,* 443.

ainim f. *soul, life,* 468.

ainm n,n. (later m.) *name, reputation,* 9, 14, 314, etc. gen. sg. anmæ, 281.

129

ainré *long period.* gen. sg. aenré, 126.

airbe io,[n.?] (later f.) *hedge, fence.* With meaning *phalanx, serried rank* (of fighting men). acc. plu. airbiu, 195.

airde io,n. *sign, token.* nom. plu. airdi, 364.

airdech ā,f. *cup, vessel.* nom. sg. 49, 55, 58 etc.; airidech, 79; airideog, 34; airdeog, 96; airedeog, 134.

airdirc, airderc adj. *well-known, famous,* 84. aurderc, 282.

airdircus u (later o), m. *eminence, renown, nobility.* dat. sg. uirdercus, 39.

áirem ā,f. *act of counting, reckoning.* nom. sg. árim, 12.

airiugad *act of noticing, detection.* acc. sg. airegud, 5.

aislinge orig. io? (later f.) *vision, dream.* nom. sg. aislingi, 56.

alaile adj. *other.* As subst. *the other, the second.* nom. sg. m. alaili, 260.

álaind adj.,i *lovely, splendid,* 409.

al(l) prep. with acc. *beyond,* 115, 229.

amal prep. and conj. *like, as.* In phrase amal sodain *so, in that case,* 20.

amein *thus, then.* amni, 431.

amrae adj.,io/iā *wonderful.* Comparative form used for superlative amru, 266. As subst. *renowned person,* amra, 284.

án adj.,o/ā *fiery, splendid, brilliant,* 258, 459. gen. sg. áin, 113.

anaid *ceases, stops,* 28. fut. 3rd sg. rel. ainfes, 327.

and, ann adv. *there, then,* 6, 22, 30, etc.

anetargnaide adj.,io/iā *unknown,* 25.

anfine *stranger kindred, foriegn people,* 106. acc. sg., 65. dat. sg., 306, 391.

anse adj.,io/iā *hard, difficult,* 59, 81, 97.

antúaid with fri *to the north of,* 163, 271. With meaning *from the north, northwards,* 205, 300.

1 ar' prep. with acc. and dat. *for, before, on account of.* acc., 178 414. dat., 23, 199, 341. Plus poss. adj. 3rd sg. m. ara, 6, 37, 122, etc.; 3rd sg. f., 33. With rel. part. ara, 306.

2 ar prep. used as conj. *for, since, because,* 36, 161, 172, etc.

ár o,m. (orig. n.?) *slaughter, destruction, defeat,* 122, 265, 365, etc. acc. sg., 157, 422. dat. sg., 76. acc. plu. áru, 278. nom. sg. in compound tromár *great slaughter,* 68. nom. plu. in compound rúaidáir *bloody slaughters,* 326.

ara conj. folld by subj. *that, so that.* neg. arna, 4.

araile *another.* gen., 50.

árbach o,m. (orig. n.?) *slaughter, carnage.* gen. sg. aurbaig, 280.

arbar o,m. *host, army.* acc. plu. airbriu, 265.

ar-berta *proposes, instigates.* impf. ind. 3rd sg. ar-bertad, 268.

ardraigidir *be apparent.* pret. 3rd sg. -arrdraigestair, 54.

ar-fich *fights, vanquishes.* pres. ind. 3rd sg. plus infix. pron. 3rd plu. Class C arda-fich, 372.

ar-gaib *seizes, captures.* fut. 3rd sg. rel. ara-ngéba, 276.

argat o,n. (later m.) *silver.* gen. sg.

arcait, 33.

argraige *journey, expedition*, 56.

armach adj.,o/ā *armed*. As subst. *one who is armed*, 263.

ar-naisc *binds, guarantees*. fut. 3rd sg. ar-nena, 122, 224.

ársid m. *warrior, champion*, 263. In compound cruindársid *sturdy champion*, 150.

ar-slig *smites, slays*. fut. 3rd sg. rel. ara-sela, 305.

art o,m. *bear* (used fig. of a hero), 382.

ar-tá *is in store for, impends*. pres. ind. 3rd sg., 343; rel. ara-thá, 139, 179. pres. ind. 3rd plu. plus infix. pron. 3rd sg. m. Class A ara-taat, 239.

ar-túaisi *listens to, pays heed to*. pres. ind. 3rd plu. ar-túaset, 124.

as-beir *says, speaks*. pret. 3rd sg. as-bert, 38, 48; as-pert, 10.

asnae io?,m. *rib*. In compound damasnæ *rib of an ox*, 45. gen. sg. damasnai, 46. In compound torcasnæ *rib of a boar*, 45. gen. sg. torcasnai, 47.

at-bail(l) (normally with infix. n. pron.) *perishes, dies*. pres. ind. 3rd sg. rel. ad-baill, 91, 244; with i n- plus infix. pron. 3rd sg. n. Class C inid-abbaill, 304. fut. 3rd sg. at-béla, 216, 435; -ebbéla, 283. Narrative tense supplied by suppletive vb ad-bath: pret. 3rd sg. at-bath, 338, 362; used for fut. 230, 273.

at-beb- [normally with n. infix. pron.] (redup. stem of fut. and pret.) *will die, died*. fut. 3rd sg. at-beba, 246, 292, 327. fut. 3rd sg. rel. ara-mbeba, 336. fut. 3rd

plu. rel. ara-mbebat, 107, 286.

at-etha *obtains, gets*. fut. 3rd plu. at-ethfat, 178.

at-reig *set forth*. impf. ind. 3rd sg. plus emph. pron. at-raigedsom, 4. With meaning *ascends*, 3rd sg. past (with infix. ro) at-raracht, 1.

attá *substantive verb (to be)*. pres. ind. 3rd sg. attá, 56. consuet. pres. 3rd sg. conj. -bí, 312. pres. subj. rel. sg. bes, 16. fut. 3rd sg. biaid, 137, 265, 288, etc.; bied, 144, 156, 213, etc.; biëd, 303; -bia, 129, 383; -bie, 433. fut. 3rd sg. rel. bias, 19, 43, 231, etc. fut. 3rd plu. -biat, 241, 433. pret. 3rd sg. rel. boí, 44. pret. 3rd plu. rel. bátar, 22. perf. 3rd sg. ro buí, 1, 12.

att *swelling, tumour*. aitt, 320. gen. sg. aitti, 469. See Murray (1999a).

at(t)ba (usually in phrase éc at(t)bai) *death (by tumour)*. gen. sg. atbai, 197, 273, 292, etc.; átbai, 225, 247, 424; atbui, 295. See Murray (1999a).

aurchor m. *cast, shot*. nom. sg. erchor, 26. acc. plu. aurchuru, 26.

aurdrach *sprite, phantom*, 39.

aurscartad u,[m.] (orig. n.?) *act of removing, driving out*, 465.

bachall ā,f. *crozier*. acc. plu. bachla, 183.

bádud o,m. *act of drowning, destroying*. dat. sg., 349.

báegul o,n. *unguarded condition, surprise attack*. gen. sg. baíguil, 397.

baïd *dies*. pres. ind. 3rd sg. -ba, 306. pres. ind. 3rd plu. -baat,

83. fut. 3rd sg. bebaid, 132, 139, 182, etc.; bebais, 320, 423.

bóid adj.,i *affectionate, tender*, 434.

baile m. and f. *vision, frenzy, madness*, 56.

band o *exploit, deed.* acc. plu. bandæ, 325. gen. plu. band, 227, 231.

bárc ā,f. *ship.* nom. plu. bárca, 444.

barr o,m. *tiara, diadem*, 32.

bás o,n. (later m.) *death*, 372. dat. sg., 39.

bath o,n.? *death, destruction.* In compound rígbath *kingly-death (royal-slaughter)*, 144.

bé n. (later f.) *woman.* acc. sg., 459.

becc adj.,o/ā *small.* nom. sg. n., 458. gen. sg. m. bic, 396. nom. plu. becca, 112.

beirid *brings, secures, gets.* fut. pass. sg. bérthair, 206, 295. perf. 3rd sg. ruc, 420. With meaning (in pass.) *is born.* perf. pass. sg. rucad, 386.

bél o,m. *lip, mouth.* dat. plu. in phrase ar bélaib *in front of*, 33, 307.

bélrae io,n. *language.* nom. plu. in compound ilbélrae *many languages*, 180.

ben ā,f. *woman*, 433. gen. sg. mná, 341. nom. plu. mná, 194.

benaid *strikes, cuts*, 196.

benn *mountain, peak.* dat. sg. in compound Cúalg[n]iubeinn, 393.

bertaid *brandishes, shakes, makes quake.* fut. 3rd sg. bertfaid, 396.

bile io (orig. n.?) *large tree, tree-trunk*, 30. With meaning *scion, hero* in compound gríanbili (lit: *sun-hero*), i.e. *great hero*, 425. In compound lóegbili *darling hero*, 435.

bir u,n. *horn, antler.* dat. sg., 454.

bith u,m. *the world*, 130. acc. sg., 282.

blíadain ī,f. *year*, 231, 360. dat. sg., 18. nom. plu. blíadnai, 99, 118, 131, etc.; blíadnæ, 234; blíadna, 272. gen. plu. blíadnae, 78, 95, 105, etc. gen. plu. blíadan (Mid. Ir.), 293.

blogaid i,m.? *breaker, destroyer.* In compound clethblugaid *breaker of spears*, 263.

bodb ā,f. Name of a war-goddess, *scald-crow.* gen. sg. bodbai, 313.

bóraime iā,f. *cattle-tribute.* gen. sg. bórime, 127; bóramai, 142.

brat o,m. *cloak, mantle*, 33.

bráth u and o,m. *doomsday.* In phrase co bráth/co brád *till doomsday*, i.e. *for ever*, 16, 20, 43, etc.

bráthair r,m. *brother, kinsman.* acc. plu. bráithri, 364.

brécach adj.,o/ā *lying, deceitful*, 363.

brécad u,m. *act of deceiving, enticing*, 370.

breccaid *speckles, scatters.* fut. 3rd sg. rel. breccfus, 422.

breth ā,f. *act of carrying, taking.* nom. sg. breith, 108.

breó d,f. (also m.) *flame.* In compounds mórbreó *a great flame*, 182; caínbreó *a fair flame*, 341.

breóach adj.,o/ā (from breó) *flaming*, 389. As subst. *fiery one, flame*, 379.

brethach adj.,o/ā *pertaining to judgement.* As subst. (acc. sg.) in compound mórbrethach *great judge*, 103.

bris(s)id *breaks, smashes.* With
meaning *wins, gains,* fut. 3rd sg.
brisfid, 368, 439. fut. 3rd sg. rel.
brisfess, 323, brissfes, 390. perf.
3rd sg. ro bris, 369.
bróen o,m. *rain, shower,* 384. acc.
sg., 363.
brogaid *proceeds, advances (on).*
fut. 3rd sg. brogfaid, 457.
brónach adj.,o/ā *sorrowful.* nom.
plu. m. brónaig, 398.
brú *edge, bank, border.* dat. sg.,
148, 183, 289, etc.
bruig i,m. (later form of mruig)
land, holding, region. gen. sg.
bruigi, 341.
bruth u,m. *heat, valour.* Ext.
meaning in compound caínbruth
fair valorous one, 389.
búadach adj.,o/ā *victorious, trium-
phant.* As subst. in compound
dálbúadach *victorious one in
encounter, battle-victor,* 426.
búaid i,n. (perhaps earlier ā,f.)
victory, triumph. acc. sg. búed,
323. dat. sg., 327. nom. dual
búed, 324. In compound cath-
búaid *battle-victory, booty,* 206.
buiden ā,f. *company of troops.* nom.
plu. budni, 121.
buidnech adj.,o/ā *having troops,
bands.* In compound mórbuid-
nech *having many troops,* 438.
As subst. *leader of troops,* 251,
450. In compound ollbuidnech
great leader, 403.
buillech adj.,o/ā *striking blows.*
As subst. (o,m.) in compound
láechbuillech *heroic blow-
striker,* i.e. *heroic warrior,* 377.
In compound mórbuillech *great
blow-striker,* i.e. *great warrior,*
378.

bunad o,[n.?] *origin, stock,* 155.
cach, cech adj. *each, all, every,*
283. nom. sg. f. cech, 466. acc.
sg. f. cach, 50. acc. sg. n. cech,
76. dat. sg. f. cach, 143. dat. sg.
n. cech, 84, 319; cach, 188, 287.
gen. sg. m. cach, 77, 232. gen.
sg. f. cacha, 43, 53. gen. sg. n.
cach, 198; cech, 464.
cách *everyone,* 314.
cáem adj.,o/ā *dear, precious.* As
subst. o,m. *comrade, noble.*
nom. plu. coím, 90.
cád adj.,o/ā (later i) *holy, noble,
pure,* 372.
cailech o,m. *cock* (used as nick-
name), 266. acc. sg., 262.
caíme iā,f. *beauty, loveliness.* gen.
sg., 37.
cáin i,f. *law, rule.* dat. sg., 447.
caín adj.,i *good, fair,* 132. Used
adverbally, 218.
caínid *laments, regrets, weeps at.*
pres. ind. 3rd plu. plus suff.
pron. 3rd sg. m. coíntit, 90, 343.
fut. pass. sg. cuínfider, 393.
calland iā,f. *calends, first day of
month.* acc. dual callaind, 394.
can interrogative *whence,* 10.
canaid *sings, recites.* pres. ind.
pass. sg. with meaning *foretells*
canair, 447.
cani neg. interrog. compound of ní,
conj. part. with infix. pron. 3rd
plu. Class A canis, 68.
casar ā,f. *shower.* nom. plu. cassra,
342.
cass adj.,o/ā *(of hair) curly.* As
subst. o,m. *curly-haired one.*
acc. sg., 395.
cath u,m. *battle, fight,* 60, 61, 62,
etc. acc. sg., 101, 122, 239, etc.
dat. sg., 162, 366. gen. sg. catha,

222, 276, 283. nom. dual, 68, 86, 87, etc. acc. dual, 228. nom. plu. catha, 66, 68, 160, etc. acc. plu. catha, 69, 100, 239, etc. gen. plu. catha, 81, 137, 220, etc. In compounds cétchath *first battle*, 237; mórchath *great battle*, 302. With meaning *troop, battalion*. gen. sg. catha, 334. nom. plu. catha, 260. dat. plu. in compound borrchathaib *mighty battles, great battalions*, 302.

cathach adj.,o/ā *warlike*, 192. As subst. *warlike one*, 378. As subst. in compound trénchathach *strongly warlike one*, 329.

cathaír f. *chair, seat*. dat. sg., 32.

caur d,m. *hero, warrior*, 449. In compound mórchaur *great warrior*, 184.

céile io,m. *companion, cleric*. nom. sg. in phrase céili [Dé] *culdee*, 393. With meaning *spouse*, acc. sg. céili, 433.

céim n,n. *stride, step*, 175, 176.

céin conj. *as long as* (followed by nas. rel. clause), 16, 130.

cel o *concealment, extinction*. In phrase cingid ar chel *dies*, 255, 468.

cen' prep. with acc. *without*, 5, 113, 144, etc. With aff. pron. 3rd sg. m. chena *besides*, 72.

cend o,n. (later m.) *head*. dat. plu. cendaib, 310; cennaib, 370. In phrases co cend *for the duration of, till the end of*, 11, 318; ar chiund *in front of, before* 35, 44; *awaiting, on arrival*, 6; ar chend *towards, in the direction of*, 24.

ceó f. (later as k-stem) *mist*. nom. sg. plus demonstr. pron., 25. acc. sg. cíaig, 22.

cerb *one who cuts*. nom. sg. cáirb, 196?

cern ā,f.? *angle, corner*. dat. plu. cernaib, 33.

cernach adj.,o/ā *victorious, triumphant*, 323.

cert o,n. *right, entitlement*, 318.

cét o,n. *hundred*, 60.

cétaín (*a battle on a*) *Wednesday*, 145, 435. dat. sg., 361.

cethair num. adj. *four*. nom. f. cethair, 45, cethir, 52. acc. m. form used for nom. m. cethri, 68. acc. f. cetheóra, 52. dat. plu. cethraib, 33.

cétudach adj.,o/ā *seated*. As subst. *seated one*, i.e. *chief*, 378, 403.

1 cía interrogative *what?*, 9. Stressed form (with rel.), *where?* 23; *who?*, 58. *to whom?*, 48, 58, 79, etc. As indef. with pres. subj. 3rd sg. of cop. in phrase cip hé *whoever*, 27.

2 cía' conj. *although*. neg. cini, 97; ceni, 324.

cían (archaic *cén*) adj.,o/ā *far, distant*. Used adverbally, *céin*, 118. In phrase *cén mair* *prosperity*, 203.

cicharda adj.,io/iā *fierce, keen*, 183.

cid interrogative *what?*, 9; *why?*, 10.

cimbal o,m. *bell*. gen. plu., 469.

cin d,m. *guilt, crime*, 93. With extended meaning *affection, love*. acc. sg., 432.

cingid *proceeds, walks, goes*. pres. ind. 3rd sg. rel. cinges, 468. fut. 3rd sg. cichis, 230; cichiss, 255. fut. 3rd plu. cichsit, 176.

cith u,m. *trial, hardship, battle*. nom. plu. citha, 328.

cland ā,f. *descendants, people.* dat. sg. claind, 16, 125.

clár o,n. and m. *board, plank, of a variety of flat articles normally made of wood,* e.g. *breastwork of a chariot.* acc. sg., 336.

clé adj.,io/iā *left.* As subst. *left-side.* acc. sg., 334, 336.

cléirech o,m. *cleric,* 357.

cles u and o,n. and m. *feat.* acc. sg. in compound clíabchless *basket-feat?,* 421.

clí f. Apparently indecl. *champion.* gen. plu., 268.

clíab o,m. *basket,* 421.

clíabach adj. (from clíab *basket*). As subst. *basketed-one?,* 421.

cloch ā,f. *stone,* 7, 9, 467. acc. sg. cloich, 7. gen. sg. cloche, 14.

cloïd *repels, vanquishes.* fut. 3rd sg. clóifid, 423, 452.

clú orig. n. (later f.) *fame, reputation,* 365. dat. sg., 370.

cluiche io,[n.?] *game, sport.* gen. sg. cluchi, 16.

cnes o,m. *skin (of body), body.* gen. plu., 335.

1 co prep. with acc. *to, till,* 100, 107, 119, etc.

2 co n- prep. with dat. *with,* 33, 306, 310, etc. With def. art. cosin, 79, 134; cosind, 96. With geminating part. coa, 231.

3 co n- conj. *so that, until,* 6, 7, 190, etc.; neg. cona, 22.

cóel adj.,o/ā *thin, slender,* 365. As subst. (usually o-stem) *slender one,* 357.

cóic num. adj. *five,* 47, 78, 158.

colaind i,f. *body, corpse.* acc. sg., 288.

comaimser *contemporaneity, contemporary,* 313.

comarb(b)a io,m. *heir, successor,* 194, 392.

comdána *very bold, fearless.* dat. dual m. comdáni, 432.

comdíne *contemporary generation, coeval(s).* nom. plu. comdíni, 399.

comnart adj.,o/ā *very strong.* In compound lethchomnart *half as strong,* 74.

comrac o *encounter, battle, combat.* dat. sg., 74.

con-beba *will die.* fut. 3rd sg. con-beba, 272. fut. 3rd plu. con-bibsat, 214.

con-gair *calls, summons.* pret. 3rd sg. con-gart, 28.

Conn Proper name, 12. nom. Cond, 1, 9, 24. dat. Cunn, 45. gen. Cuinn, 50; Cuind, 97, 104, 462.

Conn Cétchathach Proper name *Conn of the Hundred Battles.* dat., 76. gen., 56.

con-ranna divides (with fri) *shares (with), has an equal right (with).* fut. 3rd sg. con-rainnfi, 437.

con-saídi (usually used with fri) *incites, stirs up a quarrel (against).* fut. 3rd sg. con-saídfi, 242; con-saídfe, 310. pret. 3rd sg. con-sóid, 434.

con-úala *ascends, goes to.* pret. 3rd sg. plus infix. pron. Class B 3rd sg. m. cot n-úallai, 381.

corr adj.,o/ā, *peculiar, odd,* 435.

cos ā,f. *foot.* dat. plu. cosaib, 6, 7; plus emph. pron., 18.

coscrach adj.,o/ā *victorious, triumphant,* 163, 193, 196, etc.

costudach o,m. *protector, custodian,* 150, 251.

cotá *as far as, till,* 138, 182, 316, etc.

crésen adj.,o/ā *pious*, 357. As subst. o,m. *believer, pious one.* dat. sg. crésion, 372. gen. sg. créssin, 468; créissin, 470. gen. plu. crésien, 447.

cretair f. *relic, blessed object.* dat. sg., 470.

críchach adj.,o/ā *of many territories.* As subst. *one of many territories,* 449.

cride io,n. *heart.* nom. sg. cridi, 415. dat. sg. cridiu, 350.

crothaid *brandishes.* fut. 3rd sg. rel. croithfes, 390.

crú *gore, blood.* gen. sg. cróu, 301, 384.

1 crúach adj.,o/ā *bloody.* As subst. *bloody one,* 359.

2 crúach o,n.? *slaughter, carnage,* 464.

crúaid adj.,i *harsh, stern,* 323, 327, 449. acc. plu. crúaidai, 390.

crúas m. (orig. ā,f.?) *bravery, valour,* 240, 417.

cruth u,m. *form, appearance.* gen. sg. crotha, 37.

cú n,m. *hound (laudatory of person).* gen. sg. con, 396. nom. plu. in compound duinechoin *manhounds,* i.e. *warriors,* 83.

cúaine io,n. (later m. and f.) *litter, family,* 371.

cúairt i?,m. *circuit, journey.* nom. sg. cúaird, 353. dat. sg., 190.

cúanach adj.,o/ā *attended by troops.* As subst. *one attended by troops.* nom. plu. cúanaig, 456.

cucligid *protector/protecting,* 173; coicligid, 298.

cuimnech adj.,o/ā *memorable, famous,* 240.

coirm orig. prob i,n. (later n,n.) *ale, beer,* 222.

cuit i,f. *share, part,* 463.

cúl o,m. *back, rear,* 334.

cummascach ā,f.? *disturber?,* 173, 347.

cumma io,n. *act of cutting, hacking.* gen. sg. cumma, 335.

dá' num. adj. *two.* 67, 68, 85, etc. used for fem., 46. nom. f. dí, 210. acc. f. dí, 393, 452. In phrase meaning *twice,* fo dii, 325; co fo dí, 377; fo dí, 406.

dabach ā,f. a *large tub or vat with two handles,* 33, 55.

daig i (later d),f. *blaze, fire.* dat. sg., 199.

daiger ā,f. *flash.* dat. sg. daigir, 441.

dáilid *pours (out), bestows.* impv. 2nd sg. dáil, 59, 80, 97, etc. fut. pass. sg. -dáilfider, 58, 79, 96, etc.

1 dál ā,f. a *dispensing/division of food or drink.* dat. sg. dáil, 48.

2 dál ā,f. *meeting.* In compound brécdál *deceitful meeting,* 459.

3 dál o,n. *sept, tribe.* nom. plu. in compound fírdál *true tribe.* nom. plu., 214.

dalta io,m. *foster-son,* 402.

dám ā,f. a *company (of poets).* acc. plu. dáma, 214.

dardaín *Thursday.* dat. sg., 292. With día *day* (plus qualifying gen.) día dardaín, 94.

datta adj.,io/iā *beautiful, stately, noble,* 426.

de' (see **di**) prep. with dat. *from.* Plus 3rd sg. pron. (m. or n.) de, 59, 80, 97, etc. With meaning *of,* 39.

dechraid *becomes furious with anger (or excitement).* pres. ind. 3rd sg. rel. dechrass, 414.

dédenach adj.,o/ā *last, final*, 17, 26.
degaid i (old vn. of do-saig *seeks, searches*). In phrase i ndegaid *after, following*, 50.
deich n- num. adj. *ten.* gen. déac, 46; déc, 226, 348.
deired o,n. *end.* dat. sg. deriud, 260. In phrase i nderiud *at the end*, 373.
deithbir adj.,i *fitting, proper*, 36.
delb u,m. (orig. ā,f.) *form, appearance*, 466. gen. sg. delba, 37.
delgnaide iā,f. *distinction, remarkableness*, 36.
demin adj. *sure, certain*, 69.
dénum u,m. *doing, making.* dat. sg., 169.
dérach adj.,o/ā *tearful, sad*, 129.
descert o,n. (later m.) *southern part, south.* dat. sg. descurt, 216.
di' (see **de**) prep. with dat. *from, of*, 17, 33, 34, etc. Plus poss. adj. 2nd sg. ditt', 19. Plus def. art. m. sg. din, 9, 28; f. sg. dind, 401. With rel. part. dia, 6, 87, 129, etc.; die, 383.
1 día *day*, 4, 77, 94, etc.; die, 166, 255, 354; dië, 310, 320.
2 Día *God*, 182. gen. sg. Dé, 466.
dían adj.,o/ā *swift, rapid*, 177, 181.
dias (orig. disyll) ā,f. *pair, couple, two of them.* In dat. with poss. adj. in apposition a ndiis, 259.
díbaircaid *casts, throws.* pres. ind. 3rd sg. rel. díbercess, 27.
díbrucud u,m. *casting, throwing.* dat. sg., 28.
díchetal o and u,n. *incantation, spell*, 51.
díden ā,f. *end.* In phrase oín díden *end fast*, i.e. *Friday*, i n-oín dídin, 177; aín díten, 207; i n-aín dídin, 244, 262; oín díden, 343.

didiu *then, therefore*, 48.
dígal ā,f. *avenging, punishment.* nom. sg. dígail, 283. dat. sg., 189.
dirsan *sad, alas*, 76, 91, 93, etc.
díth orig. n.? *loss, destruction, fall*, 207. dat. sg., 1, 361.
díthat ā,f. *repast, meal.* acc. sg. díthait, 45.
diúltad u,m. *refusing (to acknowledge/to believe in).* acc. sg., 191.
díummus, dímus o,m. (orig. u,m.) *arrogance, pride.* gen. sg. dímeis, 113.
do' prep. with dat. *to, for*, 45, 51, 76, etc. Plus aff. pron. 1st sg. dam, 20; dom, 39; 2nd sg. and 2nd sg. emph. pron. duit-siu, 42; 3rd sg. m. dóu, 11, 13, 98, etc.; dáu, 277; dó, 42, 313; 3rd sg. f. dí, 49; 1st plu. dún, 24; 2nd plu. dúib, 39; 3rd plu. dóib, 38. Plus poss. adj. 1st sg. dom', 39; 2nd sg. dot', 16; 3rd sg. m. dia, 29, 189; dá, 432. With def. art. m. sg. dond, 12; sg. f. don, 48; m. plu. dona, 1. With following vn. in phrases expressing purpose, 27, 169. With rel. part. dia, 48, 444.
do-aidlea *comes to, visits, attacks.* pres. ind. 3rd sg. plus infix. pron. 3rd sg. m. Class A da-n-aidli, 102. fut. 2nd sg. do-aidlibe, 98. perf. (with infix. ro) 3rd sg. -táraill, 10.
do-airissedar *stays, remains.* pres. ind. 3rd sg. -tairiss, 15.
do-airngir *prophesies, foretells.* perf. 3rd sg. do-rairngert, 19.
do-beir *gives, brings.* pres. subj. (corresponding to perf. do-uccus) 3rd sg. with ro of poss., prosthetic 'f' and infix. pron. 1st plu.

Class A run-fucca, 24. fut. pass.
sg. -tibérthar, 48. pret. 3rd sg. do-
bert, 44.

dochum n- prep. governing gen. *to,
towards*, 176. dochom, 121.

do-cing *approaches*. fut. 3rd sg.
(with force of rel.) plus infix.
pron. 3rd sg. f. Class C doda-
cich, 78, 95, 99, etc.; doda-ciig,
168.

do-cuirethar *put, places*. As transi-
tive vb (from root *to-ro-la) with
meaning *happens upon, comes*.
With co n- plus perf. 3rd sg.
plus infix. pron. Class C 3rd plu.
conda-rala, 30. perf. pass. sg. do-
ralad, 10; -torlad, 15.

do-éccai *looks*. impf. ind. 3rd sg.
-décad, 6.

do-fich *punishes, avenges*. pres.
subj. 3rd sg. du-phé, 398.

do-fócaib *raises, lifts*. fut. 3rd plu.
-tuicébat, 444; prot. used indep.
with meaning *carry off*, tuicébat,
452.

do-fortai *pours, sheds*. With ár *to
commit slaughter*. fut. 3rd sg.
with infix. pron. 3rd plu. Class
A dos-foirtbi, 326. With meaning
overwhelms, destroys. pres. ind.
3rd plu. do-fortat, 183. fut. 3rd
sg. do-foirtbe, 324; do-fortbi,
328.

do-gní *does, makes*. pret. pass. sg.
do-gníd, 357.

do-goa *chooses, selects*. fut. 3rd sg.
plus infix. pron. 3rd sg. m. Class
A da-ṅgega, 161.

do-icc *comes*. pres. ind. 3rd sg. tic,
459. pres. ind. 3rd plu. tecait,
364. pres. subj. 3rd sg. -tí, 461.
fut. 3rd sg. ticfa, 119, 181, 298.
fut. 3rd sg. with prosthetic 'f' do-

ficfe, 334. pret. and perf. 3rd sg.
with infix. pron. 3rd plu. Class A
with prosthetic 'f' dus-fánic, 23,
26.

do-imgair *claims, summons*. pres.
ind. 3rd sg. timgair, 391. fut. 3rd
sg. timgéra, 198.

doirr (orig. perhaps dorr ā,f.) *anger,
displeasure*. In compound dercc-
duirr *red-anger*, 122.

do-léci *throws, casts*, 25.

do-meil of time: *spend, live out*. fut.
3rd sg. plus infix. pron. 3rd sg. n.
Class A da-méla, 420. fut. 3rd sg.
neg. plus infix. pron. 3rd sg. m.
nín-toiméla, 397.

domnach o,n. (later m.) (*a battle on
a*) *Sunday*, 372, 393, 418. dat. sg.
249. With día *day* (plus qualify-
ing gen.) día domnaig *Sunday*,
102; dië domnaich, 310.

dond o,m. *chief, noble, ruler*, 320,
327. dat. sg., 304; dund, 305. gen.
sg. duind, 312. nom. plu., 351.

do-nessa *spurns*. fut. 3rd sg. rel.
plus infix. pron. Class C 3rd sg. f.
doda-nesfa, 345.

dorcha io,n. *darkness, gloom*, 361.
gen. sg., 23.

do-roich *reaches, attains*. fut. 3rd
sg. plus infix. pron. 3rd sg. m.
Class A da-rii, 286.

dórtad u,m. *pouring, shedding*. In
compound cráudórtad *shedding
of blood*, i.e. *bloodshed*, 123.
Extended meaning *destroying*. In
compound slúagdórtad *destruc-
tion of hosts*, 352.

do-saig *comes, goes, approaches*.
fut. 3rd sg. do-sia, 205.

do-tét *comes*. perf. 1st sg. do-
deochod, 39; plus emph. pron.
1st sg. do-deochad-sa, 42. fut.

3rd plu. do-regat, 300, 331.
do-tuit *falls*, i.e. *dies*. pres. ind. 3rd
sg., 213, 443, 459; du-fuit, 165;
do-fuit, 354; do-fuitt, 440. pres.
ind. 3rd plu. (plus infix. pron.
3rd sg. n. Class A?) da-thuittet,
259 (see note to l. 72); prot. form
used indep. tuitet, 350. fut. 3rd
sg. do-fóeth, 124, 129, 165, etc.;
do-fáeth, 148; do-foíth, 71; do-
tóeth, 220, 233, 249, etc.; (with
infix. pron. 3rd sg. m. Class A?)
da-fóeth, 72 (see note to l. 72).
fut. 3rd sg. -tóeth, 145, 157, 266;
prot. used indep., 228. fut. 3rd
plu. do-fóethsat, 71, 162. fut. 3rd
plu. -tóethsatt, 92; -tóethsat, 83,
325, 440, etc.; (used for subj.)
-toíthsat, 324.
drauc m. and f. *dragon* (used fig. of
a warrior or hero), 227, 231.
drech ā,f. *face, countenance*. In
compound mórdrech *broad-faced
one*, 414.
dremna iā,f. *fury*. gen. sg., 122.
drongach adj.,o/ā *attended by
throngs, companies*. As subst.
one attended by companies, 378.
druí d,m. *druid*, 21. nom. plu. druid,
2.
druimne iā,f.? *ridge* (In ogam, tech-
nical term for ridge or solid angle
from which letters were drawn).
nom. plu., 53.
dúa, doé io,m.? *mound, rampart*, 6.
dúan ā,f. *song, poem*, 353.
dubach adj.,o/ā *gloomy, sad*, 129.
dubae iā,f.? (orig. io,n.?) *gloom,
heaviness, grief*. acc. sg. dubai,
351. nom. plu. duba, 366.
dúbart *battle, raid*. nom. sg. dúbairt,
138. acc. sg., 196. acc. plu.
dúbarta, 131.

dúbartach o,m. *fighter, champion*,
109, 150, 173, etc.
dúil i,f. *being, creature, Creation*.
acc. plu. dúili, 466.
duine io,m. *person*. gen. plu. doíne,
370; daíne, 410.
dún o (later s,n.) *fort*, 54.
dúnadach *one who leads armies on
a campaign*, i.e. *military leader*,
149.
dúr adj.,o/ā *severe, resolute*, 414.
duthain adj.,i *transitory, short-lived*,
244.
é stressed form of pers. pron., 3rd sg.
m., 19; hé, 40, 75, 161, etc.
éc m. *death*, 197, 247, 292, etc. dat.
sg., 361. acc. plu. écu, 272.
echrad ā,f. *steeds, a chariot-riding
host, a cavalcade*. acc. sg.
echraid, 94.
écht u,m. (orig. n.?) *slaying, slaugh-
ter*, 153.
echtra iā,f. *adventure (voyage)*, 56.
echtrand adj.,o/ā *strange, foriegn*.
As subst. *stranger, foriegner*.
nom. plu. echtraind, 177. acc.
plu. echtranda, 179, 352. dat.
plu. echtrandaib, 368. gen. plu.
echtrand, 463, 465.
ed stressed form 3rd sg. n. of
personal pron., 16.
éicse *divination*. gen. sg. éccsi, 13.
elgna adj. *malicious*. nom. plu.
elgnæi, 351.
élúd u,m. *escape, fleeing, departure*,
117.
ém particle of affirmation *indeed,
truly*, 14.
engach adj.,o/ā *noisy, vociferous*,
443.
eochair i and k,f. *key*. nom. plu.
eochra, 13.
eó k,m. *salmon (used as complimen-*

tary epithet of leader), 402.

Ériu n,f. *Ireland.* acc. hÉrinn, 5; Érinn, 182; hÉrind, 194, 212; hÉirinn, 265. dat. hÉrinn, 20, 191, 353, etc.; hÉrind, 240; Érinn, 401. gen. hÉrenn, 44, 138, 263, etc.; hÉrend, 128, 130, 154, etc.

érnid *pays, rewards.* fut. 3rd sg. -érnfi, 218.

ernbas o,n. *lit.: death by iron,* hence *a deed of slaughter or violence, slaying,* 288.

errach o,m. *spring.* gen. sg. in compound úarerraig *cold spring,* 319.

escra io?,m. *a vessel for dispensing liquid,* 34, 55.

étach o,m. *jealousy.* gen. sg. étaig, 370.

eter, etir prep. with acc. *between,* 46, 47, 238, etc. With meaning *both,* 284.

etsecht *departure, death,* 343.

fadéin, féin adj. and pron. *self.* 3rd sg. m. fadeissin, 3, 35; féini, 371.

fáebrach adj.,o/ā *sharp-edged, keen,* 204.

fán o,m. *a slope.* In phrase i fán *laid low, prostrated,* 280.

fássach o and s,n. *a legal precedent,* 126.

fé *a rod for measuring the dead,* 383.

fer o,m. *man,* 36, 80, 136, etc. acc. sg., 136. nom. plu. fir, 4, 194, 292, etc. acc. plu. firu, 177, 324, 423, etc. dat. plu. feraib, 178. In compound dondfer *princely-man, noble-man,* 313.

feraid *pours, sheds.* fut. 3rd sg. rel. firfes, 363. With meaning *supplies,* fut. 3rd sg. firfid, 396. With cath and matan meaning

to give battle. fut. 3rd sg. firfid, 69, 101, 122, etc.; -firfe, 69; plus suff. pron. 3rd plu. firfidius, 60; rel. firfes(s), 81, 228, 232, etc. fut. pass. sg. firfidir, 270, 359, 436. fut. 3rd plu. rel. firfide, 67; firfite, 131; firfidi, 464. fut. pass. plu. firfitir, 199, 284. With meaning *effects, causes,* fut. 3rd sg. firfid, 212, 284, 367. With meaning *make,* fut. pass. sg. firfidir, 351, 436. In phrase feraid fáilti fri *welcomes,* 28.

fert o,n. *a mound over a burial place,* 351.

fescur o,m. *evening (battle),* 163, 352. nom. dual, 67, 88.

fessach adj.,o/ā *knowing, well informed,* 403. As subst. *knowledgeable one,* 415.

fíacail i,m. and f. *tooth,* 102.

fiäch o,m. *raven.* nom. plu. fiäig, 301, fiäich, 332.

fíachach adj.,o/ā *raven-like,* 443.

fían ā,f. *a band of professional fighters, a company.* nom. plu. fíanda, 131. acc. plu. fíanna, 252.

fiche d,m. *twenty.* gen. sg. fichet, 45, 52, 68. nom. plu. fichit, 78.

1 fichid *fights.* fut. pass. sg. rel. fesar, 84; fessar, 109, 138. fut. pass. plu. fessaitir, 159. part. in compound díanfichta, 352.

2 fichid *bubbles, flows.* pres. ind. 3rd sg. -fich, 381.

fidbae *venom, poison.* gen. sg. fidbai, 102.

fili d,m. *poet,* 14. nom. sg. file, 11, 19, 27. acc. sg. filid, 51. dat. sg. filid, 9, 12. nom. plu. filid, 3.

fín *end,* 271.

find adj.,o/ā *white, bright, fair, blessed,* 395, 399, 403, etc. dat.

plu. finnaib, 252.

findruine *an amalgam of copper or gold with silver*, 31.

fine iā,f. *a group of persons of the same family or kindred*, 106. acc. sg. fini, 65. dat. sg., 305, 391. In wider sense *descendants, race.* acc. sg., 218.

fíne iā,f.? *sin*. dat. sg. fíni, 306.

fingal ā,f. *kin-slaying.* acc. sg. fingail, 388. dat. sg., 244. gen. sg. fingaile, 156, 169, 351, etc.

fírinde iā,f. *justice, righteousness.* gen. sg., 392.

flaith i,f. *lordship, sovereignty, rule*, 44, 161, 298, etc. acc. sg., 211. dat. sg., 146, 172, 203, etc. gen. sg. flatha, 43. gen. plu. flathæ, 127. dat. sg. in compound comḟlaith *joint-sovereignty*, 210. acc. sg. in compound ardḟlaith *great sovereignty*, 169. dat. sg. in compound derbḟlaith *sure/certain sovereignty*, 235. Also *lord, ruler* (also m.) 18, 212, 218. acc. sg., 50. gen. sg. flatha, 43. nom. plu. flathi, 160. gen. plu. flaithi, 155. In compounds síthḟlaith *peaceful ruler*, 371; tigḟlaith *last ruler*, 462.

flaithius u and o,m. *sovereignty, rule*, 17. In compound comflaithius *joint-sovereignty*, 460.

flesc ā,f. *stick, stave.* gen. sg. flesci, 53. nom. plu. flesca, 55. acc. plu. flescæ, 52.

fo', fa' prep. with acc. and dat. *under.* Acc.: with meaning *throughout.* with def. art. fon, 8, 282. Dat.: 14, 154, 252, etc. With poss. adj. 2nd sg. fad', 18; 3rd sg. m. foa, 6, 7; 3rd sg. n. foa, 30. With meaning *about, at*, 273, 320.

fo-ácaib *leaves.* perf. pass. sg. forácbad, 54.

fo-ceird *puts, places.* fut. 3rd plu. -foíchret, 130.

fochla io,n. *The North, the champion's seat.* dat. sg. fochlæ, 309.

fodég *because, for*, 4.

fodbach adj.,o/ā *spoil-laden, well-accoutred*, 212.

fo-derga *reddens (by bloodshed).* fut. 3rd sg. fo-dercfa, 325.

fo-gaib *finds, gets.* pret. 3rd sg. -fúair, 6. pret. and perf. pass. sg. -fríth, 36. With meaning *accepts* fut. 3rd sg. -faigbi, 18.

fo-gíalla *exacts hostages or submission.* fut. 3rd sg. fu-géillfi, 160.

foglaid i,m. *plunderer.* nom. plu. foglaide, 398.

fogmar o,m. *autumn.* gen. sg. fogmair, 373.

fo-gní *serves, is subject to.* fut. 3rd plu. fo-génat, 465.

foil k,f. *a ring or bracelet.* With extended meaning *valuable*, acc. plu. foilgi, 438.

follscaide adj.,io/iā *scorched*, 114.

fomna(i)s subst. (with force of impv.) *guarding, beware*, 312, 324.

fo-naisc *binds, lays tribute on, subdues.* fut. 3rd sg. fo-nen, 194, 212; fo-nena, 232.

for prep. with acc. and dat. *on, onto, over.* Acc.: 2, 59, 80, etc. With def. art. forsin, 103, 236, 262, etc. With poss. adj. 3rd sg. m. fora, 364. With aff. pron. 3rd sg. m. or n. fair, 11; 3rd sg. f. fuirri, 7; 3rd plu. forru, 26. Dat.: 20, 61, 64, etc. (replaced by) ar, 165, 178. Plus poss. adj. 3rd sg. f. fora, 32. With rel. part. forsi, 79, 96, 103, etc.; fors', 58.

for-accai *oversees.* pres. ind. 3rd sg., 399.

foránach adj.,o/ā *aggressive, violent,* 212. As subst. *aggressive one,* 403.

forba(i)s f. (orig. ā?) *keeping a hostile look or watch (on), siege.* acc. sg. forbais, 367, 427. acc. plu. forbasa, 212.

forbba io,n. *smiting,* 410.

forbusach adj.,o/ā *victorious, conquering,* 376.

for-brissi *breaks* (in idiom 'the battle breaks before A on B', i.e. 'A defeats B'). fut. 3rd sg. arbrisfi, 100.

forggu *choice, pick,* 154.

for-ling *leaps on or over.* pres. ind. 3rd sg., 7.

formna io,m. *shoulder.* Used fig. *perfection,* 280.

fornaidm n,n. *binding,* 187.

fortbe io,n. *slaying, slaughter,* 175.

fo-ruimi *sets, places.* pret. and perf. pass. sg. fo-ruirmed, 15.

forus o and u,n. *stability,* 154.

foscad u/o,n. (later m.) *shadow.* acc. sg., 53.

fota, fata adj.,io/iā *long,* 421. As subst. in compound tóebḟota *long-sided one, tall one,* 149.

fotha o,m. and n.? *origin, basis,* 156.

fott o,n. (later m.) *length, long,* 45, 46, 53.

fo-úacair *proclaims, announces, makes known.* fut. pass. sg. rel. -foicertar, 365.

fri prep. with acc. *against, to,* 64, 65, 128, etc. Plus aff. pron. 2nd sg. fritt, 21; 3rd sg. fris(s), 11, 294, 371; 3rd plu. friu, 48. Plus poss.

adj. 3rd sg. m. fria, 119. Plus neg. frisna, 379. With meaning *facing,* 456. With meaning *during,* plus poss. adj. 3rd sg. m. fria, 154, 156. With meaning *through,* plus poss. adj. 3rd plu. fria, 469. With rel. part. frisa, 10; fris[a], 325.

fris-gair *answers, replies.* pret. 3rd sg. fris-gart, 38, 49.

fris-taít *opposes, revolts.* fut. 3rd sg. fris-tercha, 371.

frithisi in phrase a ḟrithisi *again,* 12.

fubthaire io,m. *one who terrifies or intimidates?* gen. sg. fubthairi, 116.

fuigell, fugall o,m. *judgement.* gen. sg. fugail, 119.

fuil i,f. (orig. n.) *blood, a wound,* 381. acc. sg., 295, 332.

fuiligud u,m. *blood-letting, wounding.* dat. sg., 268.

gabál ā,f. *taking.* dat. sg. in phrase gabáil láma *expelling,* 236.

gaibid *takes (hold of),* pres. ind. 3rd sg. rel. gaibess, 463. fut. 3rd sg. gébaid, 282; rel. géba[s], 305. With meaning drive, fut. 3rd sg. gébaid, 284, 340. With for *attacks, assails,* past subj. 3rd plu. (with ro) -ragabtais, 4. With for *rules over,* fut. 3rd sg. gébaid, 224. With forbais meaning *lays siege to,* 427. With fri *goes against, opposes,* pres. ind. 3rd sg. pass. rel. -gaibther, 379. With a *to proceed from,* pres. ind. 3rd sg. -geib, 455.

gaim *winter.* gen. sg., 108. dat. sg. in compound úargaim *cold winter, mid-winter,* 331.

gaimred o,n. (later m.) *winter.* gen. sg. in compound cétgaimrid *early winter,* 361.

gainithir *is born, is derived, produces.* fut. 3rd sg. gignidir, 299; gignedar, 154; rel. gignetar, 75; gignid, 446.

gair n. *a short time*, 360.

gal ā,f. *warlike ardour, valour.* dat. sg. gail, 418. gen. sg. gaile, 328.

galach adj.,o/ā *hot.* Of persons *valiant, brave.* As subst. in compound úargalach *stern valiant one*, 426.

Gall o,m. *a foriegner, Norseman.* nom. plu. Gaill, 368, 463. acc. plu. Gaullu, 352.

gamain i,m. *a calf.* acc. sg. in compound ossgamain *deer-calf, fawn*, 425.

gand adj.,o/ā *scanty.* With extended meaning *mean, evil*, 145.

garb adj.,o/ā *rough.* In compound foltgarb *rough-haired*, 456.

garg adj.,o/ā *fierce, rough*, 215. nom. plu. garcca, 328.

gáu ā,f. *lie, false judgement*, 233.

géim n,n. (later m.) *shout, roar.* gen. plu. gémind, 19.

geinne adj.,io/iā *born, begotten.* Used substantivally in compound óenguine *only-begotten one*, 188.

geinti i,m. *the (heathen) Norsemen.* acc. plu. 346. gen. plu., 342.

géisid *cries out, roars.* pret. 3rd sg. géisis, 7. perf. 3rd sg. ro géisi, 9, 19; ro gési, 18.

gercc o,m. fig. of *a king or champion.* acc. sg., 322. gen. plu. gárcc, 413; garc, 464.

gíall o,m. *a human pledge, a hostage*, 158. nom. plu. géill, 158, 159. acc. plu. gíallu, 198, 224, 232, etc.; gíalla, 122; gíallæ, 391. gen. plu., 187.

gilla *youth.* gen. plu., 405.

glainide adj.,io/iā *made of glass or crystal.* dat. sg. glanidi, 32.

glanaid *clears.* Of slaughter after a battle *completes.* fut. 3rd sg. glanfaid, 205, 278; rel. glanfus, 376. fut. 3rd plu. glanfait, 157.

glasmes u,m.? *unfavourable judgement?*, 370.

1 glé adj.,o/ā *clear, bright*, 169.

2 glé indecl.? (cf. *ZCP* 20, 364) *a fight, a combat*, 145. acc. sg., 147. dat. sg., 75. gen. sg., 308.

glond o,m. and ā,f. *a deed, an exploit.* gen. plu., 136, 165, 180.

gním u,m. *a deed*, 213, 306.

Goídel o,m. *an Irishman.* nom. plu. Goídil, 133, 272; Goídeil, 225. acc. plu. Góedelu, 284; Goídelu, 340. gen. plu. Goídel, 365; Gaídel, 122, 188, 425; Góedel, 177, 218, 224.

golgaire io,n. (later iā,f.) *wailing, lamentation.* nom. sg. golgairi, 319.

gonaid *wounds, kills.* fut. pass. sg. géntair, 77, 189, 306.

gorta iā,f. *hunger, famine*, 407.

grád o,n. *rank, order.* gen. sg. gráid, 181.

grafand o,n. (later ā,f.) *a band of horsemen.* gen. plu. graphand, 328.

graifnech adj.,o/ā *fond of horse-racing.* As subst. *horseman*, nom. sg. graiphnech, 359, 415.

gres ā,f. an attack. In compound úargres *hostile attack.* acc. plu. húargresa, 101.

grés in adv. phrase do grés *always, as usual*, 6.

grían ā,f. *sun*, 392. gen. sg. gréine, 2. nom. plu. gríana, 467.

gríb ā,f. *a fierce warrior, a chieftain,*

165.

grith u,m. *shaking, collapse, shout.* acc. sg., 130. With meaning *seizure, attack.* acc. sg., 282. Used fig. of that which causes fear or panic. gen. sg. in compound with ord. number cét (with allied meaning *primary, great*) fer cétgretha *a great fear-rousing man,* 80.

grúac ā,f. *hair of the head.* nom. plu. grúaca, 370.

guba io,m. *mourning, lamenting.* In compound fálguba *royal-lamentation,* 278.

gubadán from guba *mourning, lamenting,* 117.

guin i,n. *(act of) wounding or slaying by wounding,* 153. dat. sg., 27, 347. gen. sg. gona, 316.

gúr adj.,o/ā *sharp, keen.* gen. plu., 425.

gus u,m. *fierceness, impetuosity, anger.* gen. sg. gossa, 351.

guth u,m. *voice, sound.* acc. sg., 469.

i n- prep. with acc. and dat. *in, into.* Acc.: 388; hi, 25, 52, 53, etc. Plus def. art. n. assa, 30; issa, 31. Dat.: 1, 15, 32, etc.; hi, 17, 36, 43, etc.; a, 75, 162, etc. Plus def. art. issind, 247; m. sg. hisin, 148; isin, 265, 331, 366. f. sg. issin, 18. n. sg. isin, 35, 44; isind, 277. Plus poss. adj. 3rd sg. m. inna, 35; ina, 106, 118, 137, etc.; 'na, 172, 294, 364, etc.; 3rd sg. n. inna, 260. With rel. *in which* in, 384.

í stressed form of pers. pron. 3rd sg. f. hí, 15.

íadaid *closes in, draws near.* pres. ind. 3rd sg., 361.

íar n- prep. with dat. *after,* 1, 76, 77, etc. With poss. adj. 3rd sg. m. íarna, 264, 348. (of place) *beyond, on the western side of,* 94. With meaning *across, along,* 198, 451. With meaning *according to,* 447. In phrase íar sein *after that,* i.e. *then,* 53, 117, 131, etc. With def. art. sg. íarsin, 287.

íarmi-foich *seeks after, asks.* 3rd sg. perf. ro íarfacht, 9, 12.

íarnóin *late afternoon, evening.* Used of *evening battle,* 440

íarum adv. *thereafter, then,* 7, 11, 18, etc.

íath orig. u,n. (later o,m.) *land, country.* acc. sg., 100.

ibar o,m. *a yew, yew wood.* gen. sg. iphair, 52.

ibid *drinks.* fut. 3rd sg. plus infix. pron. 3rd sg. f. Class C nodasíbai, 58; noda-íba, 78, 95, 99, etc.; noda-íobæ, 164; doda-íba, 221; noda-íbæ, 385. fut. 3rd plu. íbait, 301, 332.

il adj.,i (orig. u) *many.* nom. plu. m. ile, 92, 172; ili, 294, 311, 364. As subst. *many, a multitude,* nom. plu. ili, 87, 178; ile, 90.

ilar o,n. (later m.) *a multitude.* gen. sg. ilair, 136, 180, 227, etc.

ille (adv. of place) *hither,* 383.

imdergad u,m. *act of shaming, insulting.* nom. sg. imdercad, 116.

imguin i,m. and f. *waging war, slaughter, conflict,* 253.

im(m)' prep. with acc. *about, around,* 75, 120, 288, etc.; him, 183. Plus aff. pron. 3rd sg. f. impe, 33. With def. art. m. sg. immon, 266.

immach *out(wards).* With meaning

onwards, himach, 420.

im(m)ed o,n. (later m.) *abundance*, 392, 464. dat. sg. immud, 303.

imm-ric (usually with a petrified infix. pron.) *occurs, befalls*. pres. ind. 3rd sg. rel. imma-ric, 207.

immurgu *indeed, then*, 54, 239.

in definite article *the*. nom. sg. m. in, 4, 11, 19, etc.; an, 14, 28; int, 26, 55, 153, etc. nom. sg. f. an, 7, 283; ind, 12, 44, 48, etc.; in, 9, 25, 59, etc. nom. sg. n. a, 17, 19, 51, etc.; in, 49, 59, 80, etc. acc. sg. f. in, 7, 205. acc. sg. n. a, 35. gen. sg. m. in, 23; ind, 116, 319, 365; int, 241. gen. sg. f. na, 2, 14, 127, etc. gen. sg. n. an, 54; in, 23, 56; ind, 260. nom. plu. m. in, 3, 83, 162, etc.; ind, 112; na, 157. nom. plu. f. na, 55. gen. plu. m. na, 410. gen. plu. f. na, 126. nom. dual m. na, 277, 445.

indala indecl. *one (of two)*. Used substantively before gen. of 3rd plu. pron. indala n-aí *one of them*, 259.

in-deich *avenges*. pres. ind. 3rd sg. in-dech, 468.

indiu *today, the present time*, 269.

indna io,m. *spear, weapon*. acc. plu. indnu, 390.

indredach adj.,o/ā *given to invading or attacking*. As substantive in compound slógindredach *host-attacker*, 330.

ingantae iā,f. *wondrousness*. dat. sg. inganti, 37.

ingen ā,f. *girl, maiden*, 44, 48, 59, etc. acc. sg., 32. acc. dual, 452. With meaning *daughter*, 354. gen. sg. ingeni, 358; ingine, 413. gen. plu. in compound rígingen *princesses*, 126.

ingnad adj.,o/ā *wonderful*, 445.

inis ī,f. *island*. gen. sg. insi, 298.

inonn (adv. of place) *yonder, thither*. innund, 383.

is *copula*. pres. ind. 1st sg. neg. nímda, 38. pres. ind. 3rd sg. is, 9, 10, 15, etc.; iss, 16; rel. ass, 266; neg. ní, 20, 269. pres. ind. 3rd plu. rel. ata, 353. With ceni, pres. ind. 3rd sg. cinid, 462. With cía, pres. subj. 3rd sg. cith, 74; cid, 409; neg. cinip, 198. fut. 3rd sg. bid, 107, 116, 127, etc.; neg. nípa, 125, 245; nípi, 233; níba, 294. fut. 3rd sg. rel. bas, 16; bass, 272, 314; m̀bess, 130. fut. 3rd plu. bit, 121, 178; biat, 311, 398, 399. fut. 3rd plu. neg. nípat, 112. pret. 3rd sg. ba, 12, 36, 44, etc. modal. pret. ba, 93, 178; neg. níbu, 434. perf. 3rd sg. ropu, 35.

ith u,n. (later m.) *corn, grain*. gen. sg. etha, 407.

la prep. with acc. *with, by, on account of*, 51, 55, 69, etc. With aff. pron. 3rd sg. m. leis, 28, 351; lais, 270, 300, 332. With def. art. f. plu. lassna, 252.

lá (earlier form laithe) io,n. (later m.) *day*, 17, 451; laa, 1. acc. sg., 215. gen. sg. laí, 260. gen. plu. laithe, 11. dat. sg. in compound óenlóu *same day, one day*, 277. nom. plu. in compound samlaithi *summer days*, 467.

labar adj.,o/ā *talkative, boastful*, 444.

láech o,m. *warrior*, 398.

láechda adj.,io/iā *warrior-like, heroic*, 382.

laíd ī?,f. *poem, lay*. nom. plu. laídi, 353.

láim (orig. ā,f.) *hand*. gen. sg. láma,

236.

laith *ale, liquor.* With lenited prosthetic 'f' f̓laith, 96. dat. sg. in compound dergf̓laith *red ale*, 34, 49, 58 etc.; derclaith, 135.

lán adj.,o/ā *full, complete*, 12, 34.

lár o,n. *middle.* In phrase for lár *in the middle of, in*, 269. In phrase di lár *from within*, 308; *from the centre*, 313.

lecc ā,f. *flat slab of rock or stone, flagstone, tombstone, altar-stone.* dat. plu. lecaib, 252.

lecht u?,m. *grave, tomb, resting place*, 447.

légaid *reads, studies.* fut. pass. plu. rel. légfaitir, 353.

leth o and s,n. *side, half*, 281, 397, 401. dat. sg. leith, 385. gen. dual leithi, 401.

lí *beauty, lustre, glory.* nom. sg. lii, 409.

lín u,n. and m. *number, complement*, 4, 19, 445, etc. dat. sg., 220.

línaid *fills, flood, covers.* fut. 3rd sg. línfaid, 428; rel. línfus, 182, 195, 265.

loimm n. *sip, mouthful.* acc. plu. in phrase lommæ cróu *gushes of blood*, 301.

loinges, longas ā,f. *fleet, ships, naval expedition*, 100, 118. With meaning *invasion by sea*, gen. sg. loingsi, 463.

loiscid *burns, lays waste by fire.* pres. ind. 3rd sg. rel. loiscess, 458. fut. 3rd sg. loiscfid, 377, 453.

lo(i)sctech adj.,o/ā *burning.* As subst. *burner*, 414, 427.

lomm *bareness, poverty.* With intensive prefix imm- *great poverty.* gen. sg. imluim, 408.

lúaidre io,m.? *advantage, benefit?*

nom. plu. lúadri, 112.

lúan o,m. *Monday*, 259, 383, 409.

má' conj. *if*, 24, 398.

macc o,m. *son*, 72, 93, 170, etc. gen. sg. maic, 143, 170, 185, etc. gen. plu., 93. With meaning *descendant*, 401.

maccdacht indecl. adj. *young, of marriageable age.* maccthacht, 32.

mag s,n. *plain.* acc. sg., 30, 76, 313. dat. sg. maig, 188, 282, 319. gen. sg. maigi, 92, 198. nom. plu. maigi, 159. acc. sg. in compound hÉrendmaig *the plain of Ireland*, 176.

maidid In phrase m. re A for B *it breaks before A on B*, i.e. *A defeats B.* fut. 3rd sg. memais(s), 131, 253, 279, etc.; memaid, 278. In phrase m. A la B *A is defeated by B.* pres. ind. pass. plu. maidtir, 94.

maidm n,n. and m. *defeat.* In compound bandmaidm *deed of defeat*, i.e. *defeat*, 404.

maín, moín i,f. *benefit*, 125. With meaning *treasure*, gen. plu. maíni, 445.

maínech, moínech adj.,o/ā *wealthy, precious*, 266.

mairg, maircc indecl. subst., m. and f. *sorrow, woe*, 116, 287. gen. sg. 24, 166.

máirt i,f. *(a battle on a) Tuesday*, 130, 139, 197, etc. dat. sg., 196. With día *day* (plus qualifying gen.), 77, 132, 441; with die / dië, 320, 354.

maith adj.,i *good*, 161, 172. As subst. i,n. (later m.) *good (person).* gen. plu. maithe, 154.

marb adj.,o/ā *dead*, 132, 417. Used

with cop. as periphrasis for verb *to die*, 428. As subst. o,m. *a dead person*, nom. plu. mairb, 92, 311. gen. plu., 225.

marbaid *kills.* perf. 3rd sg. ro marb, 210. perf. pass. sg. ro marbad, 366, 384.

marcach o,m. *rider, horseman*, 25, 28. gen. sg. marcaig, 24.

martrae iā,f. *martyrdom, violent death.* acc. sg. martrai, 178.

matan, maiten ā,f. *morning (battle)*, 1, 92, 114, etc. nom. sg. madan, 89, 448; maten, 303. acc. sg. matin, 119. In compound dergmaten *red*, i.e. *bloody morning (battle)*, 229. nom. plu. dercmaitni, 239. acc. plu. der[g]maitni, 69.

máthair r,f. *mother*, 355, 374, 389, etc.

mén i *mouth, opening.* acc. sg., 305.

mend adj.,o/ā *stammering, inarticulate.* As subst. *stammerer.* acc. sg., 363.

mé(i)t f. *greatness, size, amount*, 31. dat. sg. méid, 23. gen. sg. méti, 36.

meth o and i, n. and m. *decline, failure.* acc. sg., 144.

mí s,m. *month.* dat. sg. mís, 331.

míad o,n. and m. *honour, dignity, status*, 413.

mid u,n. and m. *mead.* gen. sg. meda, 417.

milliud u,m. *the act of destroying, ruining*, 397.

minn o,n. and m. *an insignia, a crown.* dat. plu. minnaib, 252.

mo' poss. adj. 1st sg. *my*, 40.

moch adj.,o/ā *early*, 2.

mochtaide adj.,io/iā *great, mighty.* nom. sg. m. mochtaidi, 244.

mór adj.,o/ā *big, large, great*, 36, 123, 143, etc. acc. sg. f. móir, 22, 243. dat. sg. f. móir, 244. dat. sg. n. már, 281. gen. sg. n. móir, 181. As subst. o,n. (later m.) *a great amount, many*, 24, 179, 197, etc.

móraid *exalts, makes great(er), increases, (assembles).* fut. 3rd sg. rel. mórfass, 211. fut. 3rd plu. mórfait, 180. fut. pass. plu. mórfuitir, 106; mórfaitir, 159, 160.

mortlaid ā,f. *large number of deaths, a plague*, 240.

múcna adj.,io/iā *stern, gloomy.* As subst. *sorrow.* nom. plu., 241.

muir i,n. and m. (later also f.) *the sea*, 138, 182, 316, etc. acc. sg., 108, 284, 295, etc. dat. sg., 281, 347. Muir nIcht *The English Channel.* acc. sg., 176.

mullach o,m. (also treated as s,n.) *crown of the head.* dat. sg., 32.

ná rel. part. 3rd sg. used in neg. *which ... not*, 18.

nach disjunctive neg. conj. *nor*, 37, 54.

naiscid *binds, exacts a pledge.* fut. pass. plu. nensitir, 159.

nammá adv. *only, merely*, 78, 95, 99, etc.

nathair k,f. *snake, serpent.* gen. sg. nathrach, 415.

nech indef pron. m. *any one*, 350.

nem s,n. *heaven.* dat. sg. nim, 364.

nert o,n. and m. *power, might.* dat. sg. neort, 127.

1 ní adv. of negation, 11, 54, 59, etc.

2 ní indef pron. (n. of nech) *something*, 269. as pred. of cop. *something that is of consequence*, 277.

nia d,m. *a warrior, champion.* In compound rígniä *royal-champion*,

139.

nó conj. *or*, 393, 410, 441, etc.

noí n- indecl. num. adj. *nine*. noí, 100, 460; noii, 226.

noíbaid *blesses, sanctifies*. pres. ind. 3rd sg. rel. noíbas, 136.

nóïd, nóithid *makes known, spreads the fame of, celebrates*. fut. 3rd sg. rel. nóifidius, 182. fut. pass. sg. nóifidir, 469. fut. pass. plu. nóitfitir, 159; nóifitir, 292.

noíl k (later ā),f. *oath*. acc. sg., 382.

nóin f. *mid-afternoon*. íar nóin *late afternoon, evening*, 239.

nóithech adj.,o/ā *notable, distinguished*. As subst. *distinguished (one)*, 174.

núall o,n. and m. *acclamation*, 425.

1 ó', úa' prep. with dat. *from*, 50, 289, 364, etc. Plus 2nd sg. aff. pron. húait, 43; 3rd sg. aff. pron. m. húad, 154. Plus def. art. sg. f. ónd, 316.

2 ó conj. *after*, 49.

3 ó s,n. *(curved) handle*. dat. sg. óu, 34.

oc prep. with dat. *at (the occasion of)*, 188. ic(c), 12, 252; ig, 236; uc, 351. meaning *to*, with aff. pron. 3rd sg. m. occa, 124; denoting *possession*, occai, 421.

ocht n- num. adj. *eight*, 46, 53, 314.

ochtach ā,f. *ridge-pole*. dat. sg. ochtaig, 31.

ocus conj. *and*, 17; is, 284.

óen, oín num. adj. and pron. *one*, 360. As indef. pron. *one, an individual*, 127.

óenach o,n. and m. *assembly, gathering, fair*, 16. gen. sg. óenaich, 17.

ogum o,m. *ogham*. acc. sg., 52.

oirgid *kills, destroys*. fut. 3rd pl.

iurait, 214.

ol defective vb said, *says*, 14, 19, 20, etc. Mid. Ir. variant for, 24.

ól o and u,m. *a drink, a draught*. dat. sg. óul, 417.

olc(c) adj. and subst. As subst. o,n. (later m.) *misfortune*, 458.

oll adj.,o/ā *great*, 106, 218. nom. plu. f. ola, 121.

or, ur o,m. *boundary, extreme, end*. acc. plu. uru, 447.

ór o,m. *gold*. dat. sg. ór, 33, 34. gen. sg. óir, 34; plus demonstr. óir-se, 58, 79; óir-si, 96, 134.

órdae adj.,io/iā *made of gold, golden*, 30. órdai, 32. dat. plu. órdaib, 33.

orgun ā,f. *slaying, massacre*. nom. sg. orggain, 126.

os(s) o,m. (orig. n.?) *ox, deer*. gen. sg. ois, 454.

ós, úas prep. with dat. *over, above*, 123, 247, 383, etc.; húas, 393.

ossnadach ā,f. *groaning (one), complaining (one)*. acc. sg., 449.

rád o,m. (orig. n.?) *act of saying*, 21.

ráithe iā,f. (orig. io,m.?) *a season*. nom. sg. ráithi, 466.

ré, ría n- prep. with dat. *in front of, before*, 2, 131, 254, etc. Plus 3rd sg. m. aff. pron. ríam, 2, 292, 335; riäm, 309. Plus 3rd sg. m. poss. adj. ríana, 360; réna, 268, 360.

ré io,n. and iā,f. *(period of) time, reign*, 142, 215, 270. acc. sg., 154, 156. dat. sg., 106, 137, 220, etc.

recht u,m. *authority, rule*, 245. gen. sg. in compound duimrecht[a] *wretched rule*, 372.

réim n,n. *advance, course*, 177. acc. sg., 230.

reithid *runs, hastens*. fut. 3rd sg.

reis, 388.

rí k,m. *king,* 71, 161, 172, etc. nom. sg. rii, 107, 216, 230, etc. acc. sg. ríg, 253. dat. sg., 14, 365. gen. sg., 27, 117, 354, etc. nom. plu., 324. acc. plu. rígu, 288. dat. plu. rígaib, 1. gen. plu., 19, 274. In compound a(i)rdrí *high-king,* 128, 276.

ríam advb *at any time previously, ever,* 30.

rían o,m. *sea, way.* acc. sg., 106. gen. sg. in phrase Mag Réin, lit.: *the plain of the sea,* i.e. *the sea, ocean,* 118.

rígdál ā,f. *royal assembly.* dat. sg. rígdáil, 113.

ríge io,n. (later f.) *sovereignty, kingship.* nom. sg. rígi, 354. acc. sg., 399. dat. sg., 387, 420. gen. sg., 318.

rigid *subdues, rules.* fut. 3rd sg. riris(s), 376. With meaning *fights, wins,* 423. With meaning *binds,* 382, 456.

rígrad ā,f. *kings, chiefs, princes* (coll.), 71. With meaning *a line / host of kings, royalty,* 228, 266.

rígráith m. and f. *royal fort, royal rampart.* acc. sg., 2.

rígsuide io,n. *throne, royal seat (palace).* dat. sg. rígsudiu, 35.

ro-cluinethar *hears.* impv. 2nd sg. cluinti, 118. pret. 3rd plu. co cúalatar, 23. pret. pass. sg. co closs, 7.

róe f. *rout, battle(field).* acc. sg. roí, 205, 376, 423, etc. dat. sg. roí, 268, 354. In compound cathróe *warlike battle.* gen. plu. cadræ, 60.

ro-finnadar with stem fit-, fet- (in pret. active with force of pres.)

knows. fut. 3rd sg. plus infix. pron. 3rd sg. m. Class A ra-fiastar, 314. fut. 3rd sg. -fiastar, 350. pret. 3rd plu. -fetatar, 22.

roínid *routs, wins.* In construction roínid re A for B, i.e. A gains a victory over B. fut. 3rd sg. ruínfid, 309. fut. pass. plu. roín-fitir, 291.

roithid *sets in motion, makes run.* fut. 3rd sg. roithfid, 467.

rón o,m. *a seal,* 281.

ros o,m. *a promontory, wood.* gen. sg. rois, 77, 232.

rúad adj.,o/ā *(dark) red [often of bloodstains], mighty.* dat. sg. f. rúaid, 199. gen. sg. m., 313.

1 rúanaid adj.,i *red, blushing.* As subst. *timid (one).* acc. sg., 236.

2 rúanaid i,m. *a strong man, champion,* 308.

ruidiud u,m. *the act of turning red, blushing,* 236.

rún ā,f. *mystery, secret.* acc. plu. rúna, 350.

rúd u,m. *a wood or forest.* dat. sg. in compound méthrúd *heavy forest,* 451.

sáegul o,m. *duration, period of time.* acc. sg., 42. gen. sg., saíguil, 397.

1 saigid *goes towards, seeks.* With meaning *attacks,* fut. pass. plu. sesaitir, 160.

2 saigid i,f. (vn. of saigid) *seeking.* acc. sg., 142.

sain adj.,i *different, distinct,* 466.

sainchan advb (sometimes written as two words) *hither and thither, here and there, round about,* 288.

saltraid *treads, stamps.* pret. 3rd sg. saltrais, 7.

samain f. *The first of November, the*

festival held on that date. dat. sg.
samuin, 259.

satharn(n) o *Saturday.* With die
day (plus qualifying gen.) die
sathairn(d) *Saturday*, 166, 255.

scál o,n. *supernatural or superhu-
man being, phantom, giant, hero*,
49, 59, 80, etc. acc. sg., 35. with
emph. pron. 1st sg., 38. gen. sg.
scáil, 54, 57.

scaraid *separates, relinquishes.* fut.
3rd sg. scairfaid, 169; (later with
ē-fut.) 3rd sg. rel. scérus, 438.

scél o,n. *story, news*, 84, 126, 143,
etc. In compound fírscél *true
story*, 316.

sceo conj. *and*, 129.

scíss o and u,m. and ā,f. *fatigue,
sorrow*, 243.

Scott o,m. *Irishman.* gen. plu., 299.

scrútan o *act of examining, investi-
gating.* dat. sg., 13.

secht n- num. adj. *seven*, 66, 69.

sechtmain f. *week.* dat. sg., 17.

seiche d,f. *the human skin.* dat. plu.
seichib, 332.

sí stressed form of pers. pron. 3rd sg.
f. *she*, 44, 447; sii, 44.

síabair i,m. *phantom, supernatural
being.* nom. plu. in compound
ilsíabrai *many phantoms*, 107.

síabraid i,m.? *one who is aroused
to martial fury, magic champion*,
250.

síar adv. *westwards.* In compound
síardes *south-westwards*, 335.

1 síd, síth s,n. (later u and o,m. and
ā,f.) *fairy-mound.* gen. sg. (or
plu.) síthi, 9.

2 síd, síth s,n. (later u and o,m. and
ā,f.) *peace*, 106, 218, 458, etc.

sídaige, síthaige io,m. *a síd-dweller.*
nom. plu. síthaigi, 107.

síl o,n. *seed, race.* dat. sg. 39, 97,
462; plus emph. pron. 2nd sg.,
20.

sin adj. demonstrative *that*, 4, 12,
18, etc. Also sen, 56, sein, 53. In
phrase in sein / and sein *then*, 9,
10, 13.

sínid *stretches, spreads.* fut. 3rd sg.
sínfid, 425. With meaning *lies
(scattered or prostrate)*, pres. ind.
3rd plu. sínit, 307.

sír adj.,o/ā *long, lasting*, 94.

síthaigid *pacifies.* fut. 3rd sg. rel.
síthaigfes, 446.

slaidid *destroys.* fut. 3rd sg. rel.
selus, 451.

slóg, slúag o,m. *host, army, crowd*,
129, 205, 334, etc. gen. sg. slúaig,
241. nom. plu., 130, 160, 162,
etc. dat. plu. slúagaib, 428.

slógad, slúagad o,n. *a hosting.* nom.
sg. slóged, 282.

slógadach, slúagadach adj.,o/ā
warlike, martial. As subst. *a
warrior*, 358.

slonnud u,m. *surname, family name,
lineage*, 40.

sluindid *tells, names.* sec. fut. 3rd
sg. -sluindfed, 11. perf. 3rd sg.
plus infix. pron. 3rd sg. f. Class A
rus-sluinn, 49.

so demonstr. pron. *this*, 92.

sochaide iā,f. *host, multitude.* gen.
sg. sochaidi, 171, 193.

soïd with fri *turns to/towards,
attacks.* fut. 3rd sg. rel. sóifes,
336.

són enclitic pron. *truly, indeed*, 36.

sondchad u,m.? *stave-battler*, 431.

srath (orig. o,m.?) *meadow or grassy
place near a river.* dat. sg., 94.

sreth ā,f. *stripe, line, edging.* dat.
plu. srethaib, 33.

suide anaphoric pronoun *this, that, the thing or person just mentioned.* nom. sg. m. (used as enclitic) side, 12; sidi, 38, 50. acc. sg. m. suide, 75, 140. acc. sg. n. sodain in phrase la sodain *then*, 25.

tabart ā,f. *giving.* dat. sg. tabairt, 51.

tailc(c) adj.,i *strong, vigorous, firm.* Used adverbally, 268.

tá(i)lcend o,m. lit.: *adze-head; a nickname of St. Patrick, a cleric*, 181, 306, 446. gen. sg. táilcind, 191. nom. plu. táilcind, 184. gen. plu., 469.

tair adv. *(in the) east*, 198.

tairngertaid i,m.? *prophesied one.* nom. sg. tairngertaig, 202.

talam n,m. *ground.* acc. sg. talmain, 46, 47. dat. sg., 271, 454.

tan ā?,f. *time.* In phrase in tan(d) *when*, 48, 327, 336. In phrase nach tain *whenever*, 299.

tangnacht ā,f. *treachery, deceit.* gen. sg. tangnachte, 215.

tar, dar prep. with acc. *over, across*, 76, 108, 118, etc. With meaning *against, in violation of*, 428.

tascur o,m. *an expedition from across the sea*, 181.

tech, teg s,n. (later m.) *house*, 30, 54. acc. sg., 31. dat. sg. taig, 35, 44, 84, etc. In compound táilcentech *monastery (of Armagh).* acc. sg., 328. dat. sg. táilcentaig, 320, 367. See Murray (1999b).

techt ā,f. *act of coming, going.* dat. sg., 341. With meaning *messenger*, 364.

tegdais ī, i and ā,f. *house, dwelling.* nom. plu. in phrase tegdaisi táilcend *monasteries*, 469.

teine d,m. (later also f.) *fire.* nom. sg. teni, 412. dat. sg. tein, 347. gen. sg. tened, 76, 458. In phrase teine gelán *lightning*, 441.

téit *goes, proceeds.* fut. 3rd sg. regaid, 253, 469. fut. 3rd sg. rel. regus, 316. sec fut. 3rd sg. no regad, 10. pret. 3rd sg. luid, 48. pret. 3rd plu. lotar, 31, 53. perf. 3rd plu. do-cótar, 30; rel. do-chótar, 23.

tercae iā,f. *scarcity, lack.* gen. sg. tercai, 408.

termann o,m. *the lands of a church or monastic settlement within which rights of sanctuary prevailed*, 328.

tessbaid f. *lack, loss*, 407.

tes(s) adv. *(in the) south (of)*, 108, 312, 431, etc. As adj. *southerly*, 352; *southern*, 401.

tíchtu n,f. *act of coming.* gen. sg. tíchtan, 342.

tigerna io,m. *lord, chief.* nom. plu. tigernai, 286.

timchell o,n. (later m.) *act of going round, surrounding.* dat. sg. timchiul, 77. As adv. *around*, 300.

tind adj.,i *severe*, 312.

tír s,n. *land, territory*, 15, 16. dat. sg., 198. gen. sg. tíre, 15. acc. plu. tíri, 25; tíre, 295. nom. plu. in compound iltíre *many lands*, 180.

tocad o,[m.?] *good fortune, prosperity.* gen. sg. tocaid, 342.

*****tocaid** (used only in passive with ro) *destines.* ro thocad, 21.

tóe ā,f. *silence.* acc. sg. taí, 451.

tóeb o,m. (later ā,f. and u,m.) *side.* In phrase hi tóeb *beside, near*, 132.

togach adj.,o/ā *choice.* As subst. *chosen one,* 390.

togal ā,f. *besieging, destroying,* 175.

toichmech adj.,o/ā *marching, preceeding.* As subst. *head of marching column,* i.e. *leader, invader,* 151.

toicthech adj.,o/ā *prosperous, wealthy,* 371.

toísech adj.,o/ā *first.* As subst. o,m. dat. sg. toísiuch, 27.

tóla io,n. *inundation, incursion,* 128, 463.

tolgach adj.,o/ā *strong.* As subst. tolcach *strong one,* 414.

toll adj.,o/ā *pierced, perforated.* nom. plu. tuill, 433.

tond ā,f. *wave, abundance,* 136.

1 tor o,m. *tower, fortified building.* gen. sg. tuir, 175. With meaning *champion, hero,* 446. nom. plu. tuir, 159.

2 tor o,m. *host, multitude.* nom. plu. tuir, 343. acc. plu. turu, 414.

torad o,n. *produce, crop.* gen. sg. toraid, 392, 464. acc. plu. toirthiu, 458.

torc o,m. *boar.* Used fig. of a *chieftain, hero.* acc. plu. turcu, 452.

torcbál ā,f. *rising.* dat. sg. turcbáil, 2.

tosach o,n. (later m.) *first.* In phrase hi tosuch *at the start, beginning,* 260; hi tossach, 314.

tothaim(m) n,n. *act of falling, a fall, death,* 113, 143; tathaimm, 163; toitimm, 179; totim, 186. acc. sg., 190.

tráethaid *subdues, vanquishes.* fut. 3rd sg. tróethbaid, 302.

traig d,f. *foot.* nom. dual., 46. nom. plu. traigid, 31, 45, 46, etc.

trait adj.,i *quick.* comparative form

(used adverbally) traidiu, 26.

tre' prep. with acc. *through, by means of,* 52. With poss. adj. 3rd sg. m. tria, 432. With meaning *on account of,* with poss. adj. 3rd sg. m. tria, 191.

treb ā,f. *house, abode.* dat. sg. treiph, 29.

tregtach adj.,o/ā *painful, wounded.* nom. plu. tregtaig, 433.

treise iā,f.? *period of three days.* treissi, 11.

trén adj.,o/ā *strong, powerful,* 426. gen. sg. tríuin, 298.

tress u,m *contention, fight,* 312.

tressach adj.,o/ā *warlike, fierce.* As subst. in compound dergthresach *bloody fierce one,* 329.

trethan o,m. *thundering, fury.* acc. sg., 23.

trí num. adj. *three.* nom. m., 2, 157, 440. acc. m., 25. nom. f. teóra, 131, 144, 348, etc. acc. f., 101; deóra, 69. In adverbial phrase meaning *thrice* fo thrí, 116, 160, 467; fa thrí, 112; co fo thrí, 66, 114; co fo thrii, 107.

trom adj.,o/ā *heavy, difficult, grievous,* 51. gen. sg. truimm, 166. nom. plu. truim, 326.

trú k,m. and f. *a doomed person, a wretch,* 18. gen. plu. troch, 123, 310. In compound íartrú *black-wretch?* acc. sg. íartróg, 455.

túaid adv. *(in the) north.* As adj. *northern,* 401. As prep. (with acc.) túath, 240. In phrase fa thúaith *northwards,* 253.

túaim n,n. *peak, tip* (exact meaning uncertain). acc. sg. 46, 47.

túaiscert o (orig. n.?) *north.* dat. sg. túaiscirt, 283.

túaruscbáil (orig. ā,f.) *account,*

description, report, 342, 458.
túath ā,f. *people, tribe*, 402. acc. plu.
túatha, 100. With meaning *country,*
territory. dat. sg. túaith, 143.
tuidecht ā,f. *coming.* dat. sg., 307.
tuile io,n. *an abundance, plenty.* gen.
sg. tuile, 165.
úa io,m. *grandson*, 104; húa, 271.
úachtar o,n. (later m.) *upper part of a*
country. dat. sg. úachtur, 448.
úa(i)r (orig. ā,f.) *time, occasion.* dat.
sg. húair, 316. acc. sg. in phrase fri
oínhúair *at the same time*, 51.
úaite adj.,io/iā *few.* nom. plu. úati,
399.
úallach adj.,o/ā *proud, arrogant*, 170.
u(i)de io,n. (later m. and f.) *journey*,
74.
uile adj.,io/iā *all, every.* acc. sg. hule,
8. With meaning *whole, complete.*
nom. sg. huili, 386. dat. sg. huli,
420.
uisce io,m. *water*, 444.

153

KEVIN MURRAY

BIBLIOGRAPHY

Baumgarten, Rolf
— (1990) 'Etymological Aetiology in Irish Tradition', *Ériu* 41, 115-22.
Bănăţeanu, Vlad
— (1930) 'Die Legende von König Dathí', *ZCP* 18, 160-88.
Bergin, Osborn
— (1934-38) 'Syntax of the Verb in Old Irish', *Ériu* 12, 197-214.
Best, Richard I.
— (1928) 'Notes on Rawlinson B. 512', *ZCP* 17, 389-402.
Bhreathnach, Máire
— (1982) 'The Sovereignty Goddess as Goddess of Death', *ZCP* 39, 243-60.
Bieler, Ludwig
— (1979, Dublin) *The Patrician Texts in the Book of Armagh*, SLH 10.
Binchy, Daniel A.
— (1958) 'The Fair of Tailtiu and the Feast of Tara', *Ériu* 18, 113-38.
— (1962) 'Patrick and his Biographers: Ancient and Modern', *Studia Hibernica* 2, 7-173.
Borsje, Jacqueline
— (2002) 'Fate in Early Irish Texts', *Peritia* 16, 214-31.
Breatnach, Liam
— (1977) 'The Suffixed Pronouns in Early Irish', *Celtica* 12, 75-107.
— (1990) 'Varia v. 1: On the Nasalization of the Preverb *to*', *Ériu* 41, 139-40.
Breatnach, R.A.
— (1953) 'The Lady and the King: a Theme of Irish Literature', *Studies* 42, 321-36.
Byrne, Francis John
— (1964) 'Clann Ollaman Uaisle Emna', *Studia Hibernica* 4, 54-94.
— (1965) 'The Ireland of St. Columba', *Historical Studies* 5, 37-58.
— (1967) 'Seventh-century Documents', *IER* 108, 164-82.
— (1969, Dublin) *The Rise of the Uí Néill and the High-kingship of Ireland*, O'Donnell Lecture Series 13.
— (1971) 'Tribes and Tribalism in Early Ireland', *Ériu* 22, 128-66.
— (1973, London) *Irish Kings and High-kings*.
Byrne, Mary E.
— (1908, Halle) 'Airec Menman Uraird maic Coise', *Anecdota from Irish Manuscripts* ii, ed. O.J. Bergin, R.I. Best, K. Meyer & J.G. O'Keefe, 42-76.
Calder, George
— (1917, Edinburgh; repr. 1995, Dublin) *Auraicept na n-Éces: The Scholars' Primer.*
Carey, John
— (1981) 'The Name "Tuatha Dé Danann"', *Éigse* 18, ii, 291-4.
— (1982) 'The Location of the Otherworld in Irish Tradition', *Éigse* 19, 36-43.

154

— (1987) 'Time, Space and the Otherworld', *PHCC* 7, 1-27.

— (1989) 'Otherworlds and Verbal Worlds in Middle Irish Narrative', *PHCC* 9, 31-42.

— (1991) 'The Irish 'Otherworld': Hiberno-Latin Perspectives', *Éigse* 25, 154-9.

— (1995) 'On the Interrelationships of Some *Cín Dromma Snechtai* Texts', *Ériu* 46, 71-92.

— (1996) 'The Narrative Setting of *Baile Chuinn Chétchathaig*', *ÉC* 32, 189-201.

— (1998, Dublin) *King of Mysteries: Early Irish Religious Writings.*

— (1999) 'Varia I: *Ferp Cluche*', *Ériu* 50, 165-8.

— (forthcoming) 'Tara and the Supernatural', *The Kingship and Landscape of Tara*, ed. E. Bhreathnach.

Carney, James

— (1961, Dublin) *The Problem of St. Patrick.*

— (1989, Tübingen) 'The Dating of Archaic Irish Verse', *Early Irish Literature – Media and Communication / Mündlichkeit und Schriftlichkeit in der frühen irischen Literatur*, ScriptOralia 10, ed. S.N. Tranter & H.L.C. Tristram, 39-55.

Chadwick, Nora K.

— (1935) 'Lug Scéith Scál Find', *Scottish Gaelic Studies* 4, 1-5.

— (1967) 'The Borderland of the Spirit World in Early European Literature', *Trivium* 2, 17-36.

— (1968) 'Dreams in Early European Literature', *Celtic Studies: Essays in Memory of Angus Matheson*, ed. J. Carney and D. Greene, 33-50.

Charles-Edwards, Thomas

— (2000, Cambridge) *Early Christian Ireland.*

Charles-Edwards, Thomas & Kelly, Fergus

— (1983, Dublin) *Bechbretha: An Old Irish Law-tract on Bee-keeping.*

Connon, Anne

— (2000, Dublin) 'The *Banshenchas* and the Uí Néill Queens of Tara', *Seanchas: Studies in Early and Medieval Irish Archaeology, History and Literature in Honour of Francis J. Byrne*, ed. A.P. Smyth, 98-108.

Dillon, Myles

— (1943-6) 'The Yew of the Disputing Sons', *Ériu* 14, 154-65.

— (1946, Oxford; repr. Dublin, 1994) *The Cycles of the Kings.*

— (1948, Chicago; repr. Dublin, 1994) *Early Irish Literature.*

— (1952) 'The Story of the Finding of Cashel', *Ériu* 16, 61-73.

— (1953, Dublin) *Serglige Con Culainn*, MMIS 14.

— (1973) 'The Consecration of Irish Kings', *Celtica* 10, 1-8.

Doan, James E.

— (1985) 'Sovereignty Aspects in the Roles of Women in Medieval Irish and Welsh Society', *PHCC* 5, 87-102.

Dobbs, Margaret E.

— (1921) 'The History of the Descendants of Ir', *ZCP* 13, 308-59.

— (1930) 'The Ban-shenchus', *RC* 47, 283-339 (metrical version).
— (1931) 'The Ban-shenchus', *RC* 48, 163-233 (prose version).
— (1932) 'The Ban-shenchus', *RC* 49, 437-89 (indices).

Enright, Michael J.
— (1996, Dublin) *Lady with a Mead Cup.*

Flower, Robin
— (1926, London) *Catalogue of Irish Manuscripts in the British Museum,* vol. 2.

Fraser, John, Paul Grosjean and James G. O'Keefe
— (1931-33, London) *Irish Texts*, i-v.

Gantz, Jeffrey
— (1976, Penguin) *The Mabinogion.*

Gray, Elizabeth A.
— (1983) *Cath Maige Tuired*, ITS 52.

Gwynn, Lucius
— (1912) 'De Síl Chonairi Móir', *Ériu* 6, 130-43.

Hanna, J.W.
— (1856) 'The Battle of "Magh Rath": Its True Site Determined', *Ulster Journal of Archæology* 4, 53-61.

Henderson, George
— (1899, London) *Fled Bricrend*, ITS 2.

Hennessy, William M.
— (1875, Dublin) *The Book of Fenagh*, trans. D.H. Kelly.

Herbert, Máire
— (1988, Oxford; repr. Dublin, 1996) *Iona, Kells and Derry: The History and Hagiography of the Monastic Familia of Columba.*
— (1992, Edinburgh) 'Goddess and King: The Sacred Marriage in Early Ireland', *Women and Sovereignty*, ed. L.O. Fradenburg, 264-75.

Hudson, Benjamin
— (1996, Westport) *The Prophecy of Berchán.*
— (2001 [2002], Dublin) 'The Practical Hero', *Ogma: Essays in Celtic Studies in Honour of Próinséas Ní Chatháin*, ed. M. Richter and J.-M. Picard, 151-64.

Hull, Vernam
— (1947) 'Conall Corc and the Corco Luigde', *PMLA* 62, 887-909.
— (1952) 'Geneamuin Chormaic', *Ériu* 16, 79-85.

Jackson, Kenneth
— (1934) 'Tradition in Early Irish Prophecy', *Man* 34, 67-70.

Jaski, Bart
— (1999, [Summer]) 'Cú Chulainn, *Gormac* and *Dalta* of the Ulstermen', *CMCS* 37, 1-31.

Kelleher, John V.
— (1971) 'The Táin and the Annals', *Ériu* 22, 107-27.

Kelly, Fergus

— (1988, Dublin) *A Guide to Early Irish Law*.

Knott, Eleanor

— (1960, Cork; 2nd ed.) *Irish Classical Poetry*.

Lloyd-Jones, J.

— (1947, Cork) 'The Compounds of *Gal*', *Féilscríbhinn Torna*, ed. S. Pender, 83-9.

Loomis, Roger Sherman

— (1963, Cardiff) *The Grail: From Celtic Myth to Christian Symbol*.

Macalister, R.A. Stewart

— (1956) *Lebor Gabála Érenn* 5, ITS 44.

Mac Cana, Proinsias

— (1955-56, 1958-59) 'Aspects of the Theme of King and Goddess in Irish Literature', *ÉC* 7, i 76-114; ii 356-413; *ÉC* 8, iii 59-65.

— (1972) 'Mongán mac Fiachna and *Immram Brain*', *Ériu* 23, 102-42.

— (1975, Dublin) 'The Influence of the Vikings on Celtic Literature', *The Impact of the Scandinavian Invasions on the Celtic-speaking Peoples, c. 800-1100 A.D.*', ed. B. Ó Cuív, 78-118.

— (1976) 'The Sinless Otherworld of *Immram Brain*', *Ériu* 27, 95-115.

— (1980, Dublin) *The Learned Tales of Medieval Ireland*.

— (1987, An Cumann le Béaloideas Éireann) *'Fianaigecht* in the Pre-Norman Period', *Fiannaíocht: Essays on the Fenian Tradition of Ireland and Scotland*, ed. B. Almqvist, S. Ó Catháin and P. Ó Héalaí, 75-99 (= *Béaloideas* 54-5 [1986-7]).

MacCarthy, Bartholomew

— (1892, Dublin) *The Codex Palatino-Vaticanus no. 830*, TLS 3.

Mac Cionnaith, Láimhbheartach

— (1938, Baile Átha Cliath) *Dioghluim Dána*.

Mac Eoin, Gearóid

— (1968) 'The Mysterious Death of Loegaire mac Néill', *Studia Hibernica* 8, 21-48.

Mac Giolla Easpaig, Donall

— (1981) 'Nouns and Noun Compounds in Irish Placenames', *ÉC* 18, 151-63.

Mac Mathúna, Séamus

— (1985, Tübingen) *Immram Brain: Bran's Journey to the Land of the Women*.

MacNeill, Eóin

— (1913) 'Poems by Flann Mainistrech on the Dynasties of Ailech, Mide and Brega', *Archivium Hibernicum* 2, 37-99.

MacNeill, Máire

— (1962, London) *The Festival of Lughnasa*.

Marstrander, Carl

— (1911) 'A New Version of the Battle of Mag Rath', *Ériu* 6, 226-47.

McCone, Kim

— (1986i) 'Dubthach maccu Lugair and a Matter of Life and Death in the Pseudo-historical Prologue to the *'Senchas Már'*, *Peritia* 5, 1-35.

— (1986ii [Winter]) 'Werewolves, Cyclopses, *Díberga,* and *Fíanna:* Juvenile

Delinquency in Early Ireland', *CMCS* 12, 1-22.

— (1990, Maynooth) *Pagan Past and Christian Present in Early Irish Literature.*

— (2000, Maynooth) *Echtrae Chonnlai and the Beginnings of Vernacular Narrative Writing in Ireland.*

McManus, Damian

— (1991, Maynooth) *A Guide to Ogam.*

Meek, Donald

— (1986 [Summer]) 'The Banners of the Fian in Gaelic Ballad Tradition', *CMCS* 11, 29-69.

Meyer, Kuno

— (1901) 'Baile in Scáil', *ZCP* 3, 457-66.

— (1905, Oxford) *Cáin Adamnáin: An Old Irish Treatise on the Law of Adamnan*, Anecdota Oxoniensia, Medieval and Modern Series xii.

— (1909, Dublin) *A Primer of Irish Metrics.*

— (1910, Halle) 'Conall Corc and the Corco Luigde', *Anecdota from Irish Manuscripts* iii, ed. O.J. Bergin, R.I. Best, K. Meyer & J.G. O'Keefe, 57-63.

— (1913i) 'Baile Bricín', *ZCP* 9, 449-57.

— (1913ii) 'The Laud Synchronisms', *ZCP* 9, 471-85.

— (1918) 'Das Ende von Baile in Scáil', *ZCP* 12, 232-8.

— (1921) 'Corrigenda Zu Band xii', *ZCP* 13, 150.

Mulchrone, Kathleen

— (1939, Dublin) *Bethu Phátraic: The Tripartite Life of Patrick.*

Murphy, Gerard

— (1952) 'On the Dates of Two Sources Used in Thurneysen's Heldensage', *Ériu* 16, 145-51.

— (1961, Dublin) *Early Irish Metrics.*

Murray, Kevin (al. Caoimhín Ó Muirigh)

— (1999i) Varia vii: 'At(t)ba / Éc At(t)bai', *Ériu* 50, 185-7.

— (1999ii) '*Táilcentech* "the Monastery of Armagh"?', *Peritia* 13, 309-10.

— (2001i [2002], Dublin) '*Baile in Scáil* and *Echtrae Chormaic*', *Ogma: Essays in Celtic Studies in Honour of Próinséas Ní Chatháin*, ed. M. Richter and J.-M. Picard, 195-9.

— (2001ii) Review of Jacqueline Borsje, *From Chaos To Enemy: Encounters with Monsters in Early Irish Texts. An Investigation Related to the Process of Christianization and the Concept of Evil*, *ZCP* 52, 302-5.

— (2001iii) 'The Finding of the *Táin*', *CMCS* 41, 17-23.

— (2002) '*Baile in Scáil* and *Baile Bricín*', *Éigse* 33, 49-56.

— (2003) 'A Reading from *Scéla Mosauluim*', *ZCP* 53, 198-201.

— (forthcoming: i) 'The Manuscript Tradition of *Baile Chuind Chétchathaig* and its Relationship with *Baile in Scáil*', *The Kingship and Landscape of Tara*, ed. E. Bhreathnach.

— (forthcoming: ii) Review of B. Ó Cuív, *Catalogue of Irish Language Manuscripts in the Bodleian Library at Oxford and Oxford College Libraries*,

Part 1: Descriptions, ZCP 53.

Ní Bhrolcháin, Muireann
— (1982) 'The Manuscript Tradition of the Banshenchas', *Ériu* 33, 109-35.

Ní Chatháin, Próinséas
— (1979-80) 'Swineherds, Seers, and Druids', *Studia Celtica* 14/15, 200-11.
— (1991) 'Traces of the Cult of the Horse in Early Irish Sources', *JIES* 19, 123-31.
— (1996, Klett-Cotta) 'Ogham Terminology in Táin Bó Cuailnge', *Irland und Europa im früheren Mittelalter: Bildung und Literatur / Ireland and Europe in the Early Middle Ages: Learning and Literature*, ed. P. Ní Chatháin and M. Richter, 212-16.

Nic Dhonnchadha, Lil
— (1964, Dublin) *Aided Muirchertaig Meic Erca*, MMIS 19.

Ní Dhonnchadha, Máirín
— (1982) 'The Guarantor List of *Cáin Ádomnáin*', *Peritia* 1, 178-215.
— (2000, Dublin) 'On Gormfhlaith Daughter of Flann Sinna and the Lure of the Sovereignty Goddess', *Seanchas: Studies in Early and Medieval Irish Archaeology, History and Literature in Honour of Francis J. Byrne*, ed. A.P. Smyth, 225-37.

Ní Dhubhnaigh, Clodagh (al. Clodagh Downey)
— (2001, National University of Ireland, Unpublished Ph.D. Thesis) *Temair Breg, Baile na Fian and Echtra mac nEchdach Mugmedóin: An Edition, Translation and Comparative Analysis*.
— (2004, Celtic Studies Publications, Aberystwyth) 'Intertextuality in *Echtra mac nEchdach Mugmedóin*', *Cín Chille Cúile: Texts, Saints and Places – Essays in Honour of Pádraig Ó Riain*, ed. J. Carey, M. Herbert & K. Murray, 77-104.

Ní Mhaonaigh, Máire
— (2002) 'Tales of Three Gormlaiths in Medieval Irish Literature', *Ériu* 52, 1-24.

O'Brien, Michael A.
— ([*c*. 1954]; printed, not published) *Irish Origin Legends*.

Ó Broin, Tomás
— (1990) 'Lia Fáil: Fact and Fiction in the Tradition', *Celtica* 21, 393-401.
— (1996) 'Doomed Kings?', *Éigse* 29, 64.

Ó Buachalla, Breandán
— (1989, Maynooth) 'Aodh Eanghach and the Irish King-Hero', *Sages, Saints and Storytellers: Celtic Studies in Honour of Professor James Carney*, ed. D. Ó Corráin, L. Breatnach and K. McCone, 200-32.

Ó Buachalla, Liam
— (1961) 'The Leinster Tribute Feud', *JCHAS* 66, 13-25.

Ó Cathasaigh, Tomás
— (1977, Dublin) *The Heroic Biography of Cormac mac Airt*.
— (1977-78) 'The Semantics of *Síd*', *Éigse* 17, 137-55.

— (1983, Cork) 'Cath Maige Tuired as Exemplary Myth', *Folia Gadelica*: *Essays presented to R.A. Breatnach*, ed. P. de Brún, S. Ó Coileáin and P. Ó Riain, 1-19.

— (1986) 'The Sister's Son in Early Irish Literature', *Peritia* 5, 128-60.

— (1989) 'The Eponym of Cnogba', *Éigse* 23, 27-38.

— (1990) 'On the Cín Dromma Snechta Version of *Togail Brudne Uí Dergae*', *Ériu* 41, 103-14.

— (1994) 'The Threefold Death in Early Irish Sources', *Studia Celtica Japonica* 6, 53-75.

— (1995) 'The Phantom's Vision', Unpublished translation of §§1-9, 'The Hero of Irish Myth and Saga: Course Materials' (Harvard University) 110-12.

Ó Cearúil, Micheál

— (2000, National University of Ireland, Unpublished Ph.D. Thesis) *Tairngreachtaí Míchinniúna agus a gCúlra*.

— (2003, An Daingean) *Torann a Dheireadh! Léas ar an Eascateolaíocht, ar an mBean Sí agus ar an Lia Fáil*, Dán agus Tallann 12.

Ó Concheanainn, Tomás

— (1971) 'Topographical Notes – I: Cermna in Meath', *Ériu* 22, 87-96.

— (1975) '"Aided Nath Í" and the Scribes of Leabhar na hUidhre', *Éigse* 16, ii, 146-62.

— (1988 [Winter]) 'A Connacht Medieval Literary Heritage: Texts Derived from Cín Dromma Snechtai through Leabhar na hUidhre', *CMCS* 16, 1-40.

Ó Corráin, Donnchadh

— (1971) 'Topographical Notes – II: Mag Femin, Femen, and Some Early Annals', *Ériu* 22, 97-9.

Ó Cróinín, Dáibhí

— (1981) 'The Oldest Irish Names for the Days of the Week', *Ériu* 32, 95-114.

— (1995, London & New York) *Early Medieval Ireland: 400-1200*.

Ó Cuív, Brian

— (1963) 'Literary Creation and Irish Historical Tradition', *PBA* 49, 233-62.

— (2001, Dublin) *Catalogue of Irish Language Manuscripts in the Bodleian Library at Oxford and Oxford College Libraries, Part 1: Descriptions*.

O'Curry, Eugene

— (1861, Dublin) *Lectures on the Manuscript Materials of Ancient Irish History*.

O Daly, Máirín

— (1952) 'A Poem on the Airgialla', *Ériu* 16, 179-88.

— (1975, Dublin) *Cath Maige Mucrama*, ITS 50.

Ó Dubhthaigh, Bearnárd

— (1966) 'A Contribution to the History of Drumsnat', *Clogher Record* 6, 71-103.

Ó Gealbháin, Séamas

— (1991) 'The Double Article and Related Features of Genitive Syntax in Old Irish and Middle Welsh', *Celtica* 22, 119-44.

O'Grady, Standish Hayes
— (1892, London) *Silva Gadelica*, i-ii.
O'Kearney, Nicholas
— (1856, Dublin) *The Prophecies of SS. Columkille, Maeltamlacht, Ultan, Seadhna, Coireall, Bearcan, etc. ... with Literal Translation and Notes.*
O'Keefe, James G.
— (1934, London) 'A Prophecy on the High-kingship of Ireland', *Irish Texts* 4, 39-41.
O'Leary, Philip
— (1986 [Summer]) 'A Foreseeing Driver of an Old Chariot: Regal Moderation in Early Irish Literature', *CMCS* 11, 1-16.
O Lochlainn, Colm
— (1940, Dublin) 'Roadways in Ancient Ireland', *Féil-sgríbhinn Eóin Mhic Néill*, ed. J. Ryan, 465-74.
Ó Máille, Tomás
— (1910, Manchester) *The Language of the Annals of Ulster.*
— (1927) 'Medb Chruachna', *ZCP* 17, 129-46.
Ó Murchadha, Diarmuid
— (2004) 'Dún Cermna: A Reconsideration', *Éigse* 34, 71-89.
Ó Néill, Pádraig P.
— (2001 [2002], Dublin) 'The Old-Irish Glosses of the *Prima Manus* in Würzburg, M.P.Th.F.12: Text and Context Reconsidered', *Ogma: Essays in Celtic Studies in Honour of Próinséas Ní Chatháin*, ed. M. Richter and J.-M. Picard, 230-42.
O'Rahilly, Thomas F.
— (1942) 'Notes, Mainly Etymological', *Ériu* 13, 144-219.
— (1943-6) 'On the Origin of the Names *Érainn* and *Ériu*', *Ériu* 14, 7-28.
— (1946, Dublin) *Early Irish History and Mythology.*
Ó Riain, Pádraig
— (1977) 'Traces of Lug in Early Irish Hagiographical Tradition', *ZCP* 36, 138-56.
— (1978, Dublin) *Cath Almaine*, MMIS 25.
Petrie, George
— (1872, Dublin) *Christian Inscriptions in the Irish Language*, vol. 1, ed. M. Stokes.
Plummer, Charles
— (1922, Oxford) *Bethada Náem nÉrenn*, 2 vols.
Pődör, Dóra
— (1999, Trinity College Dublin, Unpublished Ph.D. Thesis) *Twelve Poems Attributed to Fland Manistrech from the Book of Leinster.*
Pokorny, Julius
— (1921) 'Nachlass Kuno Meyer: Der Anfang von Baile in Scáil', *ZCP* 13, 371-82.
— (1923, Halle) *Historical Reader of Old Irish.*

Scowcroft, Mark
— (1995) 'Abstract Narrative in Ireland', *Ériu* 46, 121-58.
Sessle, Erica J.
— (1994) 'Exploring the Limitations of the Sovereignty Goddess through the Role of Rhiannon', *PHCC* 14, 9-13.
Sharpe, Richard
— (1979) 'Hiberno-Latin *laicus*, Irish *láech* and the Devil's Men', *Ériu* 30, 75-92.
Shaw, Francis
— (1947, Cork) 'Fe Ille Fe Innund', *Féilscríbhinn Torna*, ed. S. Pender, 77-82.
— (1962) 'Postmortem on the Second Patrick', *Studies* 51, 237-67.
Sims-Williams, Patrick
— (1990, Van Nuys) 'Some Celtic Otherworld Terms', *Celtic Language, Celtic Culture: A Festschrift for Eric P. Hamp*, ed. A.T.E. Matonis and D.F. Melia, 57-81.
Skene, William F.
— (1868, Edinburgh) *The Four Ancient Books of Wales*, 2 vols.
Smith, Peter J.
— (2001 [2002], Dublin) 'Early Irish Historical Verse: The Evolution of a Genre', *Irland und Europa im früheren Mittelalter: Texte und Überlieferung / Ireland and Europe in the Early Middle Ages: Texts and Transmissions*, ed. P. Ní Chatháin and M. Richter, 326-41.
Smyth, Alfred P.
— (1979, New Jersey and Dublin) *Scandanavian York and Dublin*, vol. 2.
Stokes, Whitley
— (1887, London) *The Tripartite Life of Patrick*, 2 vols.
— (1890, Oxford) *Lives of the Saints from the Book of Lismore*.
— (1891, Leipzig) 'The Irish Ordeals, Cormac's Adventure in the Land of Promise, and the Decision as to Cormac's Sword', *Irische Texte* 3.1, 183-229.
— (1894) 'The Prose Tales in the Rennes Dindšenchas', *RC* 15, 272-336.
— (1903) 'The Death of Crimthann Son of Fidach and the Adventures of the Sons of Eochaid Muigmedón', *RC* 24, 172-207.
— (1905i) 'The Evernew Tongue', *Ériu* 2, 96-162.
— (1905ii, London; repr. 1984, Dublin) *Félire Óengusso Céli Dé*, HBS.
— (1908) 'The Training of Cúchulainn', *RC* 29, 109-52.
Strachan, John
— (1904) 'The Infixed Pronoun in Middle Irish', *Ériu* 1, 153-79.
Thomson, Derick S.
— (1986, Dublin) *Branwen Uerch Lyr*, MMWS 2.
Thomson, R.L.
— (1997, Dublin) *Ystorya Gereint uab Erbin*, MMWS 10.
Thurneysen, Rudolf
— (1912) 'Zur irischen Grammatik und Litteratur', *ZCP* 8, 64-81.

— (1912-13, Berlin) *Zu irischen Handschriften und Litteraturdenkmälern*, Abhandlungen der königlichen Gesellschaft der Wissenschaften zu Göttingen, Phil.-hist. Klasse, neue Folge, Band 14 (nos 2 & 3).

— (1921, Halle) *Die irische Helden- und Königsage bis zum siebzehnten Jahrhundert.*

— (1930) 'Allerlei Keltisches', *ZCP* 18, 108-10.

— (1933) 'Zur Göttin *Medb*', *ZCP* 19, 352-3.

— (1936) 'Baile in Scáil', *ZCP* 20, 213-27.

Todd, James H.

— (1867, London) *Cogad Gaedhel re Gallaibh: The War of the Gaedhil with the Gaill.*

Tolstoy, Nikolai

— (1985, Sceptre) *The Quest for Merlin.*

Toner, Gregory

— (2000) 'Reconstructing the Earliest Irish Tale Lists', *Éigse* 32, 88-120.

Trindade, W.A.

— (1986) 'Irish Gormlaith as a Sovereignty Figure', *ÉC* 23, 143-56.

van Hamel, Anton G.

— (1933, Dublin) *Compert Con Culainn and Other Stories*, MMIS 3.

— (1941, Dublin) *Immrama*, MMIS 10.

Vendryes, Joseph

— (1953, Dublin) *Airne Fíngein*, MMIS 15.

Walsh, Paul

— (1941) 'The Ua Maelechlainn Kings of Meath', *IER* 57, 165-83.

— (1947, Dublin) *Irish Men of Learning.*

Index Nominum

All names given in italics have a full paragraph devoted to them in BS. Further information given only on those other individuals mentioned in the text.

Áed Allán (alias *Úaridnach*) *mac Domnaill* §29.

Áed Allán mac Fergaile §43.

Áed Engach §62 (see Introduction 3 & **6.2**).

Áed Finnlíath mac Néill §51.

Áed mac Ainmerech §31.

Áed mac Conchobuir §52. King of Connachta. Died in a battle against the Norse (fighting alongside Flann Sinna mac Máele Sechnaill), *AU* 888.5.

Áed mac Dlúthaig §36. Styled king of Fir Chúl, *ATig.* 688. Killed Fínnachta mac Dúnchada, *AU* 695.1. Obituary given, *AU* 701.6.

Áed Muinderg §46. Son of Flaithbertach mac Loingsich of the Cenél Conaill. His father was the last Cenél Conaill king of Tara.

Áed Oirdnide mac Néill §47.

Áed Rón mac Béicce Bairche §43. King of Ulaid. Killed in the battle of Fochairt, *AU* 735.2. See *LL* 5806.

Áed Sláine mac Díarmata §30.

Ailill Aulom §11. Father (or son) of the eponymous ancestor of the Eóganacht of Munster.

Ailill mac Domangairt §29.

Ailill Molt mac Nath Í §20.

Ailill Olgné §10.

Ainmere mac Sétna §25.

Ardgal §22. Ardgal mac Conaill Cremthainne, grandson of Níall Noígíallach. He fell in the battle

of Detnae, *AU* 520.2 or 523.1.

Aróc ingen ríg Fer Cúl, §50. See Introduction **6.5**.

Art mac Cuinn §11.

Athba §56.

Aurthuile §18.

Báetán mac Muirchertaig §26.

Blathmac mac Áeda Sláine §34.

Bloc §1. One of Conn Cétchathach's druids.

Bluiccne §1. One of Conn Cétchathach's druids.

Brandub mac Echach §28. King of Laigin. Killed Áed mac Ainmirech, *AU* 598.2. Defeated by Áed Úaridnach in the battle of Slaebre, *AU* 605.1. Slain by his own kin, *AU* 605.2.

Brían Bóruma mac Cennétig §57.

Cairpre Lifechair §14.

Carrach Calma §56. Carrach Calma 'the brave scabby one' was an epithet of Donnchad mac Murchada maic Óengusa maic Flainn Sinna. His death is recorded in *CS* 967 (recte 969; cf. *NHI* 9, 130). See Walsh (1941) 168.

Cellach (Locha Cimbi) §39. Cellach mac Ragallaig, king of Connachta, defeated Loingsech mac Óengusa in the battle of Corann, co. Sligo, *AU* 703.2. His death, after entering clerical life, is recorded in *AU* 705.3.

Cellach mac Dúnchada §46. King of Laigin from 760 to his death (recorded in *AU* 776.8).

Cenn Fáeled mac Blathmaic §38.

Cerball / Cairell §63 (see Introduction **3**).

Cessarnn §1. One of Conn Cétchathach's *fili*.

Cináed úa Conaing §42. Cináed mac Írgalaig maic Conaing, king of Tara before Flaithbertach mac Loingsich. He was killed in the battle of Druimm Corcáin by Flaithbertach, *AU* 728.1.

Colla Úais §19.

Colla, na trí §17. The three Collas (Colla Úais, Colla Menn, Colla Fo Chríth), supposed ancestors of the Airgíalla and nephews to Echu Mugmedón. A claim is made for Colla Úais as king of Tara in §19.

Colmán Mór mac Díarmata §33. *BS* mistakenly records that he was killed in the battle of Dathe. It was his brother, Colmán Becc mac Díarmata (ancestor of Caílle Follamain), who was killed in this battle, *AU* 587.1. Colmán Mór (ancestor of Clann Cholmáin) was either killed *AU* 555.2 or *AU* 558.1.

Conchobar §10.

Conchobar §17.

Conchobar mac Donnchada §48.

Congal Cinn Magair mac Fergussa §40.

Congalach Cnogba mac Maíl Mithig §55.

Conn Cétchathach §10.

Corb §1. One of Conn Cétchathach's *fili*.

Cormac úa Cuinn §13.

Cummascach and **Li[...]** §60. The last occurence of the name Cum(m)ascach in *AU* is s.a. 1004.5.

Díarmait mac Áeda Sláine §35.

Díarmait mac Cerbaill §27.

Domnall mac Muirchertaig §28.

Domnall mac Áeda §32.

Domnall Midi mac Murchada §44.

Domnall úa Néill §56.

Donnchad Donn mac Flainn §54.

Donnchad Midi mac Domnaill §46.

Dúnflaith ingen Flaithbertaig maic Loingsich, §47. See Introduction **6.5**.

Dúnflaith ingen Muirchertaig, §57. See Introduction **6.5**.

Dúngal mac Fergaile §52. King of Osraige. Death recorded in *AU* 842.13.

Dúnlang, na dá §62.

Echu Mugmedón §17.

Énna §13

Eochaid §1. One of Conn Cétchathach's *fili*.

Eochaid mac Domnaill §26.

Eochaid Tóebfota §13. Son of Ailill Aulom of the Eóganacht of Munster. His death is recorded in *AFM* 241 (i, 114) in the battle of Ferta, waged by Cormac úa Cuind.

Fergal §64 (see Introduction **3**).

Fergal mac Máele Dúin §41.

Fergus [ardrí Ulad] §13. Fergus Dubdétach, king of the Ulaid, killed by Cormac úa Cuind in the battle of Crinna.

Fergus §10.

Fergus mac Muirchertaig §28.

Fíachra mac Cathail §46. Chief of Fir Chúl, *AFM* 781 [recte 786] (i, 388). Killed in the battle of Lía Finn, waged by Donnchad Midi, *AU* 786.6.

Fíachu Sroiphtine §15.

Fíngin Corad §56.

Fínnachta §47. Probably refers to

165

Fínnachta mac Domnaill, slain in the battle of Druimm Ríg in *AU* 797.3. Could possibly refer to Fínnachta mac Follamain, however, who fell in the same contention.

Fínśnechta Fledach mac Dúnchada §36.

Flaithbertach mac Loingsig §42.

Flaithbertach mac Muirchertaig Uí Néill §58 (see Introduction **3**).

Flann Cinuch §65 (see Introduction **3** & **5.6**).

Flann ingen Dúngaili ríg Osraide, §52. See Introduction **6.5**.

Flann Sinna mac Máele Sechnaill §52.

Fogartach mac Néill §40.

Follaman mac Con Congalt §46 King of Mide, died *AU* 766.2. Eponymous ancestor of Caílle Follamain (Clann Cholmáin Bicc).

Forannán §10

Fothad §11

Fothad mac Crúaid §15

Furbaide Menn Macha §56. There seems to be some contamination here. The person for whom Carn Furbaidi in N. co. Longford is named is Furbaide Fer Benn (see *MD* iv, 30-5). The source of this contamination may be the list of Clann Chonchobuir meic Fachtna given in *Senchas Síl hÍr* (*CGH* 157, 53-4) where the 2nd and 3rd names noted are Cúscraid Menn Macha and Furbaide Fer Benn (cf. *CA* nos. 255 & 256).

Glúnḟinn §17.

Gormlaith ingen Donnchada, §51. See Introduction **6.5**.

Ioseph §54. Ioseph mac Fathaig of Dál Ríata, abbot of Armagh (also

bishop and anchorite). Died *AU* 936.1. See *LL* 6048.

Lígach ingen Ḟlaind, §55. See Introduction **6.5**.

Lóeguire mac Néill §21.

Loingsech mac Óengusa §39.

Lugaid Mac Con §12.

Lugaid mac Lóeguiri §23.

Mac Cécht §17.

Máel §1. One of Conn Cétchathach's druids.

Máel Canaig §47. Anchorite of Louth, died *AU* 815.6.

Máel Febail ingen Flaind maic Conaing, §54. See Introduction **6.5**.

Máel Mairi ingen Chináeda maic Alpín, §53. See Introduction **6.5**.

Máel Sechnaill I mac Máele Rúanaid §50.

Máel Sechnaill II mac Domnaill §57.

Máelchenn §13.

Máelmór mac Airgetáin uí Meich Í §22. He is named as the killer of Túathal Máelgarb, *AU* 544 (there called *Mael Mordha*) and again, *AU* 549.4, where his own death is also recorded. This is also related in *Bethu Phátraic* (Mulchrone, 1939, ll. 972-5). His full name is given in *LL* 3018-9.

maic Ímair §52. Sons of Ímar, king of the Norse in Ireland, died *AU* 873.3. Two of his sons were Scandinavian kings of York and Dublin (Smyth, 1979, 316) and their deaths are recorded in *AU* 888.9 (Sigfrid) and *AU* 896.3 (Sigtryggr). The raid of Armagh is mentioned in *AU* 882.1 but the leader of the Norse party is not given.

Mane mac Bríathraig §10.

Thurneysen (1935, 221.14) expands Rawl. *m- briathraigh* as M*en*briathraigh here (*recte* Menbríathrach?).

Mo Chuta §35. Hypocoristic form of the name Carthach. Saint associated with Rahan, co. Offaly and Lismore, co. Waterford. He was of the Cíarraige Lúachra. His death is recorded in *AU* 637.2.

Muirchertach Mac Erca §24.

Muiredach Tírech §16.

Murchad / Muiredach §61 (see Introduction **3**).

Murchad §59 (see Introduction **3**).

Níall Caille mac Áeda §49.

Níall Frossach mac Fergaile §45.

Níall Glúndub mac Áeda §53.

Níall Noígíallach §18.

Óengus §52. Óengus mac Flainn maic Máele Sechnaill. He is called *ridomna Temrach* on his death, *AU* 915.1.

Óengus §60 (see Introduction **3**).

Óengus Dubaigi §10.

Óengus mac Domnaill §11.

Pátraic §21. St Patrick.

Sechnussach mac Blathmaic §37.

Suibne Menn mac Fíachna §33.

Tipraite (Tírech) §10. Conn Cétchathach's demise at the hands of Tipraite Tírech is mentioned in *CGH* 136b1.

Tipraite §62. See Murray (2002) 54.

Tuathal Máelgarb mac Coirpri §22.

Uí Erthuile §56. The name Erthuile does not seem to be all that common. *CGH* gives the Clann Aurthuili of Uí Chaissine as Dál Cais; the Uí Aurthuili of Uí Chonaill Gabra as Eóganacht and the Uí Aurthuili of Clann Ailgile as Dál Cais. The death of one Ertuile m. Ferghusa Uill is given in *AU* 719.1; Erthuile ua Crundmail (of Cenél Feradaig) is listed as one of the guarantors of *Cáin Adomnáin* (Ní Dhonnchadha (1982) 207).

Index Locorum

Common abbreviations used in this index
b.: *barony*; **bb.**: *baronies*; **btl(s)**.: *battle(s)*; **co.**: *county*; **cos**: *counties*; **d.**: *diocese*; **p(p).**:
parish(es); **tl(s)**.: *townland(s)*; **tn**: *town*; **trib.**: *tributary.* **vil.**: *village.*
Many of the placenames listed in *BS* are hard to identify and locate due to lack of context.

Aí (= Mag naÍ) *A plain between Roscommon and Elphin, co. Roscommon (though earlier more extensive).* gen., §41.

A(i)che gen., §20. btl., §10. A battle of this name won by Cenél nEógain, *LL* 23502.

Aidne *Territory equivalent to d. Kilmacduagh, in bb. Kiltartan, Dunkellin and Loughrea in S.W. corner of co. Galway.* dat., §13. gen., §10. btl., §11; 7 btls. §35. A battle of this name is mentioned (i) in *AU* 533.3, fought by Muirchertach Mac Erca against the Connachta; (ii) in *LL* 23594; (iii) in *BFen.* 328, waged by Conall Gulban. None of these examples refer to the battles in question in *BS*.

Ailech *Now 'Greenan Elly', royal seat of Uí Néill, in tl. Carrowreagh, p. Burt, b. Inishowen W., co. Donegal. (orig. referred to (fortifications in?) tls Elagh More, Co. Derry and Elaghbeg, Co. Donegal).* dat., §61. gen., §53, §64. See *JRSAI* 131, 145-9.

A(i)rb (= Mag nAirb? *On borders of cos Tipperary and Kilkenny).* btls., §10. A battle in Mag nAirb is noted in *LL* 23592.

Airbre *Territory in W. part of b. Carbury, co. Kildare and adjacent to b. Warrenstown, co.*

Offaly. btl., §61.

Albu *From the ninth century, the Gaelic kingdom in Scotland, later the whole of Scotland.* dat., §53. gen., §12, §18, §53.

Allmag Liphi *Probably W. of r. Liffey, in co. Kildare.* dat., §60.

Almu *Hill of Allen, in tl. Carrick, p. Rathernan, b. Connell, co. Kildare.* btls., §41, §41, §43. This important battle (see *AU* 722.8), the subject of a famous saga (ed. Ó Riain, 1978), saw the defeat of Fergal mac Máele Dúin, Cenél nEógain overking of Uí Néill, by Murchad mac Brain, king of Laigin.

Araide (= Dál nAraide). *An Ulaid dynasty located in S. Antrim / N. Down.* acc., §16.

Ard Cam *In Munster.* btl., §13. See Appendix 2.

Ard Macha *Tn / p. / b. / d. Armagh, co. Armagh.* nom., §52. dat., §47, §49. gen., §47.

Arddmóin *In Scotland.* dat., §18.

Argatros *Territory on both sides of r. Nore, mainly in b. Fassadinin, co. Kilkenny, but partly also on the W. side in bb. Galmoy and Crannagh, co. Kilkenny, and b. Clarmallagh, co. Laois.* btl., §11. A battle of this name is mentioned (i) in *AFM* 3656 a.m.; (ii) in *BFen.* 328, a battle waged by Conall Gulban; (iii) in

FFÉ ii, 106 and *BFen.* 22, a battle in which Éber son of Míl is slain by his brother Éremón.

Assal *Territory in bb. Moyashel, Fore and Delvin, co. Westmeath.* gen., §13, §56, §59.

Áth (.i. matan Midi) btl., §57. Perhaps this refers to Brían Bórama's hosting to Athlone, *AU* 1002.1, and his taking hostages from among the men of Mide (*Slogad la Brian co Ath Luain co ruc giallu Connacht 7 fer Midhe*).

Áth Beth *Probably at Ballybay (Béal Átha Beithe), b. Cremorne, co. Monaghan.* btl., §13. See Appendix 2.

Áth Clíath *On r. Liffey, at Dublin.* btl., §53. This battle, where Níall Glúndub was slain, is noted in *AU* 919.3.

Áth Dá Charna btl., §43. A battle of this name won by Cenél nEógain, *LL* 23530, *LL* 23642.

Áth Dá Ferta *Probably on r. Fane at Knockbridge in tl. Loughantarve, p. Louth, b. Upr Dundalk, co. Louth.* dat., §47.

Áth Dairi Duib *Perhaps on r. Nore in tl. Derryduff, p. Offerlane, b. Upperwoods, co. Laois or on r. Duff, in tl. Derryduff, p. Rossinver, b. Rosclogher, co Leitrim.* btl., §11. Áth Dairi Duib is the place where Fland mac Find meic Echtaig Érand and Conán Ferdomon were slain, *LL* 28737-40.

Áth Dumai *Unidentified location, probably in E. Ulster.* btl., §13. See Appendix 2. This is the also the name of a battle between the Ulaid (Airthir) and Uí Echach Cobo, *AU* 761.2 and *AU* 776.9.

Áth Í *On r. Barrow at Athy, b. Narragh and Reban W., co. Kildare.* dat., §12.

Áth Lúain *On r. Shannon at Athlone, co. Westmeath / co. Roscommon.* acc., §27.

Áth Medóin *Unidentified location, in mid-Ulster.* btl., §43. Battle won by Cenél nEógain, *LL* 23527, *LL* 23641.

Áth Sigi *On r. Boyne in tl. / p. Assey, b. Lower Deece, co. Meath.* btl., §24. Battle where Muirchertach Mac Erca defeated the Laigin, *AU* 528.2, *AU* 533.4 and *LL* 23596.

Áth Tálmaige btl., §20. Battle fought by Nathí mac Fíachrach, *ZCP* 18, 183. See *HDGP* s.n.

Bairche *Probably area around Mourne Mountains, S. co. Down.* gen., §53.

Banna *R. Bann in Ulster, flowing from L. Neagh into the sea N. of Coleraine, co. Derry.* gen., §63.

Benn Bairche (Benna Bairche = *Mourne Mountains, co. Down*). Unusual to see it given in the sg. Perhaps it refers to *Slieve Donard* (highest peak in Mourne Mountains). acc. sg., §13.

Berbae *R. Barrow in Leinster, flowing into the sea at Waterford Harbour.* gen. – Beruhai, §63.

Bérre *In b. Bear, S.W. co. Cork.* btl., §13. gen., §39. See Appendix 2.

Bóann *R. Boyne in N. Leinster, flowing into the sea at Drogheda Bay.* dat., §37.

Brea (= Dún mBrea?) *Bray Head, b. Rathdown, co. Wicklow.* gen., §63.

Brecc Fánat *Probably in Fanad Peninsula, N.E. of b. Kilmacrennan, co. Donegal.* dat., §46.

Brega *People and plain in E. co. Meath, S. co. Louth and N. co. Dublin.* dat. plu., §44. In compound Bregmag *the plain of Brega.* dat., §2. gen., §48, §64.

Bregonn *In E. part of Mag Femin; near Clonmel, co. Tipperary.* btl., §22. A battle of this name, waged by Érimon, is mentioned in *FFÉ* ii, 106.

Bréifne *People and territory co-extensive with d. Kilmore, cos Leitrim and Cavan.* acc., §63. Bréifnech *a person from Bréifne.* acc. plu., §52, §61.

Bretain *Inhabitants of Britain, British.* gen. – Bretan, §18.

Brí Chobthaig Coíl *In Brega.* btl., §11.

Brí Éile *Croghan Hill, p. Croghan, b. Lower Philipstown, co. Offaly.* btl., §10. btl., §56. Won by Ailill Molt, *AU* 473, 475, 478. This is not the battle in question here.

Brí Léith *Hill, c. 1 mile S.W. of Ardagh, co. Longford; in tl. Garrycam, p. Kilglass, b. Moydow.* btl., §61. Cf. *Ainm* 7, 4-5.

Búas *R. Bush, co. Antrim; flowing into the sea N. of Bushmills.* btl., §10.

Camas *Perhaps the r. Camus (trib. of r. Bann), b. Coleraine, co. Derry.* btl., §10. See note to l. 64.

Caisel *Cashel, co. Tipperary.* acc., §59.

Caisse *Unidentified river in Mag Life, co. Kildare.* gen., §21.

Calann *Callan r., b. Oneiland W., co. Armagh.* dat., §49.

Carn Aisi = Ard Aise?; *perhaps Mullyash Mt, p. Muckno, b. Cremorne, co, Monaghan*, §60.

Carn Fíachach *Tl. Carn, p. Conry,*

b. Rathconrath, co. Westmeath. gen., §46. This battle was fought, *AU* 765.5, between Donnchad and Murchad, two sons of Domnall Midi mac Murchado.

Carn Fordroma *Perhaps tl. Carnane, p. Fedamore, b. Smallcounty, co. Limerick.* btl., §57. This battle, won by Máel Sechlainn over Túadmumu, is given in *AU* 990.3. The battle is called *cath Fordroma* in *ATig.* (*RC* 17, 347).

Carn Furbaidi *In co. Longford; perhaps tl. Carn, p. Kilglass, b. Shrule.* dat., §56.

Carn Lugdach *Probably Corran Hill in p. Desertserges, b. E. Carbery, co. Cork.* gen., §64. Cf. *Ainm* 8, 42-3.

Carn maic Cáirthinn *Unidentified location, probably in co. Meath.* btl., §46. Donnchad mac Domnaill routed Áed Ingor from Tailltiu to Carn maic Cáirthinn, *AU* 791.5.

Cenannas *Kells, co. Meath.* dat., §53. btl., §43; btl., §60. The battle of Kells in §43 probably refers to the battle in Seredmag (mentioned later in the same paragraph) as the battle of Seredmag is glossed *.i.* Ceanannas in *AU* 743.4. Another battle in Kells is mentioned in *AU* 718.3.

Cenn Dairi *In co. Armagh; perhaps in tl. Canary, p. Clonfeakle, b. Oneilland W.* btl., §13. See Appendix 2. Cf. *Ainm* 7, 7.

Cenn Tíre *Kintyre, Argyll and Bute, Scotland.* btl., §10. Battles in Cenn Tíre are recorded in *AU* 576.1 and *AU* 577.1.

Cerna *In E. co. Meath, N.E. of*

Tara. dat. §55. gen., §47. See Ó Concheanainn (1971) and Ó Murchadha (2004).

Cithamair gen., §36.

Cláire *In E. co. Limerick.* gen., §47, §53. 4 btls., §10. btl., §57. Battles in Cláire are recorded in *AFM* 4169 a.m., *AFM* 4694 a.m. and *BFen.* 328.

Clasach *Apparently in Munster; perhaps tl. Classagh, p. Killaloe, b. Tulla Lower, co. Clare.* btl., §13. See Appendix 2.

Cleitech *In E. co. Meath, near r. Boyne.* gen., §13, §24.

Clochar btl., §10. Battle in Clochar recorded in *BFen.* 328.

Clóenloch *Perhaps Coole L., b. Kiltartan, co. Galway.* acc., §46. Cf. *Ainm* 7, 8.

Clúain dat., §50.

Clóitech *Clady, p. Urney, b. Strabane Lower, co. Tyrone.* gen., §51, §58. 2 btls., §47. Battle waged by Áed Ordnide mac Néill against Domnall mac Áeda, *LL* 23645; won by Cenél nEógain over Cenél Conaill, *AU* 789.12.

Clúain btl., §63.

Clúain Iraird *Vil. / p. Clonard, b. Moyfenrath Upper, co. Meath.* dat., §40, §46, §48.

Clúain mac Nóiss *Clonmacnoise, co. Offaly.* dat., §43, §50, §52.

Cnámchaill (1) *Unidentified location in Connacht.* btl., §58. Another battle of this name given in *AFM* 3656 a.m.

Cnámchaill (2) *Probably tl. Cleghile, p. Kilshane, b. Clanwilliam, co. Tipperary.* acc., §64. btl., §65.

Cnámros *Unidentified location in Leinster.* dat., §15. Named as one of the *Bóraime* battles, *LL*

38265.

Cnogba *Knowth, p. Monknewtown, b. Slane Upper, co. Meath.* gen. – Cnogbai, §56.

Codal (.i. Grellach Eilti) *Grellach Eilti was W. of Crossakeel; perhaps near Creeve L., p. Loughcrew, b. Fore, co. Meath.* Perhaps Codal (cf. Loch Codail, *MD* i, 40) = *Creeve L.* gen., §54. btl., §53. A defeat of Níall Glúndub there in a surprise attack by Óengus mac Máele Sechnaill, *AU* 914.7. Cf. *Ainm* 7, 17.

Coidlim btl., §11.

Colla gen., §55.

Collobair (= Collamair?) *Between Gormanstown and Turvey, co. Dublin.* btl., §11.

Conaille *In N. co. Louth.* dat. plu., §47.

Connachta *(People of) Connacht.* acc., §43, §53. gen., §47.

Corann *In b. Corran, co. Sligo (seems to once have included part of co. Mayo).* btl., §39. This is listed in *AU* 703.2 as the battle in which Loingsech died at the hands of Cellach of Loch Cimbe.

Crinna *On borders of cos Meath and Louth, not far from Dowth.* btl., §13.

Crinna Fregabuil *Unidentified location on the Ravel Water, co. Antrim.* btl., §13. See Appendix 2.

Crúachu (.i. Leth Cam) *Leth Cam is E. of Armagh city.* btl., §49. Uí Chremthainn and Ulaid beaten there by Níall mac Áeda, *AU* 827.4. Crúachu is also the name of a battle waged by Conall Gulban, *BFen.* 328.

Crúachu *Vil. Rathcroghan, b. / co.*

Roscommon. gen., §51, §52, §53 etc.

Cruithne *The Picts.* btl., §32; btls., §35.

Cúailnge *Cooley peninsula, b. Lower Dundalk, co. Louth.* 7 btls., §10. btl., §13. In compound Cúal[n]giubenn, §54. See Appendix 2.

Cúalu *In S. co. Dublin and N. co. Wicklow.* acc., §53. gen., §54, §57. btl., §54.

Cuib (= Mag Coba) §35. *In bb. Upper & Lower Iveagh, co. Down.* gen., §53.

Cúil Chaichir btl., §13. Seems to be written here in mistake for the battle of Cúl Tóchair – see Appendix 2. Cúil Chaichir is the name of a battle fought by Éber (son of Míl) in which Caicher fell at the hands of Amorgen Glúingel. See Macalister (1956) 161, *FFÉ* ii, 106 and *AFM* 3502 a.m.

Cúil Choíláin *Perhaps tl. Kilkeelan, p. Athboy, b. Lune, co. Meath.* btl., §36. btl., §38. Given as a battle won by Díarmait mac Áedo Sláine in *AU* 635.2. In *AU* 675.1 we find: *Bellum Cind ḟaeladh filii Blathmaic filii Aedho Slane in quo Cind Faeladh interfectus est. Finechta mc. Dunchada uictor erat.* This information matches the information we have in §§36 & 38 about the battle of Cúil Choíláin.

Cúl Dreimne *Probably tls Cooldrumman Lower / Upper, p. Drumcliff, b. Carbury, co. Sligo.* Battle referred to in the line *cath fáebrach for Díarmait Dreimni,* §27. Díarmait mac

Cerbaill was defeated there by Forgus and Domnall, two sons of Muirchertach Mac Erca, *AU* 560.3 and *AU* 561.1-2. Waged by Cenél nEógain, *LL* 23605. For further details, see Byrne (1965, 44), Herbert (1988, 27-8) and Charles-Edwards (2000, 294-5).

Dá Dule btl., §10.

Daball *River Blackwater, Ulster, which flows into Lough Neagh.* acc., §54. gen., §16, §62.

Daire btl., §13.

Daire Calcaig *Derry.* btl., §49. Battle won against the Norse by Níall and Murchad, *LL* 23655; same information given, *AU* 833.4.

Dam Derg *In Brega.* btl., §10. A battle of this name won by Indrechtach úa Conaing, *AU* 743.2.

Dathe *Perhaps in b. Farbill, E. co. Westmeath.* btl., §33. Won by Cenél nEógain, *LL* 23501. Listed in *AU* 587.1 (*Bellum Doæthe*) as battle won by Áed mac Ainmirech over Colmán Bec mac Díarmato. In *AU* 593.3 this battle is also called *cath Bhealaig Dhaithe.* The battle is misplaced here in §33. It did not occur during the reign of Suibne Menn (615-628) but during the reign of Áed mac Ainmerech (586-598). For information about this battle and its identification with the battle of Cúl Feda, see Byrne (1965) 45. Cf. *Ainm* 7, 4.

Dercluachair (.i. **Druim Ríg**) Druim Ríg = *tl. Drumree, p. Knockmark, b. Deece Lower, co. Meath.* dat., §47.

Dermag *Durrow, b. Ballycowan, co.*

Offaly. dat., §41. gen., §41.

Detnae *Perhaps tl. Deenes, p. Duleek, b. Lower Duleek, co. Meath.* btl., §22. Followed in *BS* by the death of Ardgal – both occur during the reign of Tuathal Máelgarb. All other sources give the battle and the death of Ardgal under the reign of Muirchertach Mac Erca. See *AU* 520.2 and *AU* 523.1; *LL* 23510 and *LL* 23595; *ATig.* (*RC* 17, 128). Cf. *Ainm* 7, 12.

Dollad *Perhaps r. Dolla, N. co. Tipperary.* dat. sg., §36. Cf. *Ainm* 7, 16-17.

Dorcha *Name of a mound at Tara, co. Meath.* btl., §11.

Drúag btl., §11.

Druimm nAlban *Chain of mountains in Scotland (that separated the Irish settlers from the Picts).* dat., §18.

Druimm nArbelaig *Tl. / p. Drumreilly, b. Carrigallen, co. Leitrim.* btl., §22.

Druimm Cailli dat., §53.

Druimm Corcáin *N. of Tara, co. Meath.* btl., §42. Cináed slain there by Flathbertach find Fáil, *LL* 24115-8. Battle between Flaithbertach mac Loingsich and Cináed mac Írgalaig (in which Cináed died), *AU* 728.1.

Druimm nDígais *Probably tl. Drumdigus, p. Kilmurry, b. Clonderalaw, co Clare.* btl., §11.

Druimm nDub btl., §10.

Druimm [Fi]unnglaissi *Perhaps Dromfinglas in tl Cregmoher & Killeen, p. Rath, b. Inchiquin, co. Clare.* btl., §11.

Druimm Ríg *Tl. Drumree, p. Knockmark, b. Deece Lower, co.*

Meath, §47. Battle implied in ll. 291-2: *Fo-dercfa bandæ fo dii, / fris[a] tóethsat slúaig Midi .i. Fíndachta* and given as a gloss in §47. Battle won by Áed Oirdnide over Clann Cholmáin, *LL* 23647 and *AU* 797.3. See Derclúachair (above).

Drummat 3 btls., §11.

Dub Combair *In co. Meath; perhaps where r. Blackwater joins r. Boyne, near Navan.* dat. sg., §17.

Dubach §10.

Dubad *Tl. / p. Dowth, b. Upper Slane, co. Meath.* 3 btls., §13. See Appendix 2.

Dubaiche btl., §10.

Dublinn *Dublin.* dat., §52.

Dún Cethirn *Perhaps tl. Lisachrin, p. Desertoghill, b. Coleraine, co. Derry.* btl., §32. A battle there between Uí Néill and Cruithne, *Vita Columbae,* 93. Won by Cenél nEógain, *LL* 23507. Listed in *AU* 629.2 as a battle won by Domnall mac Áedo over Congal Caech, where Guaire mac Forindáin was killed. For more on this battle, see Byrne (1965) 45. Cf. *Ainm* 7, 14.

Dún Cúair (= Ráth Cúair?) *Tl. / p. Rathcore, b. Moyfenrath, co. Meath.* btl., §18.

Éile *In S. co. Offaly and N. co. Tipperary.* btl., §35. Batle of this name won by Cenél nEógain, *LL* 23516.

Eillne *In co. Antrim, W. of r. Bush and Liberty of Coleraine, co. Derry (between r. Bann & r. Bush).* btl., §13. See Appendix 2.

Elpa *The Alps.* acc., §20. dat., §20. gen., §20.

Eochinn btl., §43.

Eolarcca acc., §20.

Érennmag *(The plain of) Ireland.* dat., §20.

Ergoll *In Ros Guill, N. b. Kilmacrenan, N. co. Donegal.* btl., §10. A battle of this name listed in *LGen.* 49.

Ériu *Ireland.* btl., §14.

Escir Ḟorchai (Alias for Achad Forchai). *Probably tl. Agheragh, p. Moybolgue, b. Lr Kells, Co. Meath.* dat., §23.

Ess Rúaid *Falls of Assaroe (on r. Erne) at Ballyshannon, co. Donegal.* acc., §62. dat., §58. gen., §39.

Étan Tairb (= Áth Dá Ḟerta; cf. TBC[1] 4151-2). *Probably on r. Fane at Knockbridge in tl. Loughantarve, p. Louth, b. Upper Dundalk, co. Louth.* btl., §46. More unlikely (but also possible) the place in question might be tl. Edenterriff, p. Annagh, b. Loughtee Lower, co. Cavan.

Étar *Howth, b. Coolock, co. Dublin.* gen., §57, §59. btl., §10. Battle waged by Conall Gulban, *BFen.* 328.

Eth *Near Kells, co. Meath.* btl., §13. See Appendix 2. Cf. *Ainm* 7, 15.

Euo *Probably in Mag nAí, co. Roscommon.* btl., §13. See Appendix 2.

Fálmag *The Plain of Fál* (A poetic name for Ireland). dat., §39. gen., §31.

Febail *Perhaps r. flowing near Slieve Gorey (in p. Knockbride, b. Clankee), co. Cavan.* btl., §54.

Femen It could refer to *the plain which extends from Cashel to Clonmel, co. Tipperary* but more likely refers to the place of the same name *in Brega* (see Ó Corráin, 1971). gen., §17. btl., §10. A battle of this name given in *AU* 446.

Ferne *A river in b. Tireragh, co. Sligo.* dat., §53.

Fidga dat., §63.

Finncharn *Perhaps in Slíab Fúaid* (cf. Fúat), *co. Armagh.* dat., §64.

Finnmag *Unidentified location.* btl., §11. A battle of the same name is mentioned in *AU* 1054.4.

Fir Chúl Fir Chúl Breg: *People and territory in N. co. Meath, N. of r. Blackwater*; Fir Chúl Tethba: *In N.W. of co. Westmeath.* gen., §50.

Fochairt *Tls Faughart Upper / Lower, p. Ballymacscanlan, b. Lower Dundalk, co. Louth.* btl., §43. This battle, in which Áed Rón fell, is listed in *CGH* 330d35. Described in *AU* 735.2 as *bellum in regionibus Murtheimhne.*

Forach *Tl. Farrow, p. Leny, b. Corkaree, co. Westmeath.* gen. – Forchai, §50. This battle was won by Máel Sechnaill against the Norse, *AU* 848.4. The importance of this battle, in which seven hundred Norse allegedly fell, is discussed by Ó Cróinín (1995) 247-8.

Forad Lúain §18. See note to l. 162.

Forcalad *Perhaps in p. Ballyloughloe, b. Clonlonan, co. Westmeath* (cf. *AFM* i, 378). btl., §46. This battle, in which Congalach mac Conaing was slain by Donnchad Midi mac Domnaill, is noted in *AU* 778.1.

Franc *A Frank.* gen. plu., §18.

Fremainn *Frewin hill in tl. Wattstown, p. Portloman, b.*

Corkaree, co. Westmeath. btl., §10. btl., §11. Listed as a battle won by Failge Berraide in *AU* 510. *Cath Fremand Mide* given as one of the Bóraime battles, *LL* 38301.

Fúat (= Slíab Fúaid) *An extent of mountainous country lying between Newtownhamilton, Keady, Markethill and the Fane Valley, co. Armagh.* btl., §46. See *Ainm* 7, 162-70.

Fúat Líamna Líamain (gen. – Líamna) *was near Dublin; probably Lyons Hill, tl. Lyons, p. / b. Newcastle, co. Dublin.* gen., §30.

Gaibthine btl., §10.

Geinned *Unidentified location, perhaps in Britain.* btl., §20.

Goll *Now Ros Guill, a promontory in N. b. Kilmacrennan, co. Donegal.* btl., §10.

Granard *Granard, co. Longford.* btl., §13. See Appendix 2.

Grellach Eilti *Grellach Eilti was W. of Crossakeel; perhaps near Creeve L., p. Loughcrew, b. Fore, co. Meath.* dat., §22. btl., §52. A defeat of Níall Glúndub in a surprise attack by Óengus mac Máele Sechnaill, *AU* 914.7. See Codal (above).

Grían *Perhaps Pallas Grean, p. Grean, b. Coonagh, co. Limerick.* btl., §10. btl., §13. See Appendix 2. Battle waged by Conall Gulban, *BFen.* 328.

Grophtine btl., §56.

Í Coluim Cille *Iona.* acc., §45.

Ibar *Perhaps Newry, co. Down.* btl., §10.

Imlech (= Imlech Fía?). *The designation 'ós Bóaind' may refer to r. Moynalty (a late name for this trib. of the Boyne) which flows through p. Emlagh.* dat. – Imbliuch, §37.

Imlech Fía *Tl. / p. Emlagh, b. Lower Kells, co. Meath.* dat., §44. See note to ll. 292-3.

Immar gen., §10. See note to 1. 70.

Inber Domnann *On sea-coast, near Swords, co. Dublin; most probably Malahide Bay.* gen., §65.

Inda, in dá *Perhaps in or near tls / p. Downings, b. Clane, co. Kildare.* §35.

Inis Dornglaissi *On r. Moy, N. Connacht.* btl., §11.

Inis Fáil *The Island of Fál* (A poetic name for Ireland) Here, however, it represents the mythical island whence the Lía Fáil was brought, §4.

Irlúachair *N.E. co. Kerry along with the adjoining parts of cos Limerick and Cork.* btl., §11.

Iroros Near Áth Féine (see *HDGP* s.n.): *In p. Tyfarnham, b. Corkaree, co. Westmeath.* §57.

Laigille dat. plu. – Laigillib, §46.

Laigin *(People of) S. Leinster.* nom. – Laigin, §29. acc. – Laigniu, §24, §41, §61, etc. dat. – Laignib, §55. gen. – Laigen, §43.

Lége *Tl. / p. Lea, b. Portnahinch, co. Laois.* btl., §22.

Lethet Lachtmuige *Tl.* Knocklayd, *p. Armoy, b. Cary, co. Armagh.* btl., §11. See *PNNI* vii, 41-3.

Lettir Ainge (.i. Cell Móna) Ainge: *The Nanny r., co. Meath.* Cell Móna: *Tl. / p. Kilmoon, b. Skreen, co. Meath.* btl., §56. The battle of Cell Móna was won, *AU* 970.4, by Domnall mac Congalaig and

Amlaíb over Domnall úa Néill.

Lettir Daigri (.i. **Cell úa nDaigræ**)
Cell úa nDaigre: *Tl. Killineer,
p. St Peter's, b. Drogheda, co.
Louth*. btl., §51. Waged by Áed
Finni, *LL* 23546. Fland mac
Conaing was slain at the battle
of Cell úa nDaigræ by Áed
Finnlíath, *LL* 23671. Won by Áed
mac Néill over Uí Néill of Brega,
the Laigin and a force of foreigners, *AU* 868.4.

Line (Also Mag Line) *Extending
from Lough Neagh to near
Carrickfergus, co. Antrim*. gen.,
§41, §53, §59. 2 btls., §11. Battle
waged by Conall Gulban, *BFen*.
328.

Linn Néill lit.: *Níall's pool on Callan
r., co. Armagh*. dat., §49.

Liphe *(The plain of) r. Liffey*. gen.,
§17, §39, §43, etc. 2 btls., §11.
Won by Cenél nEógain, *LL*
23518. Also the name of a battle
waged by Conall Gulban, *BFen*.
328. In compound Liphemag. dat.
– Liphemaigh, §31. btls., §14.

(Loch) Ainnin *Lough Ennell, co.
Westmeath*. btl., §52.

Loch Bricrenn *Loughbrickland, p.
Aghaderg, b. Upper Iveagh, co.
Down*. btl., §58. There is a rout
of the Ulaid and Uí Echach here,
AU 1005.6.

Loch Cimbi *Lough Hackett, near
Headford, co. Galway*. gen.
– Locha Cimbi, §39.

Loch Dá Cháech *Waterford
Harbour*. §63.

Loch Daim *Perh. in tl. Loughduff,
p. Carncastle, b. Upper Glenarm,
co. Antrim*. btl., §11.

Loch Lébinn *Lough Lene, between
Fore and Drumcree, co.*

Westmeath. gen., §53. btl., §58. A
battle of this name waged against
Domnall Úa Máelsechlainn, *AFM*
1094.

Loch Léin *Lough Leane, Killarney,
co. Kerry*. btl., §13. See Appendix
2.

Loch Luglochtau *Perhaps nr Lusk,
N. co. Dublin* (see note to l. 301).
gen., §46.

Loch Sailchitain *Tl. Loughsallagh,
p. / b. Dunboyne, co. Meath*. gen.,
§43.

Lúachair (all Maig Slecht) *Mag
Slecht: In p. Templeport, b.
Tullyhaw, co. Cavan* (see *Ainm* 6,
30). btl., §13. See Appendix 2.

Lúachair Ailbi *Ailbe: In pp.
Clonalvy and Moorechurch, b.
Upper Duleek, co. Meath*. btl.,
§22. This battle, won by Túathal
Máelgarb against Cíanachta Breg,
is given in *AFM* 528.

Lúachmag *Loughmoe, p. Loughmoe
West, b. Eliogarty, co. Tipperary*.
btl., §59.

Luimnech *Limerick*. acc., §63. btl.,
§13. See Appendix 2. Given as
the name of a battle waged by
Conall Gulban, *BFen*. 328.

Macha *Armagh*. acc., §57. btl., §10.
Battle waged by Conall Gulban,
BFen. 328.

Machaire *Machaire Arda Macha:
the plains around Armagh*. acc.
– Machairi, §57.

Máel btl., §10. There is mention
of a *maidm Maile dergi* in *AU*
1077.5, where the Fir Manach
were defeated by Cenél nEógain
of Telach Óc.

Mag nAilbi *A plain in S. co. Kildare
and N. co. Carlow*. btl., §52. This
battle is better known as *cath*

Belaig Mugna. It was fought (*AU* 908.3) between the men of Mumu, Leth Cuinn and the Laigin. Flann Sinna and his allies (including the Laigin) were victorious.

Mag Cruinn §60. *Cruithin territory won by Cenél nEógain.*

Mag Cuinn *Perhaps a poetic name for Ireland.* dat., §56.

Mag Fáil *The plain of Fál* (A poetical name for Ireland). acc., §13.

Mag Laigen *The plain of Leinster.* dat., §43.

Mag Line *Extending from Lough Neagh to near Carrickfergus, co. Antrim.* 7 btls., §10.

Mag Mucramai *Between Athenry and Galway.* btl., §11. Cath Mucrama, waged by Muirchertach Mac Erca, *LL* 23587. Famous battle of this name – see O Daly (1975).

Mag Muí (recte Mag nAí?). btl., §10.

Mag Ratha 2 btls., §15, **Mag Roth** 2 btls., §32. *Tl. / p. Moira, b. Lower Iveagh, co. Down.* Battle listed under the reign of Domnall in *AU* 637. See Byrne (1965) 47; Marstrander (1911); Hanna (1856).

Mag Techt *Perhaps between the Camus and Moyola rivers, co. Derry.* btl., §13. See Appendix 2.

Mainister *Probably refers to Monasterboice, co. Louth.* dat., §55.

Maistiu *Around tl. Mullamast, p. Narraghmore, b. Kilkea and Moone, co. Kildare.* btl., §11, btl., §57. btl., §62. Battle waged by Conall Gulban, *BFen.* 328.

Martartech *Tl. / p. Martry, b. Lower Navan, co. Meath.* dat., §53.

Mibthine btl., §10.

Mide *Nearly co-extensive with modern diocese of Meath.* 2 btls., §10. btl., §15. btl., §64.

Móen (= Móenmag) *Around Loughrea, co. Galway.* btl., §11. There is a *Bellum Moin* listed in *AU* 727.6.

Móenmag (= Móen) *Around Loughrea, co. Galway.* dat., §13. gen., §17. btl., §10.

Móin Tuircc btl., §61.

Mórmag *Along banks of r. Blackwater, Ulster.* btl., §16.

Muir nIcht *The English Channel.* acc., §20.

Muirescc *Apparently in Munster; perh. = Muiresc Eógain, co. Limerick.* dat., §13.

Muirned btl., §18.

Mumu *(People of) Munster.* acc. – Mumain, §13, §36, §43, etc. gen. – Muman, §13.

Ocha *Tl. Faughanhill, p. Martry, b. Lower Navan, co. Meath.* btl., §62. Waged by Ailill Molt (where he was slain by Crimthainn), *LL* 23579. Also given in *AU* 482.1 and *AU* 483.2. Won by Cenél nEógain, *LL* 23502.

Óenach Fánat Fánat: *Fanad peninsula, N. b. Kilmacrenan, co. Donegal.* gen., §60.

Olarba *R. Larne, co. Antrim.* btl., §10. Name of battle, in which Fothad Airgthech was slain, *AFM* 285.

Orc *The Orkney Islands, Scotland.* gen. plu., §12. 27 btls., §12.

Orgain btl., §53.

Osraige *People and territory nearly co-extensive with the diocese of Ossory, cos Kilkenny and Laois.*

acc., §63. gen., §52. btl., §35.

Ráith Adomnæ *In co. Louth?* dat., §51.

Ráith Becc *Tl. Rathbeg, p. Donagore, b. Upper Antrim, co. Antrim.* dat., §27.

Ráth (al Machi) Macha: *Armagh.* btl., §32.

Ráth Crúachan *Rathcroghan, p. Elphin, b. / co. Roscommon.* btl., §20. Battle of this name given in *LL* 2315-6.

Renna *Tl. Rinn, p. Ardcarne, b. Boyle, co. Roscommon.* btl., §10. See *Ainm* 5, 30.

Roigne *Extensive territory in co. Kilkenny.* btl., §11. Name of battle where Énna Airgdech fell by Rothechtaid, *LL* 2308-11.

Róim *Rome.* dat., §52.

1. Ross btl., §10. Battle waged by Conall Gulban, *BFen.* 328.

2. Ross *Perh.* = *Crích Roiss, Brega.* gen., §50. btl., §50.

Ross Corcu Búain *In Dál mBúain territory, at border of cos Antrim and Down.* btl., §35.

Roth (= Mag Roth) *Tl. / p. Moira, b. Lower Iveagh, co. Down.* btl., §64.

Rúadair *Perhaps tl. Rudder, p. Duleek Abbey, b. Upper Duleek, co. Meath.* btl., §53.

Sabralla acc., §20.

Sáiltíre *Kinntyre, Scotland.* btl., §43. The battle of Sáiltíre is recorded in *ATig.* (*RC* 17, 184), *LL* 23653 and *AU* 637.1. For further information on the battle, see Charles-Edwards and Kelly (1983, 127).

Saimne *Perhaps = Cnoc Samna; tl. Knocksouna, p. Tankardstown, b. Coshma, co. Limerick.* btl., §11.

There is a *cath Samhna* given in *AFM* 4169 a.m. Battle waged by Fergus Dubdétach, *FFÉ* ii, 290. See Appendix 2.

Saxain *Saxons.* gen., §18.

Scaleda btl., §10.

Séile *R. Blackwater, co. Meath.* gen., §20.

Selca *Probably in Mag nAí, co. Roscommon.* btl., §61. Battle listed in *LGen.* 50 and *The Book of Lecan*, fo. 8a.

1. Selg *In E. Co. Wicklow?* btl., §10. A battle of this name (against Uí Cheinnselaig) is listed in *AU* 709.2.

2. Selg *Perhaps tl. Shallee, p. Kilnamone, b. Inchiquin, co. Clare.* btl., §35.

Senchúa btl., §11. btl., §35.

Seredmag *Area around Kells, b. Upper Kells, co. Meath.* btl., §43. btl., §44. Battle won by Domnall mac Murchada over Áed Alláin, *AU* 743.4.

Slabre *Perhaps nr Kells, co. Meath?* btl., §13. See Appendix 2. (Also, name of a battle in *LL* 23613, won by Áed Allán over Brandub mac Echach, rí Laigen).

1. Sláine *Tn / p. Slane, b. Upper Slane, co. Meath.* btl., §11. A victory by Ruaidrí úa Canannáin, *AU* 947.1.

2. Sláine *River Slaney, co. Wexford.* btl., §63.

1. Slíab *Perhaps in or near tls / p. Downings, b. Clane, co. Kildare.* btl., §35.

2. Slíab *Perhaps equivalent to p. Killoe, bb. Granard / Longford, co. Longford.* btl., §64. See *Ainm* 6, 27.

Slíab mBetha *Slieve Beagh, in Ulster*

(on border of cos Monaghan, Fermanagh and Tyrone). btl., §11. A battle of this name waged by Conmaol mac Emhir in *AFM* 3579 a.m.

Slíab Cailggi *Perhaps old name for Slievecallan, b. Ibrickan, co. Clare* (see *AFM* i, 48g). gen., §53.

Slíab Cúa *Knockmealdown mountains, on border of cos Tipperary and Waterford.* btl., §11. btl., §56. Won by Cenél nEógain, *LL* 23490. Waged by Muirchertach Mac Erca, *LL* 23577. Listed in *AU* 597.2 as a battle won by Fíachna mac Báetáin.

Slíab Fúait §60. *An extent of mountainous country lying between Newtownhamilton, Keady, Markethill and the Fane Valley, co. Armagh*

Slige Midlúachra *Road from Tara to Emain Macha*, §59. See O Lochlainn (1940).

Srath Cluithi *Strathclyde, Scotland*. btl., §20.

Srúb mBrain *Tl. Stroove, p. Moville Lower, b. Inishowen East, co. Donegal*. dat., §43, §47.

Srúbair btl., §46.

Sruthair *Any one of a number of places of this name*. btl., §13. See Appendix 2. (There is a battle of this name given in *AU* 766.3 between Uí Briúin and Conmaicne).

Tailtiu *Tl. / p. Teltown, b. Upper Kells, co. Meath*. acc. – Tailtin, §54. dat. – Tailtin, §53. gen. – Tailten, §4, §4, §20, etc.

Tarbgna dat. sg., §59.

Telchinn dat. plu., §57.

Telenmag *Perhaps plain around*

Teelin, p. Glencolumbcille, b. Banagh, co. Donegal. dat., §61.

Temair *Tara, co. Meath*, §4. acc. – Temraig, §3, §64. dat. – Temraich, §1; Temraig, §2, §4, §4, etc. dat. – Temair, §5; Temuir, §48, §65. gen. – Temrach, §13, §13, §54, etc; plus len., §13; Temra, §17, §20, §27. In compound Temairmag *The plain of Tara*. dat. – Temairmaig, §29; btl., §38.

Tesgabar (Also known as Laigin Desgabair) *Refers to S. Leinster in general*. acc., §63.

Tír Fáil *The Land of Fál* (A poetic name for Ireland). gen. – Tíre Fáil, §4.

Tlachtga *Hill of Ward, N.E. of Athboy, b. Lune, co. Meath*. acc., §47. gen., §17.

Torrach *Tory Island, co. Donegal*. gen. – Toirrchi, §17.

Tortíne btl., §11.

Tortu *Perhaps in p. Ardbraccan, b. Lower Navan, co. Meath*. btl., §10. Given in *AU* 543.1 and *AU* 548.3 as battle in which Muirchertach Mac Erca fell at the hands of the Laigin.

Trácht Eóthaile *Now Trawohelly Strand near Ballysadare, co. Sligo*. btl., §53. Battle in *LL* 23695 won by Ardgar of Cenél nEógain against the Connachta. The actual battle in question seems to be listed in *AU* 913.6 though its name is not given there.

Trom(m) *Trim, co. Meath*. gen., §25.

Túath Imrois *A district near Tara, co. Meath*. dat., §10, §22.

Tuithme btl., §12.

Uchbad btl., §43. A victory over the

Laigin by Áed Allán. It is listed in *LL* 23499. Uchbad is given as an alternate name for the battle of Áth Senaig – see *AU* 738.4, *FFÉ* iii, 148.

Uinnsiu *The river Unshin, co. Sligo, flowing into Ballysadare Bay*, §39. For a large part of its course, the r. Unshin acts as the border between the modern baronies of Corran and Tirerrill.

Uisnech *Ushnagh Hill, p. Conry, b. Rathconrath, co. Westmeath.*

gen., §56, §63.

Ulaid *(People of) Ulster*, §13. acc. – hUltu, §16. gen. – Ulad, §13, §43.

Umal *Territory around Clew Bay, co. Mayo (b. Burrishoole).* 3 btls., §12. Battle waged by Conall Gulban, *BFen.* 328.

IRISH TEXTS SOCIETY

Cumann na Scríbheann nGaedhilge

2004

OBJECTS • SUBSCRIPTION
OFFICERS AND COUNCIL
LIST OF PUBLICATIONS

IRISH TEXTS SOCIETY,
c/o THE ROYAL BANK OF SCOTLAND PLC,
DRUMMONDS BRANCH, 49 CHARING CROSS,
ADMIRALTY ARCH, LONDON SW1A 2DX

IRISH TEXTS SOCIETY

The Irish Texts Society, founded in 1898, is established to advance public education by promoting the study of Irish literature, and as ancillary thereto to publish texts in the Irish language, accompanied by such introductions, English translations, glossaries and notes as may be deemed desirable.

MEMBERSHIP

Membership is open to individuals and libraries.

The Annual Subscription is payable on the 1st January.

INDIVIDUAL MEMBERSHIP:

*Annual subscription £15 stg., €23, US$25.

Where payment is made by Banker's Order a preferential rate of £9 stg., €12 & US$15 shall continue to apply. This is in recognition of reduced administration.

*Benefits: – Entitled to all new publications at a special price.
– Any two back volumes of main series at half price plus postage in any one year.
– Volumes supplied in response to orders.

LIBRARY MEMBERSHIP (two options:)

Option 1: Full Library Membership
(directly or through agents)

*Annual subscription £15 stg., €23, US$25.

Where payment is made by Banker's Order a preferential rate of £9 stg., €12 & US$15 shall continue to apply. This is in recognition of reduced administration.

*Benefits: – Entitled to all new publications at a special price.
– Any two back volumes of main series at half price plus postage in any one year.
– Volumes supplied in response to orders.

Option 2: Library Circulation Membership
(directly or through agents)

*No Annual Subscription

*Benefits: – All new publications automatically sent directly to library. Payment against invoice.
– Full retail price to apply. Society to bear the cost of postage.
– All existing publications available on request at full retail price. Society to bear the cost of postage. Payment against invoice.

Non-members can obtain the Society's publications by placing an order with their usual bookseller.

In case of difficulty, they should contact the Honorary Secretary of the Society or ÁIS (Book Distribution Centre), 31 Fenian Street, Dublin 2, Ireland.

3

PRICES OF VOLUMES

(for currencies not quoted please use the sterling equivalent)

Volume 49 (members only)   **£14 stg., €20, US $24**

Volumes 4, 8, 9, 11, 13, 15, 17, 18, 19, 20, 21, 24, 25, 26, 27, 29, 29a,
30, 31, 32, 33, 37, 38, 40, 46, 47, 48, 50, 51, 53, 54, 55   **£20 stg., €30, US $36**

Volumes 1, 34, 35, 39, 41, 42, 45, 52   **£24 stg., €35, US $42**

Volumes 2, 3, 5, 6, 7, 10, 12, 14, 16, 22, 23, 28, 36, 43, 44, 56, 57   **£32 stg., €50, US $60**

OTHER PUBLICATIONS

Dinneen's IRISH-ENGLISH DICTIONARY
£25 stg., €40, US $48 (members – £20 stg., €30, US $36)

Father Dinneen – His Dictionary and the Gaelic Revival
£2 stg., €3, US $4 (incl. postage)

Foras Feasa ar Éirinn: History of Ireland. Foreword to 1987 reprint.
£3 stg., €5, US $6 (incl. postage)

A New Introduction to the Bardic Poems of Tadhg Dall Ó hUiginn (1550-1591)
£2 stg., €3, US $4 (incl. postage)

Historical Dictionary of Gaelic Placenames – Fasicle 1 (Names A –)
£20 stg., €30, US $36 (members – members £16 stg., €26, US $30)

SUBSIDIARY PUBLICATION SERIES

Nos. 1, 2, 3, 4, 7, 8   **£5 stg., €8, US $10 (members £4 stg., €6, US $7)**

Nos. 5, 9, 11, 12   **£12 stg., €18, US $22 (members £10 stg., €16, US $19)**

Nos. 6, 10, 13   **£20 stg., €30, US $36 (members £16 stg., €26, US $30)**

SPECIALLY BOXED GIFT SETS

FORAS FEASA AR ÉIRINN (volumes 4, 8, 9, 15)
£130 stg., €200, US $240 (members – £100 stg., €150, US $180)

CINNLAE AMHLAOIBH UÍ SHÚILEABHÁIN (volumes 30, 31, 32, 33)
£130 stg., €200, US $240 (members – £100 stg., €150, US $180)

BEATHA AODHA RUAIDH UÍ DHOMHNAILL (volumes 42, 45)
£75 stg., €100, US $120 (members – £60 stg., €75, US $90)

LEBOR GABÁLA ÉRENN (volumes 34, 35, 39, 41, 44)
£150 stg., €220, US $260 (members – £110 stg., €165, US $195)

DUANAIRE FINN (volumes 7, 28, 43)
£130 stg., €200, US $240 (members – £100 stg., €150, US $180)

POSTAGE PER VOLUME

Britain & Ireland: £3 stg. (SS Series £2 stg.), €4 (SS Series €3),
Surface Mail USA: $6 (SS Series $4).
All other countries: £4 stg. (SS Series £3stg.) or equivalent

PAYMENT METHODS

Subscriptions: The Society has a preference, where possible, for Bankers Orders. Other methods, as listed under volumes, are also acceptable.

Volumes: Cheques, Bank Drafts, and Credit Cards (Visa, Access, Eurocard, Mastercard) may be used to pay for volumes.

Order Forms: See pp. 15, 16 below.

COMMUNICATION

The official address of the Society is as shown on the front page of this List of Publications.
To expedite correspondence, please use the following:

For orders of books, applications/queries re membership, write to:
M. J. Burns, Hon. Treas. I.T.S., Elsemere, Tibradden Road, Rockbrook, Dublin 16, Ireland.
(E-Mail: *Hon.Treas@irishtextssociety.org*)

All other correspondence, write to:
Seán Hutton, Hon. Sec. I.T.S., 69A Balfour Street, London SE17 1PL, United Kingdom.
(E-Mail: *Hon.Sec@irishtextssociety.org*)

WEBSITE ADDRESS: *www.irishtextssociety.org*

LIST OF IRISH TEXTS SOCIETY'S PUBLICATIONS

Issued

1 **GIOLLA AN FHIUGHA**
The Lad of the Ferule
Eachtra Cloinne Rígh na h-Ioruaidhe
Adventures of the Children of the King of Norway
DOUGLAS HYDE, ed.
xx + 208 pp.   ISBN 1 870 16601 9   1899

2 **FLED BRICREND**
The Feast of Bricriu: an Early Gaelic Saga transcribed from older mss.
into the Book of the Dun Cow... with conclusion from Gaelic ms. xl.
Edinburgh Advocates Library.
GEORGE HENDERSON, ed.
lxviii + 218 pp.   ISBN 1 870 16602 7   1899

3 **DÁNTA AODHAGÁIN UÍ RATHAILLE**
The Poems of Egan O'Rahilly
PATRICK S. DINNEEN, TADHG O'DONOGHUE, ed.
lxii + 360 PP.   ISBN 1 870 16603 5   1911

4 **FORAS FEASA AR ÉIRINN**
The History of Ireland by Geoffrey Keating, D.D.
Vol. 1 (See Vols. 8, 9, 15).
DAVID COMYN, ed.
This volume contains Breandán Ó Buachalla's new introduction (1987)
xviii + 238 pp.   ISBN 1 870 16604 3   1901

5 **CAITHRÉIM CONGHAIL CLÁIRINGHNIGH**
Martial Career of Conghal Cláiringhneach
PATRICK M. MACSWEENEY, ed.
lxviii + 234 pp.   ISBN 1 870 16605 1   1904

6 **IMTHEACHTA AENIASA**
The Irish Aeneid being a Translation, made before A.D. 1400, of the
xii Books of Vergil's Aeneid into Gaelic.
GEORGE CALDER, ed.
This volume contains Erich Poppe's new introduction (1995)
xx + 238 pp.   ISBN 1 870 16606 X   1907

7 **DUANAIRE FINN**
The Book of the Lays of Fionn
Irish Text with Translation. Part I (See Vols. 28, 43)
EOIN MACNEILL, ed.
lxviii + 208 pp.   ISBN 1 870 16607 8   1908

See page 4 for prices of Volumes

5

8 **FORAS FEASA AR ÉIRINN**
The History of Ireland by Geoffrey Keating, D.D.
Vol. II (See Vols. 4, 9, 15)
PATRICK S. DINNEEN, ed.
xxxvi + 426 pp.   ISBN 1 870 16608 6   1908

9 **FORAS FEASA AR ÉIRINN**
The History of Ireland by Geoffrey Keating, D.D.
Vol. III (See Vols. 4, 8, 15)
PATRICK S. DINNEEN, ed.
viii + 388 pp.   ISBN 1 870 16609 4   1908

10 **TWO IRISH ARTHURIAN ROMANCES**
Eachtra an Mhadra Mhaoil, Eachtra Mhacaoimh-an-Iolair
The Story of The Crop Eared Dog, the Story of Eagle Boy
R. A. STEWART MACALISTER, ed.
This volume contains a new introduction by Joseph Falaky Nagy (1997)
x + 208 pp.   ISBN 1 870 16610 8   1908

11 **DUANAIRE DHÁIBHIDH UÍ BHRUADAIR**
The Poems of David Ó Bruadair
Part I, containing poems down to the year 1666. (See Vols. 13, 18)
JOHN C. MACERLEAN, ed.
lii + 208 pp.   ISBN 1 870 16611 6   1910

12 **BUILE SUIBHNE**
(The Frenzy of Suibhne)
Being the Adventures of Suibhne Geilt: A Middle Irish Romance
J. G. O'KEEFFE, ed.
This volume contains a new introduction by Joseph Falaky Nagy (1996)
xxxviii + 198 pp.   ISBN 1 870 16612 4   1913

13 **DUANAIRE DHÁIBHIDH UÍ BHRUADAIR**
The Poems of David Ó Bruadair
Part II, containing poems from the years 1667 till 1682. (See Vols. 11, 18)
JOHN C. MACERLEAN, ed.
xl + 288 pp.   ISBN 1 870 16613 2   1913

14 **AN IRISH ASTRONOMICAL TRACT**
Based in part on a Medieval Latin version of a work by Messahalah
MAURA POWER, ed.
xviii + 176 pp.   ISBN 1 870 16614 0   1914

See page 4 for prices of Volumes

15 **FORAS FEASA AR ÉIRINN**
The History of Ireland by Geoffrey Keating, D.D.
Part IV (see Vols. 4, 8, 9) containing the Genealogies, Synchronisms
with an Index, which includes the elucidation of place names and
annotations to the text of Vols. I, II and III.
PATRICK S. DINNEEN, ed.
484 pp.   ISBN 1 870 16615 9   1914

16 **LIFE OF ST. DECLAN OF ARDMORE
AND LIFE OF ST. MOCHUDA OF LISMORE**
P. POWER, ed.
xxxii + 202 pp.   ISBN 1 870 16616 7   1914

17 **AMHRÁIN CHEARBHALLÁIN**
The Poems of Carolan, together with other N. Connacht and
S. Ulster Lyrics
TOMÁS Ó MÁILLE, ed.
xviii + 424 pp.   ISBN 1 870 16617 5   1916

18 **DUANAIRE DHÁIBHIDH UÍ BHRUADAIR**
The Poems of David Ó Bruadair
Part III, containing poems from the year 1682 till the poet's death in 1698.
(See Vols. 11, 13)
JOHN C. MACERLEAN, ed.
xvi + 276 pp.   ISBN 1 870 16618 3   1917

19 **GABHÁLTAIS SHEARLUIS MHÓIR**
The Conquests of Charlemagne
DOUGLAS HYDE, ed.
xvi + 128 pp. + iv   ISBN 1 870 16619 1   1919

20 **IOMARBHÁGH NA BHFILEADH**
The Contention of the Bards, Part I
L. MCKENNA, ed.
This volume contains a new introduction by Joep Leerssen.
xxx + 177 pp.   ISBN 1 870 16620 5   1920

21 **IOMARBHÁGH NA BHFILEADH**
The Contention of the Bards Part II
L. MCKENNA, ed.
178-284 pp.   ISBN 1 870 16621 3   1920

22 **A BHFUIL AGUINN DÁR CHUM TADHG DALL Ó HUIGINN**
The Bardic Poems of Tadhg Dall Ó hUiginn (1550-1591)
Vol. I, Text.
ELEANOR KNOTT, ed.
This volume contains a new introduction by P. A. Breatnach (1997).
cviii + 280 pp.   ISBN 1 870 16622 1   1922

See page 4 for prices of Volumes

7

23 **A BHFUIL AGUINN DÁR CHUM TADHG DALL Ó HUIGINN**
The Bardic Poems of Tadhg Dall Ó hUiginn (1550-1591)
Vol. II, Translation.
ELEANOR KNOTT, ed.
viii + 360 pp.   ISBN 1 870 16623 X   1926

24 **TÓRUIGHEACHT GRUAIDHE GRIANSHOLUS**
The Pursuit of Gruaidh Grian-Sholus
CECILE O'RAHILLY, ed.
xxx + 158 pp.   ISBN 1 870 16624 8   1924

25 **ROSA ANGLICA SEU ROSA MEDICINAE JOHANNIS ANGLICI**
An Early Modern Irish Translation of Part of John of Gaddesden's
Text-Book of Medieval Medicine
WINIFRED P. WULFF, ed.
lviii + 436 pp.   ISBN 1 870 16625 6   1929

26 **CAITHRÉIM THOIRDHEALBHAIGH**
The Triumphs of Turlough
Vol. I, Text
STANDISH HAYES O'GRADY, ED.
xvi + 238 pp.   ISBN 1 870 16626 4   1929

27 **CAITHRÉIM THOIRDHEALBHAIGH**
The Triumphs of Turlough
Vol. II, Translation
STANDISH HAYES O'GRADY, ed.
vi + 252 pp.   ISBN 1 870 16627 2   1929

28 **DUANAIRE FINN**
The Book of the Lays of Fionn.
Irish Text with Translation. Part II. (See Vols. 7, 43).
GERARD MURPHY, ed.
xx + 410 pp.   ISBN 1 870 16628 0   1933

29 **INSTRUCTIO PIE VIVENDI ET SUPERNA MEDITANDI**
Instruction in Holy Life and Heavenly Thought.
Vol. I, Latin and Irish versions with Glossary of Irish Words.
JOHN MACKECHNIE, ed.
xiv + 230 +8   ISBN 1 870 16629 9   1934

29a **INSTRUCTIO PIE VIVENDI ET SUPERNA MEDITANDI**
Instruction in Holy Life and Heavenly Thought.
Vol. II, English Translation of the Irish version.
JOHN MACKECHNIE, ed.
xvi + 112 pp.   ISBN 1 870 16699 X   1946

See page 4 for prices of Volumes

30 CINNLAE AMHLAOIBH UÍ SHÚILEABHÁIN
The Diary of Humphrey O'Sullivan.
Part I, containing the Diary from 1st January, 1827 to the end of August, 1828.
MICHAEL MCGRATH, ed.
lii + 336 pp.   ISBN 1 870 16630 2   1936

31 CINNLAE AMHLAOIBH UÍ SHÚILEABHÁIN
The Diary of Humphrey O'Sullivan.
Part II, containing the Diary from 1st September, 1828 to the end of December, 1830.
MICHAEL MCGRATH, ed.
vi + 374 pp.   ISBN 1 870 16631 0   1936

32 CINNLAE AMHLAOIBH UÍ SHÚILEABHÁIN
The Diary of Humphrey O'Sullivan.
Part III, containing the Diary from 1st January, 1831 to the end of December, 1833.
MICHAEL MCGRATH, ed.
xvi + 272 pp.   ISBN 1 870 16632 9   1937

33 CINNLAE AMHLAOIBH UÍ SHÚILEABHÁIN
The Diary of Humphrey O'Sullivan.
Part IV, containing the Diary for 1834-1835 (to July), Poems,
Miscellaneous Sketches, Vocabularies, etc.
MICHAEL MCGRATH, ed.
xlvi + 392 pp.   ISBN 1 870 16633 7   1937

34 LEBOR GABÁLA ÉRENN
The Book of the Taking of Ireland, Part I.
R. A. S. MACALISTER, ed.
This volume contains John Carey's new introduction (1993)
xxxiv + 270 pp.   ISBN 1 870 16634 5   1938

35 LEBOR GABÁLA ÉRENN
The Book of the Taking of Ireland, Part II.
R. A. S. MACALISTER, ed.
viii + 274 pp.   ISBN 1 870 16635 3   1939

36 SGÉALTA THOMÁIS UÍ CHATHASAIGH
Mayo Stories told by Thomas Casey
Hull Memorial Volume
DOUGLAS HYDE, ed.
xxiv + 388 pp.   ISBN 1 870 16636 1   1939

37 AITHDIOGHLUIM DÁNA
A Miscellany of Irish Bardic Poetry, Historical and Religious, including
the Historical Poems of the Duanaire in the Yellow Book of Lecan.
Vol. I, Introduction and Text
LAMBERT MCKENNA, ed.
xxxvi + 362 pp.   ISBN 1 870 16637 X   1939

See page 4 for prices of Volumes

38 **STAIR ERCUIL OCUS A BÁS**
The Life and Death of Hercules
GORDON QUIN, ed.
xl + 264 pp.   ISBN 1 870 16638 8   1939

39 **LEBOR GABÁLA ÉRENN**
The Book of the Taking of Ireland, Part III.
R. A. S. MACALISTER, ed.
vi + 206 pp.   ISBN 1 870 16639 6   1940

40 **AITHDIOGHLUIM DÁNA**
A Miscellany of Irish Bardic Poetry, Historical and Religious, including
the Historical Poems of the Duanaire in the Yellow Book of Lecan.
Vol. II, Translation, Notes, Vocabulary.
LAMBERT MCKENNA, ed.
vi + 364 pp.   ISBN 1 870 16640 X   1940

41 **LEBOR GABÁLA ÉRENN**
The Book of the Taking of Ireland, Part IV.
R. A. S. MACALISTER, ED.
vi + 342 pp.   ISBN 1 870 16641 8   1941

42 **BEATHA AODHA RUAIDH UÍ DHOMHNAILL**
The Life of Aodh Ruadh O Domhnaill
Part I, Text and Translation
PAUL WALSH, ed.
xii + 350 pp.   ISBN 1 870 16642 6   1948

43 **DUANAIRE FINN**
Part III (see Vols. 7, 28), Introduction, Notes, Appendices, Indexes and
Glossary.
GERARD MURPHY, ANNE O'SULLIVAN, IDRIS L. FOSTER, BRENDAN JENNINGS, ed.
cxxii + 452 pp.   ISBN 1 870 16643 4   1953

44 **LEBOR GABÁLA ÉRENN**
The Book of the Taking of Ireland, Part V.
R. A. S. MACALISTER, ed.
viii + 580 pp.   ISBN 1 870 16644 2   1956

45 **BEATHA AODHA RUAIDH UÍ DHOMHNAILL**
The Life of Aodh Ruadh O Domhnaill
Part II, Introduction, Glossary, etc.
PAUL WALSH, COLM O LOCHLAINN, ed.
viii + 468 pp.   ISBN 1 870 16645 0   1957

See page 4 for prices of Volumes

See page 4 for prices of Volumes

55 STAIR NICOMÉID
The Irish Gospel of Nicodemus
IAN HUGHES, ed.
xlvi + 138 pp.   ISBN 1 870 16655 8   1991

56 OIDHEADH CHLOINNE hUISNEACH
The Violent Death of the Children of Uisneach
CAOIMHÍN MAC GIOLLA LÉITH, ed.
220 pp.   ISBN 1 870 16656 6   1992

57 BEATHA BHARRA
Saint Finbarr of Cork: The Complete Life
PÁDRAIG Ó RIAIN, ed.
xviii + 322 pp.   ISBN 1 870 16657 4   1994

SUBSIDIARY PUBLICATION SERIES

In the case of all publications in this series, the intention is to introduce the relevant text to a non-specialist readership in a way calculated to make the content more accessible and also to convey an application of its status and significance within its particular genre, literary, historical, etc. Additionally, in the case of texts already published by the Society, the intention of the Subsidiary Series (published in conjunction with the main series of texts) is to take the opportunity of a reprint to update the original introduction by noting the main developments in the field since the original publication. In such circumstances, these publications are included as additional introductory material. They are also published independently as moderately priced booklets with a view to making them available to interested readers who may not necessarily wish to acquire the reprint of the relevant text.

1. John Carey

A New Introduction to Lebor Gabála Érenn, The Book of the Taking of Ireland, Edited and Translated by R. A. Stewart Macalister, D.Litt.
22 pp.   1993.   ISBN 1 870166 80 9.

2. Joep Leerssen

The Contention of the Bards (Iomarbhágh na bhFileadh) and its Place in Irish Political and Literary History.
72 pp.   1994.   ISBN 1 870166 81 7.

See page 4 for prices of Volumes

3. Erich Poppe
A New Introduction to Imtheachta Aeniasa: The Irish Aeneid – the Classical Epic from an Irish Perspective.
40 pp.   1995.   ISBN 1 870166 82 5.

4. Joseph Falaky Nagy
A New Introduction to Buile Suibhne (The Frenzy of Suibhne) being The Adventures of Suibhne Geilt: A Middle Irish Romance.
32 pp.   1996.   ISBN 1 870166 83 3.

5. Pádraig Ó Riain
The Making of a Saint: Finbarr of Cork 600-1200.
152 pp.   1997.   ISBN 1 870166 84 1.

6. Diarmuid Ó Murchadha
The Annals of Tigernach: Index of Names.
ix + 222 pp.   1997.   ISBN 1 870166 85 X.

7. Joseph Falaky Nagy
A New Introduction to Two Irish Arthurian Romances.
18 pp.   1998.   ISBN 1 870177 86 8.

8. Maire Ní Mhaonaigh
A New Introduction to Giolla an Fhiugha (The Lad of the Ferule) and Eachtra Cloinne Rígh na h-Ioruaidhe (Adventures of the Children of the King of Norway).
32 pp.   1998.   ISBN 1 870166 87 6.

9. Pádraig Ó Riain, ed.
Irish Texts Society: The First Hundred Years
142 pp.   1998.   ISBN 1 870166 88 4.

10. Pádraig Ó Riain, ed.
Fled Bricrenn: Reassessments
114 pp.   2000.   ISBN 1 870166 89 2.

11. Pádraigín Riggs, ed.
Dáibhí Ó Bruadair: His Historical and Literary Context
119 pp.   2001.   ISBN 1 870166 90 6.

12. Pádraig Ó Riain, ed.
Beatha Aodha Ruaidh: The Life of Red Hugh O'Donnell, Historical and Literary Contexts
164 pp.   2002.   ISBN 1 870166 91 4.

13. John Carey, ed.
Duanaire Finn: Reassessments
xi + 23 pp.   2003.   ISBN 1 870166 92 2.

See page 4 for prices of Volumes

13

OTHER PUBLICATIONS

Patrick S. Dinneen, ed.

FOCLÓIR GAEDHILGE AGUS BÉARLA: An Irish-English Dictionary.

1340 pp. 1927. ISBN 1 870 16600 0.

Noel O'Connell

Father Dinneen – His Dictionary and the Gaelic Revival. 8 pp.

Breandán Ó Buachalla

FORAS FEASA AR ÉIRINN: HISTORY OF IRELAND.

Foreword to 1987 Reprint. 8 pp. 1987.

Pádraig A. Breatnach

A NEW INTRODUCTION TO THE BARDIC POEMS OF TADHG DALL Ó HUIGINN (1550-1591). 8 pp.

HISTORICAL DICTIONARY OF GAELIC PLACENAMES
FOCLÓIR STAIRIÚIL ÁITAINMNEACHA NA GAEILGE

This volume, which marks the beginning of a new Historical Dictionary of Gaelic Placenames, prepared by the Locus Project at University College Cork, is the first of its kind to appear for almost 100 years. Limited to names beginning with *A*-, it will be followed at regular intervals by volumes devoted to names beginning with the other letters of the alphabet. Preparations are already underway for the publication of names beginning in *B*-, and work has begun on names beginning in *C*-. Accompanying the present volume is an index of anglicised forms of its Gaelic names.

FASICLE 1 (Names A –)

eds. Pádraig Ó Riain, Diarmuid Ó Murchadha, Kevin Murray
xxxiv + 172pp 2003. ISBN 1 870166 70 1.

See page 4 for prices of Volumes

Cumann na Scríbheann nGaedhilge
IRISH TEXTS SOCIETY

IRISH TEXTS SOCIETY
c/o THE ROYAL BANK OF SCOTLAND PLC,
DRUMMONDS BRANCH, 49 CHARING CROSS,
ADMIRALTY ARCH, LONDON SW1A 2DX

APPLICATION FOR LIBRARY MEMBERSHIP

To: The Honorary Secretary   Date: _____

I wish to apply for Full*/Circulation* Membership of the Irish Texts Society
(**delete as appropriate*)

Name of Library: _____
(BLOCK CAPITALS)

Address: _____

_____

Authorised by: _____

Title: _____

Date: _____

Payment of Full Membership Subscription and Order for Volumes

Volume numbers _____

Amount for Volumes   _____

Postage & Packing   _____

Subscription   _____

Total Amount   _____

If you wish to pay future annual subscriptions by Bankers Order
please tick the box and the appropriate form will be sent to you.   ☐

(*Only complete the following if different from information given above or if you are an existing member*).

Name: _____

Address: _____

_____

We enclose herewith Cheque/Bank Draft in the amount of _____ re the above order.
Please debit our Credit Card.

Number: _____ Exp. Date: _____ CV2 No: _____*

Visa ☐   Access ☐   Eurocard ☐   Mastercard ☐

Signature: _____

*CV2 Number is the last 3 digits above the signature stripe and only applies to Visa & Mastercards which bear these 3 digits. If number is not on card or is illegible please indicate so in space provided.

Cumann na Scríbheann nGaedhilge
IRISH TEXTS SOCIETY

IRISH TEXTS SOCIETY
c/o THE ROYAL BANK OF SCOTLAND PLC,
DRUMMONDS BRANCH, 49 CHARING CROSS,
ADMIRALTY ARCH, LONDON SW1A 2DX

APPLICATION FOR INDIVIDUAL MEMBERSHIP

To: The Honorary Secretary   Date: _____

I wish to apply for Individual Membership of the Irish Texts Society
(*delete as appropriate*)

Name: _____
(BLOCK CAPITALS)

Address: _____

_____

Occupation: _____

Signature: _____

Payment of Full Membership Subscription and Order for Volumes

Volume numbers _____

Amount for Volumes   _____

Postage & Packing   _____

Subscription   _____

Total Amount   _____

If you wish to pay future annual subscriptions by Bankers Order
please tick the box and the appropriate form will be sent to you. ☐

(Only complete the following if different from information given above or if you are an existing member).

Name: _____

Address: _____

_____

We enclose herewith Cheque/Bank Draft in the amount of _____ re the above order.
Please debit our Credit Card.

Number: _____ Exp. Date: _____ CV2 No: _____*

Visa ☐   Access ☐   Eurocard ☐   Mastercard ☐

Signature: _____

*CV2 Number is the last 3 digits above the signature stripe and only applies to Visa & Mastercards which
bear these 3 digits. If number is not on card or is illegible please indicate so in space provided.*

PRINTED BY ELO PRESS LTD., DUBLIN 8, IRELAND.